Cucina Rustica

Also by Viana La Place
and Evan Kleiman

Cucina Fresca

Pasta Fresca

Cucina Rustica

Viana La Place

and

Evan Kleiman

Illustrations by Ann Field

William Morrow and Company, Inc.
NEW YORK

It is the policy of William Morrow and Company, Inc., and its imprints and affiliates, recognizing the importance of preserving what has been written, to print the books we publish on acid-free paper, and we exert our best efforts to that end.

Library of Congress Cataloging-in-Publication Data

La Place, Viana.
    Cucina rustica/Viana La Place and Evan Kleiman.
        p.   cm.
    ISBN 0-688-07764-1
    1. Cookery, Italian. I. Kleiman, Evan. II. Title.
TX723.L25   1990
641.5945—dc20   89-27853   CIP

Printed in the United States of America

        7 8 9 10

BOOK DESIGN BY RICHARD ORIOLO

*To our
families and friends
for sharing many happy
moments around
the table*

Contents

Acknowledgments

Over the last six years, ever since the initial stages of our first book, we have been fortunate enough to develop a warm supportive relationship with our editor, Ann Bramson. We would like to thank her for her steadfastness through all the necessary changes and, especially, for her innate understanding of our philosophy and style. It is impossible to imagine *Cucina Fresca*, *Pasta Fresca*, and *Cucina Rustica* coming to fruition without her guidance and enthusiasm.

Maureen and Eric Lasher, our agents, are always there to bolster us during the difficult moments of struggling with the manuscript. Seven years ago they took a chance on two young would-be authors and have been cheering us on ever since. For all of this and much more, we feel a special closeness and gratitude.

In addition, there are those who deserve mention for their help in preparing this book. Thank you to Kathy Ternay, Kathleen Venezia, Jeanie Manchester, and Ronda Kamihira. Special thanks from us to Teresa Joseph for her technical expertise.

Introduction

Cucina rustica translates as the "simple kitchen." The word *rustica* in Italian means simple, unadorned, basic. *Cucina* means kitchen, cooking, cuisine, and food itself. *Cucina rustica* describes a style of cooking whose elements are kept at their most basic. There is a pared-down elegance about *cucina rustica* that results from the best ingredients treated respectfully and prepared skillfully, but without artifice. Although rooted in country cooking, it is perfectly suited to modern life.

In *Cucina Rustica* we continue our personal exploration of the fresh, light style of Italian cooking that captivated us and inspired our first two books, *Cucina Fresca* and *Pasta Fresca*. The food we prepare has the ability to satisfy and nourish, yet in its spare structure it makes modest demands on the cook. It is not our goal to impress or to jar you with strange combinations of flavors, nor do we rely on culinary embellishments. Our cooking philosophy is based on the understanding that a few carefully chosen ingredients in simple combinations create richly flavorful food.

We embrace the Italian kitchen for its ability to embody, even in our industrial, urban age, the values of rustic country life, unadulterated foods, and the joy of friendly social time spent over a meal. We seem to be finding our way back to one another through caring about what we prepare for ourselves and those who are important to us. The basic acts of preparing simple rustic food and serving it in an unpretentious and accepting manner brings us closer to time-honored life rhythms. It is comforting and reassuring to be able to reclaim such an integral part of life—cooking.

Our cooking is based on tradition, which for us almost magically imparts a sense of belonging and rootedness. Our senses are served by beautiful colors and shapes, heady aromas, smooth, rough, or velvety textures. This style of cooking represents a return to basic, almost primitive, pleasures that seem to have been lost until now. With this recaptured simplicity comes reawakened tastes. We now want bread that looks like the archetypal loaf, is rich with the aroma of yeast, and is coarse, chewy, and life-sustaining. The lettuces we prefer are tender to the bite and taste peppery or sweet, with delicate leaves in beautiful patterns that range in color from creamy yellow to bottle green to deep crimson. Real tomatoes, heavy with sweet, succulent flesh, are still touched by the spicy smell of green leaves. Grilled foods perfectly represent this direct, reductionist cooking. By simply grilling vegetables, meat, or fish we return to basics—where the direct correlation between the raw material and the fuel (fire) is not obscured.

Our way of cooking is a bridge between old traditions and modern concerns—modern in its clean lines, simplicity, and leanness, and traditional in its adherence to classic combinations of ingredients. Using fresh vegetables, herbs, extra-virgin olive oil, fruits, fish, simple meats, reflects a healthful style of eating and living. There is a relaxed quality about the recipes we present in these pages. It is in this spirit that we share food with our friends and family. Italian food has always conjured up images of warmth and love, of the family, of closeness. When we eat *cucina rustica*, we become part of the family, loved, and embraced. The food transports us to sunny terraces overlooking the sea or to meadows encircled by olive groves—places where families and friends gather at the table. It brings images of children playing in narrow cobblestoned streets, and of mothers and grandmothers, sitting on small wooden chairs, deftly shaping pasta with nimble fingers, shelling fava beans, or patting a dusty child on the head.

Different paths led us both to Italy, but our individual discoveries brought us to a shared philosophy. In *Cucina Rustica,* as in our first books, we have gathered together our recipes, our memories, our adventures, in the hope of sharing our dream of a beautiful life where food is an expression of love and sharing, a reflection of nature, and a return to innocence. Few demands are placed on the cook or the eater except to succumb to the pleasures of the table.

Menus

Antipasti Buffet for 20

Hot Bath for Raw Vegetables
Rich Antipasto
Crostini of Bresaola and Arugula
Olives Marinated with Citrus and Fennel
Goat Cheese with Sun-Dried Tomatoes
Rice Salad with Shrimp
Thinly Sliced Prosciutto
Leek Frittata
Assorted Breads and Breadsticks*
Basket of Stem Berries*
Tiramisù

Antipasti Dinner for 6

Sardines with Fennel
Anchovy and Roasted Yellow Pepper Antipasto
Prosciutto, Butter, and Green Olives
Provola with Mushrooms
Green Salad
Ice Cream with Raisins Macerated in Dark Rum

Antipasti Picnic

Basket of Raw Vegetables*
Chicken Salad with Peppers and Pine Nuts
Vegetables Marinated in Oil and Lemon
Salad of Green and Yellow Beans, Prosciutto,
and Cherry Tomatoes
Potato Pizza
Crusty Country Bread*
Simple Pound Cake with Fruit

Outdoor Concert Picnic

Assorted Cheeses with Country Bread*
Thinly Sliced Chicken Breast with Green Sauce
Festive Rice Salad
Stuffed Yellow Peppers
Pine Nut Tart

Spiedini Party

Grilled Country Bread with Tomatoes and Arugula
Skewered Chicken Wrapped in Prosciutto
Lamb and Sausage Skewers
Mixed Grill of Seasonal Vegetables
Green Salad
*Watermelon Slices**

Gone Fishin'

Grilled Country Bread with Garlic and Oil
*Assorted Salame**
Grilled Whole Fish with Herb Paste
Grilled Antipasti Eggplant with Sweet Onion
*Fresh Fruit**

Lunch for 1

Baby Frisée with Poached Egg and Pancetta
*White Grapes and Biscotti**

New Year's Eve Dinner

Salmon Carpaccio
Mixed Seafood Risotto
Mixed "Wild" Greens
Mascarpone Parfait
*Champagne**

Brunch

Prosciutto and Melon*
Spaghetti alla Carbonara
Pizza Frittata
Cappuccino*

Easter Dinner

Clear Beef Broth with Thin Frittata Strips
Leg of Lamb with Ginger and Rosemary
Asparagus with Anchovy Sauce
Fava Beans Cooked with Mortadella
Rosemary Roasted Potatoes*
Mixed "Wild" Greens
Carmelized Pears with Mascarpone

Elegant Dinner for 6

Baked Stuffed Zucchini Flowers with Tomato Sauce
Risotto with Red Pepper Puree
Veal Tagliata with Wild Mushroom Sauté
Polenta-Encrusted Tomato Slices
All-White Salad
Tiramisù

Sunday Family Dinner for 4

Tuscan-style Roast Chicken
Zucchini Sautéed with Basil and Pecorino Romano Cheese
Baked Eggplant Rolls with Mozzarella and Mint
Honey-Wine Braised Figs Served over Ice Cream

Winter Dinner for 4

Grilled Polenta with Wild Mushroom Sauté
Thin Beef Scallops with Herbs
Sautéed Spinach with Prosciutto
Mixed Salad
Chocolate Mascarpone Pudding

Informal Sunday Lunch

Soup from the Green Grocer
Salad of Mixed Greens and Prosciutto
Anise-Scented Chocolate Cookies

Summer Lunch for Friends

Tasty Mozzarella
Festive Pasta
Sicilian Salad
Espresso Ice

Simple Winter Supper

Radicchio Salad from Vicenza
Red Squash and Rice Soup
Walnut Almond Biscotti

At the Beach

Seafood Salad "Our Way"
Grilled Fish Steaks with Marinade
Baked Sliced Potatoes with Tomato and Oregano
Green Salad
Mixed Fruit Salad

In the Country

Grilled Country Bread with Oil and Garlic
Grilled Game Hens in Lemon and Black Pepper
Spicy Baked Tomato Halves
Mixed "Wild" Greens
Ricotta Pudding

Summer Morning Breakfast

Cappuccino*
Olive Oil Cake
Peaches

Breakfast for 4

Crostini with Ricotta and Sausage Topping
Frittata Drowned in Tomato, Peas, and Prosciutto Sauce
Biscotti and Fruit*
Espresso*

Pasta Party for 12

Prosciutto and Melon*
Spaghetti with Oil and Garlic
Linguine with Colorful Sauce
Orecchiette with Broccoli and Sausage
Linguine with Fresh Tuna Puttanesca Style
Mixed Salad

Afternoon Tea

Semolina Cake
Mixed Fresh Berry Salad
Tea*

Summer Party

Thin Pasta with Inflamed Italian Parsley Pesto
Fried Squid
Tomato Salad
Vanilla Ice Cream Drowned with Espresso

*Asterisks mark simple recipes or foods not included in this book.

The Italian Kitchen

A n c h o v i e s —flat fillets packed in oil

A r b o r i o   r i c e —imported Italian rice characterized by a roundish short grain; used in risotti

B a l s a m i c   v i n e g a r —highly aromatic, slightly sweet aged vinegar

B r e a d —a staple for which quality is of paramount importance. Look for heavy crusty loaves, baked in a European style. Bread is an intrinsic part of many Italian dishes.

B r e a d   c r u m b s —preferably homemade from good-quality country bread

C a p e r s —the unopened buds of a shrub that grows in the Mediterranean; select small capers cured in vinegar or salt

C h e e s e s —use imported Italian Parmigiano-Reggiano or Grana Padano wherever Parmesan cheese is called for in the recipes, and use imported Pecorino Romano. (See pages 30–33 for more information on Italian cheeses.)

G a r l i c —use young, firm bulbs that have not sprouted; store in a dry, dark place.

H e r b s , d r i e d —bay leaves, Greek or Mediterranean oregano; check occasionally for pungency. Replace once a year.

H e r b s , f r e s h —there is no substitute for the lively flavors and aromas of fresh herbs. Try to incorporate fresh herbs into your daily cooking by finding a market that stocks a wide selection of fresh herbs or, even better, grow your own.

L e m o n s —look for thin-skinned lemons full of juice.

E x t r a - v i r g i n o l i v e o i l —experiment with oils from different Mediterranean countries until you find an oil that suits your taste.

P u r e o l i v e o i l —a lesser grade of oil primarily for frying

O l i v e s —keep a supply of green olives cured in brine, black Calamata olives cured in red wine vinegar, and Moroccan-style black olives cured in oil.

O n i o n s , y e l l o w a n d r e d —look for firm, unsprouted onions and store in a dry, dark place.

P a s t a , d r i e d i m p o r t e d I t a l i a n —keep a variety of shapes on hand.

B l a c k p e p p e r c o r n s —use whole peppercorns and grind as needed using a peppermill.

P e p p e r s —dried red chile peppers or red chile pepper flakes.

C o a r s e s a l t —use sea salt or kosher salt.

T o m a t o e s , f r e s h —try to find a source for organic, vine-ripened tomatoes.

T o m a t o e s , i m p o r t e d I t a l i a n c a n n e d —the only substitute for fresh, vine-ripened tomatoes.

T o m a t o e s , s u n - d r i e d —use sun-dried tomatoes packed in olive oil.

R e d w i n e v i n e g a r —use imported aged Italian or French vinegar.

W i n e , r e d a n d w h i t e —have several bottles of good red and white wines on hand. It goes without saying that wine is the ideal accompaniment to Italian food.

La Salumeria

I t a l i a n C u r e d M e a t s

One of the most "rustic" or simple ways to lay a table is to use a combination of cured meats and cheeses. La salumeria, which embraces a wide variety of cured meats, is a longstanding tradition of the Italian kitchen. In its simplest form, it can be a small, coarse-textured salamini eaten by the side of a trail off the blade of a camping knife, accompanied by a slice of good sturdy bread. Or a paper-thin slice of mortadella, almost fourteen inches in diameter, can be folded like a handkerchief and tucked into a small crusty bun. These meals become memorable for their simplicity. They accompany us during special times in our lives, when we travel, on outdoor excursions, or at simple gatherings with close friends. However, salumeria can also be used as part of an antipasti buffet or as a simple single dish to begin a meal. The key is to understand the differences in flavor and texture of whatever cured meats you can obtain. While some brands are available nationally, most are regional. Anywhere there is a "Little Italy," chances are you will discover a butcher or salame maker who has a highly flavorful and interesting selection of cured meats. We encourage you to wander around your neighborhood and uncover the best sources. What follows is a guide to the most commonly available cured meats.

Prosciutto or Prosciutto Crudo

Ingredients: fresh ham from the pig's hindquarters
Process: salted and air dried
Length of aging: 10 months to 2 years
Types:

Prosciutto di San Daniele
—from the Friuli region. Characteristically cured with the pig's foot still attached. Because the animals are allowed to graze, eating grass and acorns, their meat is very lean. Considered by many to be the finest of all prosciutti.

Prosciutto di Parma
—from Parma and surrounding areas. The animals are kept indoors and are fed the whey of Parmesan and grain. As a consequence, their meat is sweeter and fattier than Prosciutto di San Daniele.

comments: American or Canadian prosciutto is in such demand these days that the companies do not allow themselves enough time to age the ham properly. The lack of aging time is the primary quality difference between our product and the Italian product. However, true Prosciutto di Parma is now available in the United States for the first time in twenty years. We should all celebrate the availability of this high-quality product.

Salame di Milano

Ingredients: finely ground pork and sometimes beef from the ham, neck, and shoulder

Process: The fat content is low in relation to the lean meat used, and the sausage meat is processed in such a way as to thoroughly blend the fat and lean meat into a smooth-grained, even-textured sausage.

Length of aging: 3 to 4 months

Comments: Referred to as "dry or Genoa salame," this is the most widely available Italian-style salame in America.

Salame Toscano

Ingredients: approximately 80% lean pork and 20% pork fat, seasoned with salt and black peppercorns

Process: The meat is packed into the casing so that the pattern of fat and meat is more distinct than in Salame di Milano. The sausage is weighted down and squeezed to produce a close, firm texture.

Length of aging: brief

Comments: Salame Toscano is made by many large-scale Italian salame companies. Its round shape is characteristically irregular.

Mortadella

Ingredients: utility cuts of pork, pork fat, seasonings, and spices

Process: Ingredients are finely ground and stuffed into casings and baked in a slow oven, much like a meat pudding.

Comments: The very best Mortadella can be more than a foot in diameter and taste very fine. Armenian sausage makers often make a very high-quality mortadella.

Pancetta

Ingredients: pork belly, pepper, and salt

Process: The pork belly is covered with spices, rolled up, stuffed into a casing, and aged.

Length of aging: a few months

Comments: The best description of pancetta is salt pork or unsmoked bacon.

In Italy aged pancetta is often sliced very thinly and served in sandwiches like prosciutto. In *Cucina Rustica* it is used primarily to enrich simple pasta sauces, vegetable dishes, and soups.

B r e s a o l a
Ingredients: filet or tenderloin of beef trimmed of all fat
Process: rubbed with salt and finely ground pepper and air dried.
Comments: The apotheosis of beef jerky. To serve bresaola properly, slice it as thin as possible. It pairs beautifully with rich cheeses, such as goat cheese or fontina.

Formaggio

C h e e s e

Cheese is a staple in Italy; traditionally found on the richest to the poorest tables—probably because a meal of bread, cheese, and wine is accessible to almost everyone. It is eaten at every meal as well as for a *merenda*, a snack. We suggest that you familiarize yourself with a good local cheese shop that carries a wide variety of imported cheeses. They can be used to round out a meal when they are served as a dessert with fruit, or they can enrich simple meals.

Parmigiano-Reggiano

Ingredients: milk from cows fed on fresh pastures. The milk from two successive milkings (evening and the following morning) is blended for each batch of cheese.

Length of aging: at least 2 years

Area of production: northern Italy, concentrated around Parma, Reggio Emilia, and Modena

Comments: One of Italy's oldest cheeses and considered to be among the world's greatest. Used both for grating or as a table cheese served with bread and/or fruit.

Grana Padano

Ingredients: partially skimmed milk from cows fed on fresh pasture and dried fodder.

Length of aging: 1 to 2 years

Area of production: the Lombardy plain

Comments: Slightly sharper, more acidic, and yellower than Parmigiano-Reggiano. A very acceptable substitute for Parmigiano-Reggiano as a grating cheese used in cooking and, if economy is a factor, at the table.

Pecorino Romano

Ingredients: whole sheep's milk

Length of aging: 8 months

Area of production: environs of Rome and in Sardinia

Comments: We know this cheese as Romano. Half of the Italian production of this cheese is exported, mostly to the U.S. for use as a grating cheese. We pair grated Pecorino Romano with pastas from southern Italian regions and/or the islands, such as orecchiette from Puglia. It has a sharp, full flavor and is whiter in color then Parmigiano.

Pecorino Fresco

Ingredients: whole sheep's milk
Length of aging: brief; a matter of weeks
Area of production: environs of Rome, Sardinia, and Tuscany
Comments: Fresh Pecorino is a rustic local cheese, usually eaten as an antipasto paired with freshly shelled fava beans or celery.

Fior di Latte

Ingredients: cow's milk
Area of production: all over Italy, but concentrated in the Abruzzi
Comments: With a wonderful name that means flower of milk, this is a mild semisoft cheese often served as mozzarella. Much of the fresh mozzarella sold here in the United States is made in the style of fior di latte.

Mozzarella di Bufala

Ingredients: water-buffalo milk
Area of production: the Battipaglia plain near Naples
Comments: This cheese dates back centuries. Because buffalo are becoming a rarity in Italy, sometimes it is made from a mixture of cow and water-buffalo milk. Ideally it should be eaten within days after it is made. In fact, in northern cities such as Milano a waiter will often apologize if the cheese is more than one day old. Mozzarella di bufala has a resilient, firm texture that dissipates as the whey seeps out of the cheese. Look for this characteristic firm bouncy texture. It is very difficult to obtain this cheese in its peak state far from its area of production.

Ricotta

Ingredients: either cow's or sheep's milk
Area of production: everywhere
Comments: A low-fat fresh cheese that is sometimes salted to increase its shelf life. It is then used as a grating cheese (in Sicily) or as a table cheese. Because of its neutral taste, ricotta is used both as an ingredient in cooking and in baking, or for other sweet desserts.

Mascarpone

Ingredients: whole cow's milk, which is made to coagulate by adding citric acid.

Area of production: Originally a Lombardy cheese, it is now made all over Italy

Comments: A triple-cream cheese, mascarpone has a very high butterfat content, and its texture is like very heavy whipped cream. It is most often used in desserts or with pastas.

Gorgonzola

Ingredients: whole cow's milk and *Penicillium glaucum*

Length of aging: 45 days to 6 months

Area of production: Gorgonzola, northern Italy

Comments: Tradition states that Gorgonzola was first produced in A.D. 879. Depending on its butterfat content and the length of aging, the cheese is labeled either *piccante* (spicy) or *dolce latte* (sweet milk). *Dolce latte* is the most commonly found Gorgonzola in the U.S., and the most appreciated for a buttery, creamy texture, that offsets the strong bite of the cheese.

Fontina

Ingredients: whole cow's milk

Length of aging: 90 to 100 days

Area of production: the Aosta Valley region (alpine)

Comments: a rich, full-fat cheese that melts beautifully

Antipasti

Antipasti present an almost inexhaustible variety of colors, textures, and tastes. It is in the arena of whetting the appetite for a meal that the Italian love of beautiful color contrasts and ingenuity in creating bold flavor statements with just a few ingredients really shine. We have been seduced by antipasti for years. Our first book, *Cucina Fresca*, had its inspiration in our fascination with this seemingly endless repertoire of foods. As a result of the deep pleasure we get from eating antipasti, we often find that we don't want or need other courses, and end up creating entire meals out of combinations of these special dishes. In the menus at the beginning of this book, there are several suggestions for meals built entirely out of antipasti. Perhaps it is a new preoccupation with health that has turned the focus away from large meat or fish courses. Whatever the impetus, we've discovered that many people prefer lighter meals made up of small plates because they provide more variety in a meal and less emphasis is placed on one centerpiece entrée.

Antipasti are small gifts from the kitchen. Sometimes rustic, sometimes sophisticated, they announce the beginning of the meal. They entice with their colors, fragrance, texture, and freshness: a rainbow of peppers, glistening with olive oil; the muted tones of mushrooms, quickly sauteed with herbs and paired with straw-colored provola; the simple charm of a plate of well-chosen cured meats—velvety pink slices of prosciutto or deep red salame edged in coarse black pepper; shiny black olives; lemon-drenched seafood; milky-white mozzarella sprinkled with pungent oregano. They stimulate our appetites without dulling them.

Use these antipasto recipes with a great deal of flexibility. Many of them could certainly become the focus of a meal, or be a first course. When you serve them as antipasti, moderate your choices with an eye to the entire menu. The repertoire of antipasti is endless; each season brings fresh ideas and inspiration. Remember, an antipasto can be as simple as a few slices of good salame or a few slivers of raw fennel dipped in olive oil. Its purpose is to reflect a mood, set a tone, and prepare the appetite for what is to come.

Affettato Misto

Literally translated as "sliced mix," this most rustic of all antipasti can vary from two well-chosen types of salame to a platter filled with a large selection of sliced cured meats. Look at the guide to salame (pages 27–30) for help in understanding the variety of textures and flavors available locally. Also, experiment with salame that may not be marketed as Italian. Often Middle-European sausage shops can be an exciting source for coarse country-style salame. Most small-diameter salame, such as salamini (little salame) or salame forte (pepperoni), should be sliced thick, from ¼ to ½ inch. All larger-diameter salame, mortadella, and prosciutto should be very thinly sliced. Your butcher will accommodate your requests. The most important consideration in Affettato Misto is to have a balance between coarse- and fine-textured meats, and between those that are hot and mild.

Prosciutto

Mortadella

Salame Toscano

Salame forte

Crusty country bread

Have the butcher or deli person slice 2 thin slices per person of prosciutto, mortadella, and salame toscano. Cut 1 whole salame forte into thicker slices. Serve with a Chianti Riserva or one of the new-style Italian wines, a light, spare vino da tavola. Follow with Insalata Verde (see page 85) dressed with red wine vinegar and oil.

Prosciutto, Burro, e Olive Verde

Prosciutto, Butter, and Green Olives

An antipasto is more often than not a simple offering of a few savory cured or pickled foods served with good crusty bread. Here salty prosciutto and briny green olives are contrasted with sweet, mild-tasting butter and bread. The subdued shades of pale pink, dusty green, and straw yellow create a delicate palette of colors. Serve with a cool white wine.

Unsalted butter, slightly softened

Green Olives

Prosciutto

Country bread

Pack the butter into small crocks. Place the olives in a bowl. Arrange the slices of prosciutto on a platter, slightly overlapping them. Serve with thickly sliced country bread.

Antipasto di Bresaola e Carciofi

Antipasto of Bresaola and Raw Artichoke

Serves 4

A classic combination of flavors. Strong, full-flavored bresaola (air-cured, salted beef fillet) is sliced paper thin and served with faintly bitter slivers of raw artichoke heart.

1 *large artichoke*

½ *lemon*

Salt

6 *tablespoons extra-virgin olive oil, divided*

¼ *pound thinly sliced bresaola*

6 *tablespoons fresh lemon juice*

Freshly ground black pepper to taste

Trim the artichoke according to the directions on page 94. Rub the cut portions with the lemon. Cut the cleaned artichoke heart into thin slivers. Toss artichoke in 2 tablespoons of the olive oil and season with salt to taste. Arrange the slices of bresaola on 4 plates, slightly overlapping the edges. Mound some of the artichoke slivers in the center of each plate. Drizzle each serving with 1 tablespoon of oil and 1 tablespoon of lemon juice. Grind black pepper over the top.

Bruschetta

Grilled Country Bread with Garlic and Oil

Bruschetta perfectly expresses the characteristics of *cucina rustica*. In fact, Bruschetta may well embody all the qualities of the term. In its simplest form Bruschetta is grilled country bread, drizzled with olive oil and sprinkled with salt and pepper. Its flavor rests strictly on the quality of each simple ingredient. It can be embellished according to state of mind, refrigerator and/or pocketbook. The bread must be of firm crumb, not full of air, with a hard crusty exterior. The olive oil must absolutely be of the best quality available: whether Tuscan, Ligurian, Pugliese, or even Greek, Spanish, Moroccan, or French. The oil can be a deep dark green and fruity with olive flavor or it can be of the palest straw and be light on the palate. It must always be extra-virgin olive oil; that is, from the first pressing, obtained from a nonchemical process of releasing the oil through pressure.

TO GRILL BREAD FOR BRUSCHETTA:

The bread must be prepared in the same way for all bruschette regardless of topping. Cut the bread into ½-inch-thick slices. The bread can then be toasted by nearly any method; you can even toast it right on top of a gas or electric burner. Ideally, grill the bread over a charcoal or gas grill, or on a ridged stovetop griddle. If those are not options, you can toast the bread in a toaster oven or under a broiler. Grill the bread until light grill marks appear on it. If you toast the bread, the surface should be a light golden brown, and the inside should remain soft. Keep a couple of peeled garlic cloves handy, and as soon as the bread is properly grilled, lightly rub the surface with garlic. Place the garlic-rubbed grilled bread on a plate and drizzle with olive oil. How much oil you use is a matter of preference, but there should be at least enough to permeate the bread. Sprinkle the bread lightly with salt and dust with a few grindings of fresh black pepper.

Bruschetta al Pomodoro e Rucola

Grilled Country Bread with Tomatoes and Arugula

Serves 4 to 6

All over Italy, grilled country bread topped with a mixture of chopped tomatoes and arugula is the most commonly served type of bruschetta. However, we strongly associate this antipasto with Rome during summer, when Bruschetta al Pomodoro e Rucola can make a meal, served with a firm, fresh piece of mozzarella di bufala.

3 large red, ripe tomatoes, blossom ends removed, diced

2 small bunches arugula, stems removed, coarsely chopped

Salt and freshly ground black pepper to taste

6 thick slices good-quality country bread

2 garlic cloves, peeled

Extra-virgin olive oil

In a small bowl gently mix together the tomatoes and arugula. Season with salt and pepper to taste. Set aside. Grill or lightly toast bread. Rub with garlic cloves. Spoon tomato-arugula mixture over each slice of bread. Generously drizzle olive oil over the Bruschetta.

Bruschetta con Zucchine Sfrante

Bruschetta Topped with Zucchini Puree and Sun-Dried Tomatoes

Serves 4 to 6

In this dish the zucchini is cooked with onion and herbs until it completely falls apart and becomes a rough puree. Then the puree is spooned onto well-toasted sturdy bread and topped with thin slices of sun-dried tomato.

¼ *cup extra-virgin olive oil*

¼ *small onion, peeled and chopped*

2 *medium zucchini, washed, ends removed, and coarsely sliced*

2 *garlic cloves, peeled and minced*

6–8 *fresh basil leaves*

2 *tablespoons chopped Italian parsley*

Salt and freshly ground black pepper to taste

6 *thick slices good-quality Italian bread*

1–2 *garlic cloves, peeled*

Extra-virgin olive oil

4–6 *sun-dried tomatoes packed in oil, drained, cut into strips*

Gently heat the olive oil in a small sauté pan. Add the onion and sauté until soft and translucent. Add the zucchini, garlic, and herbs. Cover the pan and cook over medium heat, stirring frequently, until zucchini falls apart completely. Add salt and pepper to taste. Grill or lightly toast the bread slices. Rub each with the garlic cloves and drizzle with olive oil. Spread the rough zucchini puree on the grilled bread. Garnish with the sun-dried tomatoes.

Bruschetta 'ncapriata

Grilled Country Bread with White Bean Puree

Serves 4 to 6 as a luncheon dish, or 10 to 12 as an appetizer

In the same family as Maccù, Bruschetta 'ncapriata is a traditional dish from Puglia where greens are a staple. Here a puree of white beans is spread on grilled bread and topped with garlicky greens. It is especially delicious made with spicy mustard greens.

¼ *cup extra-virgin olive oil*

¼ *medium onion, peeled and minced*

2 *garlic cloves, peeled and minced*

1 16-*ounce can cannellini beans, drained, or 2 cups cooked white beans*

Salt to taste

1 *large bunch or 2 small bunches greens (spinach, Swiss chard, or mustard greens)*

2 *tablespoons extra-virgin olive oil*

1 *garlic clove, peeled and minced*

Salt to taste

6 *thick slices good-quality country bread, or 12 thin slices baguette or other thin loaf*

2 *garlic cloves, peeled*

Extra-virgin olive oil

Heat the olive oil in a skillet. Add the onion and minced garlic. Cook over low heat until the onion is soft and translucent. Add the beans and salt to taste. Cook over low heat until beans absorb the onion flavor, approximately 15 minutes. Remove from heat. In a food processor fitted with a steel blade or in a blender, briefly process the bean mixture to a coarse puree. Set aside.

Wash the greens well and remove any fibrous stems or ribs. Stack the leaves, roll them up, and slice across to make thin strips. Heat the 2 tablespoons of olive oil in a skillet. Add the garlic, sliced greens, and salt to taste. Cover skillet and cook over moderate heat until greens wilt and are tender. Remove from pan and set aside.

Grill or lightly toast the bread slices. Rub each with garlic cloves, and drizzle with olive oil. Spoon the white bean puree onto the grilled bread. Top each slice with some cooked greens.

Bruschetta al Maccù

Grilled Bread with Fava Bean Puree

Serves 4 to 6 as a luncheon dish, or 10 to 12 as an appetizer

Maccù is an ancient Sicilian soul food made of dried fava beans and wild fennel. If you are lucky (as we are in Los Angeles) to find a hillside carpeted with wild fennel, a delicious edible plant, pick some of the feathery tops to chop up and add to the recipe. The tops of the wild plant are more pungent than those of the domesticated bulb fennel that is widely available.

1 16-*ounce can fava beans*

1 *fennel bulb*

¼ *cup extra-virgin olive oil*

¼ *medium onion, peeled and thinly sliced*

1–2 *garlic cloves, peeled and minced*

Salt to taste

6 *thick slices good-quality country bread or* 12 *thin slices baguette or other thin loaf*

2 *garlic cloves, peeled*

Extra-virgin olive oil

Drain the fava beans and place in a bowl. Carefully remove the dark outer skin of each bean. Do not be concerned if the beans break up. Set aside the shelled beans. Carefully wash the fennel and discard any woody outer layers. Cut the bulb in half lengthwise, then thinly slice crosswise.

Heat the olive oil in a skillet and add the onion. Cook the onion over low heat until it begins to wilt. Add the sliced fennel. Continue cooking the onion and fennel together until they are both very tender, approximately 10 to 15 minutes. Add the minced garlic and cook until it gives off its characteristic aroma. If using wild fennel tops, add them at this stage. Add the fava beans and ¼ cup water. Cook all ingredients together over low heat at least 15 minutes, or until the beans are soft and the flavors blend. Add salt to taste and remove from the heat. In a food processor with a steel blade or in a blender, briefly process the bean mixture to a coarse puree.

Grill or lightly toast the bread slices. Rub with garlic cloves, and drizzle with olive oil. Serve the Maccù warm or at room temperature mounded in the center of a platter and surrounded with small Crostini (see below).

Crostini

Appetizer Croutons

Serves 8 to 10

We often serve Crostini instead of bruschetta at large gatherings or cocktail parties. Crostini are smaller, less filling, and more delicate. Either use a baguette-type loaf that has a small diameter, or cut bread slices in halves or, if necessary, in quarters.

½ *cup extra-virgin olive oil*

4 *garlic cloves, peeled and minced or left whole*

½ *cup coarsely chopped Italian parsley (optional)*

1 *loaf good-quality baguette or other thin loaf, cut into thin slices*

Heat the olive oil in a skillet. Add the garlic and parsley, and gently cook over low heat until the garlic releases its aroma. Add the slices of bread and fry until golden on one side, then turn each piece and fry the other side.

(Continued)

Alternatively, brush both sides of bread with olive oil, lay slices on a cookie sheet, and place in a preheated 400° oven. If desired, sprinkle parsley over the bread slices. Bake until bread turns golden. Remove from oven and lightly rub the whole peeled garlic cloves on one side of each bread slice. Crostini can be made in advance and served at room temperature.

Crostini di Bresaola e Rucola

Crostini of Bresaola and Arugula

Serves 6 to 8

Little rounds of bread are spread with a mixture of butter and chopped arugula and topped with a thin slice of bresaola (dried salt beef). This antipasto is delicious served before dinner with an aperitif.

½ cup unsalted butter, at room temperature

1 small bunch arugula, stems removed, coarsely chopped

1 recipe Crostini (see page 45), reserve extra for another use

¼ pound thinly sliced bresaola

Place the butter and arugula in a food processor with a steel blade and process until arugula is finely chopped and evenly distributed. Alternatively, place the butter in a small bowl and finely chop the arugula. Add the arugula to the butter in the bowl and mix well with a fork. Spread a little of the butter mixture on one side of each piece of bread. Top with a slice of bresaola. Serve immediately.

Crostini con Ricotta e Salsicce

Crostini with Ricotta and Sausage Topping

Serves 6 to 8

Sausage adds richness to the fresh, lean taste of ricotta spread on lightly toasted bread rounds. These Crostini are a delightful prelude to a lunch in the countryside.

1 *cup fresh ricotta*

2 *tablespoons grated Parmesan cheese*

Salt and freshly ground black pepper to taste

2 *sweet Italian sausages*

1 *recipe Crostini (see page 45)*

Place the ricotta in a bowl. Add the Parmesan cheese, salt and pepper to taste, and beat with a wooden spoon until well mixed.

Place the sausages and a few tablespoons of water in a small sauté pan. Puncture the skin of the sausages with a fork and cook over medium heat. When the water evaporates, continue cooking the sausages until they brown. Remove from heat and, when cool enough to handle, skin the sausages and crumble the meat.

Add the crumbled sausages to the ricotta mixture and blend well. Spread the ricotta and sausage mixture on the Crostini and serve immediately.

Olive all'Orígano

Black Olives with Oregano

Makes 2 cups

Olives are the soul of the Mediterranean. They can be cured in olive oil, in salt, or in brine, and flavored with all variety of herbs. They range in color from soft ocher and sea green to pale purple and pitch black. Olives are delicious when eaten just with good bread and wine. Here black olives are warmed in white wine, which brings out their flavor and aroma, and makes them plump and juicy. Look for Moroccan oil-cured black olives, the best choice for this recipe.

2 teaspoons extra-virgin olive oil

2–3 garlic cloves, peeled and crushed

½ cup dry white wine

2 cups oil-cured black olives

1 teaspoon chopped fresh oregano leaves

Place the olive oil and garlic in a medium-sized sauté pan and cook over medium heat until garlic is very lightly golden. Add the white wine, bring to a boil over high heat, and let boil for a few seconds. Add all the olives, lower the heat to medium, and sauté until the olives have absorbed the wine. Turn down the heat to low and sprinkle olives with the oregano. Toss briefly and serve hot.

Olive all'Arancia e Limone

Olives Marinated with Citrus and Fennel

Makes 2 cups

This Sicilian treatment pairs three archetypal southern Italian flavors—the fragrant tang of citrus, the licorice sweetness of fennel, and the salty richness of black olives.

2 *cups Calamata olives*	2 *oranges*
1 *fennel bulb*	1 *lemon*

With a sharp paring knife make 1 or 2 slits in each olive down to the pit. Place the olives in a glass bowl. Remove the tough outer layer of the fennel bulb. Cut the fennel into julienne. Add to olives. Using a zester, remove the zest from the oranges and lemon, and add to the olives. Remove and discard any remaining zest and bitter white pith from the oranges and lemon. Cut the membrane away from the individual orange and lemon segments and add segments to the olives and zest. Toss gently. Cover and let marinate at room temperature or in the refrigerator for at least 1 day. Serve in a terra-cotta bowl.

Mozzarella Saporita

Tasty Mozzarella

Serves 4 to 6

This simplest of cheese preparations can be a welcome addition to a family menu. Or, accompanied by good, rough-textured country salame, bread, and a green salad, it can make a meal.

1½ *pounds mozzarella in water, drained*

1 *teaspoon dried oregano*

Salt and freshly ground black pepper to taste

½ *lemon*

Extra-virgin olive oil

Cut the mozzarella into slices, about ¼ inch thick. Arrange the slices in a circular pattern on a serving dish. Sprinkle cheese with the oregano, salt, and pepper. Squeeze the lemon over the cheese. Drizzle the cheese with olive oil and let marinate in the refrigerator for at least 1 hour before serving.

Caprini con Pumate

Goat Cheese with Sun-Dried Tomatoes

Serves 4 to 6

Believe it or not, pairing goat cheese and sun-dried tomatoes is traditional in Puglia. In our research we were amazed to find a historical basis for combining these two trendy ingredients. This simple antipasto never fails to get raves.

6 *garlic cloves, peeled*

2 *tablespoons extra-virgin olive oil, plus additional for drizzling over finished dish*

2 *4-ounce rounds fresh goat cheese*

3 *sprigs fresh oregano or 1 teaspoon dried oregano*

5 *sun-dried tomato halves packed in olive oil, drained*

2 *teaspoons small capers or 1 teaspoon large Spanish capers*

Pinch of red chile pepper flakes or freshly ground black pepper to taste

Place the garlic cloves and the 2 tablespoons of olive oil in a small skillet with a heatproof handle. Put the skillet under a preheated broiler, approximately 4 inches below the flame. Watch the skillet constantly as the garlic begins to take on color. Remove the skillet from the broiler when garlic shows deep golden-brown specks. Set the garlic and flavored oil aside.

Carefully remove the goat cheese from its wrapping and cut into ¼-inch-thick slices. Arrange the slices attractively on a serving dish just large enough to accommodate them. Remove the leaves from 2 sprigs of oregano and scatter them over the cheese, or sprinkle with dried oregano. Cut each of the sun-dried tomatoes into approximately 4 thin slices. Scatter the

(Continued)

tomato slices and capers over the cheese, and sprinkle on top either red or black pepper to taste. Scatter the broiled garlic cloves over the dish and drizzle any flavored olive oil left in the skillet. Finish by drizzling a bit more raw olive oil over the dish, if desired, and garnish with the reserved sprig of oregano. Serve with good country bread and wine.

Fave Crude e Pecorino

Antipasto of Fava Beans and Pecorino

Serves 4

Very fresh raw fava beans are combined with salty, tangy Pecorino Romano cheese and fragrant olive oil. Use only fava beans that have a tender green pod containing small to medium-sized bright green beans. The larger the bean, the tougher it will be. Discard any beans that are yellow or pale; they lack delicacy of flavor and texture, especially when eaten raw as in this recipe. Our first introduction to this antipasto was in a small Tuscan restaurant, where we saw near the entrance a large willow basket of fava beans still in their pods sitting next to a chunk of fresh Pecorino.

2 *pounds fresh fava beans, unshelled weight*	3 *tablespoons extra-virgin olive oil*
⅓ *pound Pecorino Romano cheese*	*Freshly ground black pepper*

Shell the fava beans. Carefully remove the waxy outer covering of each bean. Cut the Pecorino Romano cheese into ¼-inch dice. Mix the beans, cheese, olive oil, and plenty of coarsely ground pepper. Let marinate at least 1 hour. Serve with crusty bread as an appetizer or as a salad.

Scamorza alla Griglia

Grilled Smoked Mozzarella

Serves 4 to 6

The beauty of this dish is its simplicity. All rests on the high quality of the ingredients. Find a good source for artisan-produced cheese (produced in small batches and fire smoked) and the best organic, vine-ripened tomatoes; they are essential for this highly flavored appetizer. We first tasted grilled scamorza at La Latteria in Milan, a cheese shop-cum-*caffè* where customers eat jammed together next to the cheese cases or in the kitchen.

2 *red, ripe tomatoes*

½–1 *teaspoon dried oregano*

Salt and freshly ground black pepper to taste

¼ *cup extra-virgin olive oil, unfiltered if possible*

1 *pound smoked mozzarella*

Remove stem ends of tomatoes. Cut tomatoes into small dice, approximately ¼ inch in diameter. In a small bowl mix the diced tomatoes, oregano, salt and pepper, and olive oil. Set aside at room temperature for at least 1 hour before preparing the cheese.

Cut the smoked mozzarella into slices ¼ inch thick and place on a small heatproof platter so that they slightly overlap. Run the platter under a preheated gas or electric broiler for 1 to 2 minutes, or until the cheese begins to bubble and shows a few golden-brown spots. Use oven mitts to carefully remove the hot platter from the broiler. Top the bubbling cheese with the tomato mixture, including all the juice. Serve immediately with good country bread.

Provola ai Funghi Trifolati

Provola with Mushrooms

Serves 4 to 6

Provola is a semisoft cheese the color of straw. It is in the same family as mozzarella and provolone filate or the string cheeses. If provola is unavailable substitute smoked mozzarella. Fresh mozzarella has too high a water content to melt successfully. The mild creaminess of the cheese contrasts with the deep woodsy flavor of the mushrooms. Cook the mushrooms over very high heat without salt to achieve a pleasing crustiness.

1 *pound provola or smoked mozzarella, cut into slices ¼ inch thick*

1 *pound mushrooms*

3 *tablespoons extra-virgin olive oil*

3 *garlic cloves, peeled and minced*

2 *sprigs fresh thyme, leaves removed, or ¼ teaspoon dried whole thyme leaves*

1 *tablespoon chopped Italian parsley, plus additional for garnish*

4 *sun-dried tomato halves, packed in olive oil*

Salt and freshly ground black pepper to taste

Arrange the sliced cheese in an attractive manner on a heatproof serving platter that is just large enough to hold the slices. Set aside.

Wipe the mushrooms clean with a damp towel. Trim the stem ends with a sharp paring knife, and slice mushrooms lengthwise. Heat the olive oil in a medium-sized skillet. Add the mushrooms, garlic, thyme, parsley, and sun-dried tomatoes. Sauté over high heat until the mushrooms are just cooked through. Do not let them become too soft! Remove the skillet from the heat and add salt and pepper to taste.

Place the cheese platter under a very hot preheated broiler until the cheese melts and begins to develop golden-brown spots. Using oven mitts, carefully remove the hot platter from the broiler. Pour the mushroom mixture over the hot cheese. Garnish with a sprinkle of fresh minced parsley.

Radicchio con Scamorza

G r i l l e d   R a d i c c h i o   w i t h
S m o k e d   M o z z a r e l l a

Serves 4 to 6

A modern dish that brings together the best ingredients of northern and southern Italy. If smoked mozzarella is unavailable, you can substitute provola, a handmade string-type cheese that is basically a slightly aged mozzarella. We enjoy the play of bitter and smoky flavors in this dish.

3 *heads radicchio*

Extra-virgin olive oil

Salt to taste

1 *pound smoked mozzarella, thinly sliced*

4 *sprigs fresh thyme, divided, or* ½ *teaspoon dried whole thyme leaves*

Freshly ground black pepper to taste

Wash and dry the radicchio well. Trim stem ends and cut each head lengthwise into four wedges. Do not remove the cores. Although the radicchio core is strong-tasting, it helps keep the leaves together during grilling. Remove individual leaves from 3 sprigs of thyme and set aside.

(Continued)

Heat a cast-iron or electric griddle until moderately hot, approximately 400° if your appliance has a thermostat, or until the griddle sizzles when sprinkled with water. Drizzle olive oil on the griddle. Place the radicchio wedges on the griddle and cook for approximately 3 minutes per side. The radicchio should wilt, change color, and become tender. Using a pancake turner, remove the radicchio from the griddle, and arrange in one layer on a heatproof serving dish. Lightly salt it to taste. Cover the radicchio with the slices of smoked mozzarella, allowing the vegetable to peek through here and there. Place the dish under a very hot preheated broiler until the smoked mozzarella begins to melt, taking care not to let the radicchio burn.

Remove the dish from the broiler using oven mitts. Sprinkle with the thyme leaves, and add a drizzle of olive oil and pepper to taste. Garnish plate with the remaining whole thyme sprig. Serve immediately accompanied by a robust red wine.

Bagna Cauda con Verdura Cruda

Hot Bath for Raw Vegetables

Serves 6

This dish from Piedmont is the winter version of Pinzimonio (see our first book, *Cucina Fresca*, page 50), which pairs tender new vegetables with a dipping sauce of the finest extra-virgin olive oil seasoned with salt, freshly ground black pepper, and, if desired, red wine or balsamic vinegar.

Bagna Cauda combines butter, olive oil, garlic, and anchovies cooked over gentle heat and served warm. It is accompanied by cut-up raw fall and winter vegetables, which are dipped into the "hot bath." The dipping sauce is traditionally kept warm at the table by placing it over a small burner. The vegetables most traditionally used are red and yellow peppers, artichokes, and celery. Cardoons, which are related to artichokes, are always included. Although not widely available, cardoons can sometimes be found in Italian markets and specialty produce stores. The vegetables we suggest for this recipe have been chosen for color, texture, and availability, but feel free to select your own favorites. Remember that certain vegetables are not at their best raw. For example, cauliflower and broccoli flowerets are often wrongly served uncooked, although the peeled stalks of young broccoli are delicious eaten raw.

THE VEGETABLES:

2 *red peppers*

2 *yellow peppers*

Handful baby artichokes

Lemon for trimming artichokes

1 *celery heart*

1 *large head radicchio*

2 *heads Belgian endive*

1 *fennel bulb*

FOR THE BAGNA CAUDA:

8 *tablespoons unsalted butter*

¼ *extra-virgin olive oil*

3 *large garlic cloves, finely chopped*

6–8 *anchovies, coarsely chopped*

Salt to taste

Cut the peppers in half and remove the seeds and white membranes. Cut peppers into strips. Trim the base of the artichokes and snap off the tough outer leaves. Rub the cut surfaces with the lemon. Separate the celery stalks. Detach the leaves from the radicchio and Belgian endive. Trim the tops from the fennel and cut in half lengthwise. Cut out the core. Cut fennel into julienne. Arrange the vegetables in a basket or on a platter.

To prepare the dipping sauce, place the butter, olive oil, and garlic in a small saucepan over low heat. Heat these ingredients until the garlic turns opaque and becomes fragrant. Add the anchovies and cook over gentle heat until the anchovies melt. Add salt to taste, if needed.

Serve in a small, warmed bowl over a small tabletop burner if possible, surrounded by the prepared vegetables.

Antipasto di Acciughe e
Peperoni Gialli

Anchovy and Roasted Yellow
Pepper Antipasto

Serves 6

A recipe from Luigi Carnacina's tome on cooking, *Il Carnacina* (see Antipasto alla Casalinga, page 74), this dish stimulates the eye and the palate. Strips of roasted yellow peppers are interlaced with anchovies, sprinkled with capers and minced hard-boiled egg yolk, and drizzled with good olive oil for a dazzlingly pretty antipasto that packs a lot of flavor.

3 *yellow peppers*

1 2-*ounce can anchovies in olive oil, drained*

2 *tablespoons capers*

3 *hard-boiled egg yolks*

3 *tablespoons extra-virgin olive oil*

2 *tablespoons chopped Italian parsley*

Roast the peppers over a gas flame or under the broiler. Peel and seed them, and remove the white membranes. Cut peppers into julienne strips. Finely chop the egg yolks.

Arrange the peppers and anchovies in a lattice pattern on a serving platter. Sprinkle with the capers and egg yolks. Drizzle the olive oil over the top and sprinkle with chopped parsley.

Melanzane con Cipolla

Grilled Eggplant with Sweet Onion

Serves 4 to 6 as an appetizer

This eggplant dish is at its best when made with fresh red onions or a sweet variety such as Vidalia or Texas onions. The pungent flavor of the grilled onion complements the mild, soft flesh of the eggplant. Although you can make this dish ahead of time and refrigerate it, we recommend preparing it the day you intend to serve it. You can let it sit all day in a cool spot out of the sun, and it will be more succulent for having avoided a stay in the refrigerator.

1 *large glossy, unblemished eggplant*

1 *sweet red or white onion, peeled*

Extra-virgin olive oil

Salt to taste

2 *garlic cloves, peeled and thinly sliced*

Red chile pepper flakes

1 *bunch fresh oregano leaves or 1 teaspoon dried oregano to taste*

Red wine vinegar

Cut off and discard root and blossom ends of the eggplant. Cut eggplant into crosswise slices, approximately ⅜ inch to ½ inch thick. Set aside. Cut the onion crosswise into ¼-inch-thick slices. Heat an outdoor grill or ridged stovetop griddle until it is very hot. Lightly brush the eggplant and onion slices with olive oil. Place the slices on the grill, oiled side down, in one layer. Brush the sides facing up with additional oil. Cook until grill marks are clearly visible and the vegetables are beginning to soften. Turn the

(Continued)

eggplant and onion slices and continue cooking until they are just soft, yet not burned. When eggplant and onion slices are done, remove them from the grill and set aside separately. Continue grilling vegetables until all are cooked.

Use a serving platter for marinating the vegetables. Make a layer of half the eggplant on the platter and lightly salt to taste. Place 1 thin slice of garlic on each slice of eggplant. Sprinkle red chile pepper flakes and oregano to taste over the eggplant. Use dried oregano sparingly as a little goes a long way. Drizzle the vinegar and olive oil lightly over the eggplant. Top the layer of eggplant with half the grilled onion slices. Add the condiments just as you did on the eggplant layer, finishing with the vinegar and oil. Make a second layer of eggplant slices and another of onion slices, sprinkling each layer with the herbs and oil and vinegar. Set aside at room temperature to marinate for at least 1 hour.

Pomodori Fritti

Polenta-Encrusted Tomato Slices

Serves 4 to 6

A hot version of the classic summertime Italian salad of tomato and basil. When you use good garden-fresh tomatoes, the gentle frying brings out all their meaty goodness. The balsamic vinegar adds a sweet touch that nicely balances the acidity of the tomatoes, and the polenta imparts a pleasing heartiness. This dish with its umber-gold coating of polenta, the red of the tomato peeking through, and simple yet effective presentation typifies *cucina rustica.*

4–6 *red, ripe, yet still firm tomatoes*

½ *cup coarse polenta or yellow cornmeal*

Coarse salt and freshly ground black pepper to taste

¼ *cup extra-virgin olive oil*

Balsamic vinegar

10 *fresh basil leaves*

Cut a thin slice from the stem end of each tomato and discard. Cut tomatoes into ½-inch-thick slices. Place the cornmeal in a shallow bowl or plate and add salt and pepper to taste. Start heating the olive oil in a large, heavy skillet. Meanwhile, lightly dredge the tomato slices in the seasoned cornmeal. When the oil is very hot, carefully place the tomato slices in the skillet, being careful not to crowd them. Every minute or so gently nudge the tomato slices with a spatula to prevent them from sticking. If the pan is hot enough, the tomato slices will be easy to turn over as soon as the cornmeal coating is properly cooked. It should be nice and crunchy. Turn over the slices and fry them on the other side. Immediately remove the

(Continued)

tomato slices from the skillet, and arrange them on a serving platter. Drizzle some of the balsamic vinegar over the tomatoes. Stack the basil leaves and roll them up. Holding the basil roll, carefully cut it crosswise into thin strips. Sprinkle the julienned basil over the tomatoes. Serve immediately.

Fiori di Zucca Ripieni

Baked Stuffed Zucchini Flowers with Tomato Sauce

Serves 4 to 6 as an appetizer

This recipe seems long, but it's worth the time it takes to prepare. Italians confront the prodigiously producing zucchini plant by using the flowers ingeniously and to great effect in cooking. They are most often served in frittate or simply dipped in a flour-water *pastella* (batter) and deep-fried in olive oil. In this recipe the flowers are stuffed with finely chopped zucchini, herbs, and Parmesan cheese. They are then baked and served with a fresh tomato sauce. Elegant and beautiful.

FOR THE SAUCE:

¼ *cup extra-virgin olive oil*

2–3 *garlic cloves, peeled and minced*

12 *ripe Roma or 6 large, round tomatoes, peeled, seeded, and chopped*

6–8 *fresh basil leaves*

Salt to taste

Pinch of red chile pepper flakes

Heat the olive oil in a medium-sized skillet over moderate heat. Add the garlic and cook until it gives off its characteristic aroma. Add the tomatoes and cook over moderate heat, stirring frequently, until they break down and give off their juice. Add the basil leaves, salt to taste, and pinch of red chile pepper flakes. Continue cooking the tomatoes over moderate heat until the pulp has completely broken down and the juices have thickened into a sauce. Set the sauce aside to cool to room temperature while you prepare the zucchini flowers.

FOR THE ZUCCHINI
FLOWERS:

½ cup extra-virgin olive oil, divided

4 small, firm zucchini, ends trimmed, cut into very fine dice

2–3 garlic cloves, peeled and minced

12 fresh basil leaves, cut into julienne, divided

Small handful coarsely chopped Italian parsley

5–6 fresh mint leaves, finely chopped

1 egg, beaten

½ cup bread crumbs

¼ cup grated Parmesan cheese

Salt and freshly ground black pepper to taste

25 large, firm zucchini flowers

2 cups light chicken broth or water

Heat ¼ cup of the olive oil in a large skillet. Add the zucchini and cook over moderate heat until tender. Remove from the heat and stir in the garlic, half the basil, the parsley, and the mint. Let cool to room temperature. Add the beaten egg, bread crumbs, Parmesan cheese, and salt and pepper to taste. Mix well and adjust seasoning. If mixture seems too watery, add more bread crumbs, but mixture should not be too stiff.

Remove the pistils from inside the zucchini flowers, taking care not to tear the tender petals. Gently fill each flower with 1 to 2 teaspoonfuls of zucchini stuffing, the amount depending on the size of the flower. Lay the

(Continued)

stuffed flowers side by side in a small baking dish. Pour the chicken broth or water and remaining olive oil over the stuffed flowers. Lightly salt and pepper them, and cover with aluminum foil. Place the covered baking dish in a preheated 350° oven for approximately 15 minutes. The flowers should have swelled slightly and be a little firm to the touch. Remove the flowers from the oven and let cool until tepid.

To serve, coat the bottom of a large platter with the tomato sauce. Arrange the zucchini flowers in a random fashion over the sauce. Garnish with the remaining julienne of basil.

Marinated Vegetables

In Italy there is a strong tradition of preserving vegetables in olive oil or vinegar to make use of abundant seasonal produce. Kitchen shelves are lined with colorful jars of eggplant preserved in vinegar, red and yellow peppers preserved in oil, and mixed vegetables in vinegar, with fresh herbs, garlic, peppercorns, and tomato as seasonings. They are essential components in antipasti. They also complement boiled beef and chicken, add a jolt of flavor to sandwiches, and are good on their own with bread and fresh cheeses.

The three recipes we offer are in this tradition, although no canning is required. Verdura Mista in Marinata e Tonno—vegetables marinated in tomato, oil and vinegar, and enriched with tuna—is the authentic version of the antipasti in little jars sold in markets, and it can be eaten right away or kept for up to a week refrigerated. It makes a colorful, healthy lunch, served with plenty of bread. The next recipe—a mixture of baby artichokes, mushrooms, small peeled onions, and black olives in olive oil, lemon, and herbs—must marinate for several days in lemon and herbs. It keeps for about a week. Verdura all'Olio e Limone goes exceptionally well with a platter of sliced prosciutto, but is just as satisfying alone, again with good bread. Radicchio sott'Aceto is elegant, tart, and acidic, a perfect accompaniment to boiled meats, and lasts for months preserved in vinegar.

Verdura Mista in Marinata e Tonna

Marinated Mixed Vegetables and Tuna

Serves 6

We love to serve this antipasto on a big earthenware platter with chunks of bread at the table. What a perfect way to start an al fresco lunch, under a big shady tree on a hot summery afternoon. Feel free to use your own combination of vegetables, but remember to stagger the addition of vegetables according to the cooking time each one requires. This antipasto lasts for days refrigerated, but should always be returned to room temperature before being served.

14 *pearl or small white boiling onions*

1 *yellow bell pepper*

3 *small zucchini, about ½ pound*

2 *tender carrots*

2 *celery stalks*

¼ *pound tender green beans*

¼ *pound mushrooms*

2½ *pounds tomatoes*

¼ *cup vinegar*

5 *tablespoons extra-virgin olive oil*

1 *teaspoon sugar*

Salt and freshly ground black pepper to taste

6 *small fresh sage leaves*

8 *small fresh basil leaves*

Pinch of nutmeg

2 *tablespoons capers*

12 *cornichons, sliced lengthwise*

2 *6½-ounce cans solid tuna packed in oil or water*

½ *cup black olives in brine, pitted*

Blanch the onions in boiling water and peel them. Cut the pepper in half lengthwise. Remove the seeds and membranes. Cut pepper into ½-inch strips. Trim the ends of the zucchini and cut into ½-inch coins. Peel carrots and cut into ¼-inch coins. Trim the celery and remove the strings. Slice celery into ½-inch pieces. Trim the ends of the green beans and cut into 2-inch lengths. Wipe the mushrooms with a damp cloth. If mushrooms are large, cut in half. Peel and seed the tomatoes. In a food processor or blender, process tomatoes until they have a fine texture, but before they become completely smooth.

Put the tomato puree into a medium-sized braising pan. Add the vinegar, olive oil, and sugar, and season with salt and pepper to taste. Add the onions and carrots first, since they require the longest cooking time. If the green beans are less than very tender, add them now. Cook for 15 minutes over medium-high heat with the lid partially on. Stir mixture occasionally. Add the remaining vegetables, including the green beans if they are tender, herbs, a pinch of nutmeg, and cook for 5 minutes with the lid off. Add the capers and cornichons, and stir to combine. If the tomato sauce is still very runny, lift out the vegetables and place them in a bowl. Continue cooking the sauce until it thickens.

Drain off any water that has accumulated in the bowl holding the vegetables and stir in the tomato sauce. Let cool to room temperature. Drain the tuna, and very carefully combine with the vegetable mixture. Try to keep the tuna in fairly large pieces. Place the contents of the bowl on a platter and garnish with the olives.

Verdura all'Olio e Limone

Vegetables Marinated in
Oil and Lemon

Serves 6

An elegant mix of tender artichokes, mushrooms, and small onions flavored with lemon and thyme. It takes a few days for the lemon and thyme to permeate the vegetables, but it is well worth the wait.

2 *pounds baby artichokes, trimmed*

1 *pound small mushrooms, wiped with a damp towel, stems trimmed*

½ *pound pearl onions, peeled*

Coarse salt

3 *cups water*

Juice of 3 lemons

½ *cup extra-virgin olive oil, plus additional for drizzling*

A few sprigs of fresh thyme and Italian parsley

4 *bay leaves*

1 *celery stalk, cut in half*

Black peppercorns

Small handful oil-cured black olives

Cook separately the artichokes, mushrooms, and onions in boiling salted water until tender but crisp. For the marinade, bring to a boil 3 cups of water, the lemon juice, olive oil, herbs, celery, and peppercorns. Simmer for about 20 minutes. Place the cooked vegetables and olives in a glass jar or deep bowl. Pour the hot marinade over vegetables. Let cool. Cover and refrigerate for several days. Before serving, bring back to room temperature. Lift the vegetables out of the marinade and adjust seasonings. Drizzle vegetables with a little olive oil and serve with good bread.

Radicchio sott'Aceto

P i c k l e d   R a d i c c h i o

Makes 1 quart

It is fascinating to watch the brilliant magenta slowly seep out of the radicchio as it blanches, leaving it a beautifully subtle silver-violet and turning the vinegar nearly hot pink. The piquant tart-bitter taste of pickled radicchio makes a good accompaniment to a bollito misto or any simple roast meat.

12 *heads radicchio, cut in half lengthwise*

Coarse salt to taste

3 *tablespoons sugar*

2 *bay leaves*

2 *sprigs fresh rosemary, divided*

2 *sprigs fresh thyme, divided*

5 *peppercorns*

¼ *cup extra-virgin olive oil*

1 *quart white wine vinegar, divided*

Wash the radicchio carefully, removing any loose, discolored, or limp outer leaves. Discard any heads that are soft and black in the center. Fill a stockpot with water and add salt, sugar, bay leaves, 1 sprig each of rosemary and thyme, peppercorns, olive oil, and 1 cup of the vinegar. Bring to a full rolling boil. Blanch the radicchio in the boiling water for 1 minute. Drain quickly and let dry on a clean dish towel until cool. The radicchio will have changed color to a silvery lavender. Place the completely cool blanched radicchio in a sterilized Mason jar or other glass container with a tight seal. Cover the radicchio with the remaining vinegar. Add the remaining herbs for decoration. Seal the jar tightly, and let the radicchio mellow in a cool dark place for a minimum of 2 weeks.

Sarde al Finocchio

Sardines with Fennel

Serves 4 to 6

This dish takes about 5 minutes to prepare. Good-quality firm, fresh sardines are difficult to come by in the United States, so we often use the canned variety. Sardines have a rich, meaty taste that is especially satisfying; however, this antipasto can also become the main course of a light lunch accompanied by cold beer or a crisp white wine, and followed by a dessert of fresh figs. We love the unusual colors of this dish—the silvery flashes of sardine peeking through the covering of thinly sliced white fennel.

1 *fennel bulb*	*Pinch of red chile peppers flakes*
2 *cans high-quality sardines, packed in olive oil*	*Olio Santo (see page 71) or extra-virgin olive oil*
2 *sprigs fresh oregano, leaves only*	1 *lemon, cut in half*

Carefully wash the fennel bulb, remove any tough, fibrous outer layers, if necessary, and cut in half lengthwise. Slice each section crosswise into thin slices. Set aside. Drain the sardines. Remove them carefully from the can so they remain intact and place them on a small terracotta or other colorful serving plate. Place a layer of fennel slices over the sardines, covering them completely. Scatter the whole oregano leaves over the fennel and sprinkle on the red pepper flakes. Dress the sardines and fennel by generously drizzling first with Olio Santo or extra-virgin olive oil, and squeeze lemon juice over all. Serve with good crusty bread.

Olio Santo

H o l y   O i l

This highly flavored oil with a spicy bite is very easy to make. Once the prepared oil has properly steeped, it can be paired with roasted meats or grilled fish and drizzled on everything from simple grilled vegetables, to bruschetta, to bean soups.

1 *liter bottle extra-virgin*
   olive oil

¼ *cup red chile pepper flakes*

5–10 *bay leaves*

2 *large sprigs fresh rosemary*

Open the bottle of olive oil, carefully removing the screwtop and the stopper, being careful to save both. Using a funnel, add the red chile pepper flakes to the oil. Thread the rosemary and the bay leaves onto 2 bamboo skewers. Carefully place the herbal skewers into the bottle, making sure that the herbs are completely submerged in the oil. This will prevent mold. Replace the stopper and the screwtop. Set bottle in a cool dark spot for a minimum of 1 month.

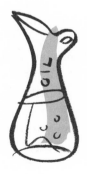

Antipasto Ricco

Rich Antipasto

Serves 6

A beautiful Sicilian antipasto garnished with deep scarlet beets, glossy black olives, and bright white and deep yellow hard-cooked eggs, Antipasto Ricco belongs in the repertoire of composed dishes found in each region of Italy. Although Italian food is generally characterized by simplicity, there are a few dishes where the Italian love for the baroque is given free rein. In the window of any *gastronomia* in Italy you will see at least one composed dish, decorated with swirls of mayonnaise forming delicate, intricate patterns. These antipasti are beautiful to behold, and because they are served cold, they do not suffer from extra time spent in decorating them. For a creative touch, put extra mayonnaise in a pastry tube with a fine tip and pipe a lacy design over the surface. However, the dish is beautiful just as it is, in its simpler form. A great addition to a buffet.

1 *bunch tender beets, all about the same size*

1½ *pounds boiling potatoes, all about the same size*

3 *tablespoons extra-virgin olive oil*

2 *tablespoons red wine vinegar*

Salt to taste

¼ *cup peas, cooked and refreshed under cold water*

3 *tablespoons chopped cornichons*

1 *heaping tablespoon capers*

1 *6½-ounce can solid tuna, packed in oil or water, drained*

½ *cup oil-cured black olives, pitted and cut in half, plus additional olives for garnish*

1 *recipe Maionese al Limone (see page 76)*

1 *tablespoon chopped Italian parsley*

3 *hard-cooked eggs, quartered lengthwise*

Lemon wedges

Trim the stems of the beets. Place in a medium-sized saucepan and cover with water. Bring to a boil and cook until tender but firm. Drain and let cool. When the beets are cool enough to handle, peel and slice them. Meanwhile, boil the potatoes in salted water to cover. Drain the potatoes when tender but firm. When they are cool enough to handle, peel and cut them into ½-inch dice. Toss the potatoes in the olive oil and vinegar, and season with salt to taste. Add the peas, cornichons, capers, tuna, and black olives, and mix gently with enough mayonnaise to hold the mixture together. Season again with salt if necessary. Mound the mixture in the center of a platter, sprinkle with chopped parsley, and garnish with the sliced beets, quartered eggs, and additional black olives. Garnish with lemon wedges.

Antipasto alla Casalinga

Antipasto Housewife Style

Serves 6

This recipe from the venerable Italian chef Luigi Carnacina has been titled by the maestro himself. Roasted green peppers are combined with sardines in olive oil, slices of slightly underripe, tart tomato, and little rings of white onion. Summery tasting and casual, this dish evokes thoughts of vacations and lazy-day eating.

3 *green peppers*

3 *medium, slightly green tomatoes*

1 *very small onion*

2 *cans sardines in olive oil, drained*

¼ *cup extra-virgin olive oil*

3 *tablespoons red wine vinegar*

Salt and freshly ground black pepper to taste

Roast the peppers over a gas flame or under the broiler. Peel and seed them, and remove the white membranes. Cut peppers into strips. Cut the tomatoes into wedges. Slice the onion into small rings.

Arrange the peppers, tomatoes, and sardines on a serving dish. Distribute the onion rings over the top. Sprinkle with the olive oil and vinegar, and season with salt and pepper to taste.

Uova Sode Ripiene Estive

Summery Stuffed Hard-Cooked Eggs

Serves 6

These stuffed eggs are just right to serve during the summer, with a filling of egg yolk, fresh tomato, capers, and anchovy, all bound with lemony mayonnaise and topped with fresh basil.

Hard-cooked eggs—the whites serving as containers, the yolks mashed and flavored—can be filled with all sorts of savory ingredients. The eggs should be cooked only until the yolks are firm, golden, and moist. Overcooking robs yolks of their flavor and creamy texture, and turns whites to rubber.

6 *eggs*

2-3 *Roma tomatoes, cut into small dice*

6 *anchovies, coarsely chopped*

1 *tablespoon capers*

1 *recipe Maionese al Limone (see page 76)*

Salt and freshly ground black pepper to taste

3-4 *large, fresh basil leaves*

Cook the eggs for about 10 minutes in simmering water to cover. Drain and refresh under cold running water. Peel the eggs and cut them lengthwise. Carefully remove the yolks without tearing the whites and place in a small bowl. Set aside the whites.

To the yolks add the tomatoes, anchovies, capers, and enough mayonnaise to bind the mixture lightly. Season with salt and pepper to taste. Carefully mound the mixture into the egg whites. Tear the basil leaves into small fragments and scatter over the tops of the stuffed eggs.

Maionese al Limone

Lemony Mayonnaise

Makes approximately 1 cup

Fresh, homemade mayonnaise is a real treat. Although legions of mayonnaise haters exist, much of that is due to the fact that most mayonnaise consumed in the United States comes in glass jars containing an industrialized product of inferior quality. Mayonnaise that is made of fresh eggs and good olive oil, seasoned with lemon juice or vinegar and salt, is an important ingredient in many composed salads (see Antipasto Ricco, page 72, or Insalata di Verdura e Pollo al Maionese, page 100). We give a blender version here, using the whole egg, which produces a consistency that is slightly lighter than mayonnaise made only with yolk.

1 *egg, at room temperature*	*¾ cup olive oil*
¼ teaspoon salt	*Juice of ½ lemon*

Combine the egg, salt, and a few tablespoons of the olive oil in a blender. Blend until the mixture is light yellow. With the blender running slowly, add the remaining oil in a thin stream. Blend until oil is incorporated, stopping when it is no longer being absorbed. Continue adding oil in a slow, thin stream until mayonnaise thickens. Add lemon juice to taste, blending briefly. Taste and adjust seasonings. Transfer to a small bowl. Cover tightly with plastic wrap and refrigerate.

Frittate

Frittate are made of beaten eggs combined with meats, vegetables, cheeses, and herbs. A frittata resembles a thick pancake. This distinguishes it from the French omelet, which is rolled and stuffed. In Italy frittate are most often served as antipasti or as the main dish of a light meal. They can be sliced into small squares or diamonds to form part of an antipasto plate or, cut into larger wedges, they can be served with a small salad to create a light summer dinner. Frittate are great for impromptu entertaining. Even when the cupboard is bare, with a few eggs, a small handful of parsley, and a tiny chunk of Parmesan cheese, you can make a delicious and satisfying dish.

When preparing frittate, keep in mind that eggs have a real affinity for peas, artichokes, spinach, zucchini, and other green vegetables that are sweet or mild. The best cheeses to use are lean and fresh and include ricotta and mozzarella. Sweet herbs such as basil, parsley, and mint complement the delicate flavor of most frittate. A fresh tomato sauce goes well with a slice of frittata when served for brunch, lunch, or a light supper.

Most supermarket eggs are terribly disappointing in terms of flavor, color, and texture. Find a source for fresh, fertile eggs so you can experience the pleasure of eating the real thing, not its pale shadow. The golden, glowing yolk and full-bodied white of a farm egg will make an infinitely better-tasting and more beautiful frittata than will a market-variety egg.

Frittata ai Porri

Frittata with Leeks

Serves 4 to 6

Leeks and pancetta are slowly cooked until tender, then they are combined with beaten eggs and Parmesan cheese and cooked until golden.

3–4 *tender leeks*

3 *tablespoons extra-virgin olive oil*

3 *slices pancetta, diced*

Salt and freshly ground black pepper to taste

6–8 *eggs*

¼ *cup grated Parmesan cheese*

2 *tablespoons extra-virgin olive oil*

Wash the leeks and cut into rings. Soak in a generous amount of cold water. Lift the leeks out of the water and rinse well under cold running water. Let drain.

Place the olive oil and pancetta in a medium-sized sauté pan and cook over low heat for about 5 minutes, or until pancetta begins to render its fat. Add the leeks and salt and pepper to taste. Cook over low heat, stirring occasionally, until leeks are very tender, about 20 to 30 minutes. Let cool.

Lightly beat the eggs. Add the leeks and Parmesan cheese and salt and pepper to taste. Heat the 2 tablespoons of olive oil in a small, nonstick, ovenproof sauté pan. Swirl the oil in the pan to coat all sides. Add the egg mixture and lower the heat. Cook slowly, stirring frequently, until the eggs have formed small curds and the frittata is firm except for the top. To cook the top, place the pan under a hot broiler or into a preheated 400° oven until the frittata browns lightly. Remove the pan from the broiler or oven. Let cool for 1 to 2 minutes. Place a plate over the top of the pan and invert the frittata onto it. Serve the frittata at room temperature, cut into wedges.

Frittata alla Pizzaiola

Pizza Frittata

Serves 4 to 6

This pizza topping on a frittata base is fun to serve as well as great tasting.

6–8 eggs

Salt to taste

2 tablespoons unsalted butter

5 ounces fresh mozzarella, sliced

4 Roma tomatoes, peeled, seeded, and diced

1 tablespoon chopped Italian parsley

1 teaspoon dried oregano

4 anchovy fillets, chopped

Freshly ground black pepper to taste

Break the eggs into a mixing bowl and beat lightly with a fork. Season with salt to taste. Beat until well amalgamated.

Melt the butter in a 10-inch ovenproof skillet, preferably one with a non-

(Continued)

stick surface. When the butter is hot, add the egg mixture. Lower the heat and with a fork gently break up mixture into soft curds. Continue stirring until frittata begins to hold together. This allows the eggs to cook evenly and prevents the bottom part from overcooking. When the eggs have set but are still slightly runny on top, arrange the mozzarella, tomatoes, herbs, and anchovies over the top. Place the skillet under the broiler and cook until eggs are set and the cheese is melted. Let sit for 1 to 2 minutes. Slide out of pan with the mozzarella and tomato side facing up and place on a platter. Grind black pepper over the frittata.

Frittata Affogata

Frittata Drowned in Tomato, Peas, and Prosciutto Sauce

Serves 4 to 6

A frittata made with herbs, vegetables, or bits of pancetta or prosciutto is a nourishing light meal. Here the frittata is "drowned" in a bright sauce of tomato, peas, and prosciutto.

FOR THE SAUCE:

¼ cup extra-virgin olive oil

2 garlic cloves, finely chopped

1 slice prosciutto, cut into thin strips

1 pound Roma tomatoes, peeled, seeded, and chopped

Salt and freshly ground black pepper to taste

½ cup tender peas, fresh or frozen

FOR THE FRITTATA:

6–8 eggs

¼ cup grated Parmesan cheese

8 fresh basil leaves, coarsely chopped or torn

Salt and freshly ground black pepper to taste

2 tablespoons extra-virgin olive oil

Prepare the sauce by placing the olive oil, garlic, and prosciutto in a medium-sized sauté pan. Warm over low heat until the garlic releases its perfume and prosciutto changes color, approximately 2 to 3 minutes. Add the tomatoes and salt and pepper to taste. Raise the heat to medium, and cook until the tomatoes break down and begin to form a sauce, about 10 minutes. If using fresh peas, add them at the same time as the tomatoes; if peas are frozen, add them a few minutes before the sauce is ready.

To prepare the frittata, lightly beat the eggs in a bowl with the Parmesan cheese, basil, and salt and pepper to taste. Heat the olive oil in a small, nonstick ovenproof skillet. Swirl the oil in the skillet to coat bottom and sides. Add the egg mixture and lower the heat. Cook slowly, stirring frequently, until the eggs have formed small curds and the frittata is firm but the top is still slightly runny. To cook the top, place the skillet under a hot broiler or in a preheated 400° oven until the frittata browns lightly. Remove the skillet from the broiler or oven. Let cool for 1 to 2 minutes. Place a plate over the top of the pan and invert the frittata onto it. Serve the frittata cut into wedges with a ribbon of tomato sauce poured over the top and some pooled around the sides.

Insalate

Salads

This chapter features two main categories of salads. First are small salads which include those meant to be served as a refresher to a traditional meal and usually begin or end a meal. The second category contains a large selection of salads to serve for luncheon or during summertime as savory main dishes when appetites shy away from hot, heavier meals.

All salads require care in preparation. Take extra time to select a tender bunch of arugula or a crisp red tomato. Make fresh mayonnaise using tart, fragrant lemon juice. Find the freshest herbs. Pause for a moment to inhale the rich bouquet of the vinegar and the warm fruity aroma of the olive oil. Prepare salads lovingly and with care, and they will reward you every time with freshness, fragrance, and beauty.

Small Salads

In Italy there are four basic small salads—Insalata Verde, Insalata Mista, Insalata di Campo, and Insalata di Pomodoro. There are also other salads which fit in this category and use a wider range of ingredients, for example, green beans, artichokes, and oranges.

Insalata Verde is composed of lettuces only. Insalata Mista contains lettuces as well as raw vegetables like tomatoes, carrots, and fennel, depending on the season. Insalata di Campo, originally composed of field greens that grew wild, is made of varied lettuces of assertive flavor. Insalata di Pomodoro is simply sliced tomatoes that are sometimes sprinkled with chopped herbs. The condiments go directly on all these salads without being combined and emulsified by shaking or stirring. There should be just enough dressing to lightly coat the ingredients. The amounts of extra-virgin olive oil, vinegar, lemon, salt, and pepper vary from one salad to the next, depending on the mix of flavors and textures. Dressing salads is a very fluid and intuitive process that is acquired through experience, and no fixed ratio can take its place.

Traditionally served after the main course, small salads are meant to refresh and cleanse the palate. In addition, any of these salads could precede the main course.

Insalata Verde

Green Salad

Serves 4

Insalata Verde usually consists of a single green such as romaine or Boston lettuce. It is always dressed with the best olive oil, imported Italian red wine vinegar or lemon juice, good salt, and sometimes freshly ground black pepper. The amounts of oil and vinegar or lemon juice will vary according to the taste and texture of the greens. Boston lettuce, for example, is sweet and soft, and requires just a touch of vinegar. Dressing a salad properly becomes an intuitive process; you season and taste until the desired balance is achieved. This salad can precede the main course or follow it.

1 *head tender romaine or 2 heads Boston lettuce*

Salt to taste

Extra-virgin olive oil

Lemon juice

Freshly ground black pepper (optional)

Detach the leaves from the romaine or Boston lettuce. Discard any leaves that are bruised or yellowed. Wash the lettuce under cold running water and dry well. Tear the leaves into bite-sized pieces. Place in a salad bowl. Sprinkle with salt to taste and drizzle with olive oil and lemon juice. If desired, grind a little black pepper over the top. Toss lettuce and adjust the seasonings.

Insalata Mista

Mixed Salad

Serves 4

Insalata Mista combines lettuces and raw vegetables. In Italy the lettuce is usually tender romaine. Raw vegetables can include tomatoes, carrots, cucumbers, radishes, fennel, and red, yellow, or green sweet peppers. Fresh herbs such as basil or parsley may be added, but never dried herbs. Sweet red onions or tender green onions are sometimes included. Keep the mix restrained, for too many ingredients would take away from this salad's simplicity and freshness. Balance textures—soft, tender, juicy, crisp—and flavors—sweet, mild, strong, and hot. Insalata Mista is dressed with the best olive oil, red wine vinegar or lemon juice, and salt; sometimes freshly ground black pepper is added. The ingredients are then tossed and the seasonings adjusted.

½ head tender romaine

1 crisp, red tomato

1 small carrot, peeled

½ small fennel bulb

4–5 crisp radishes

Salt to taste

Extra-virgin olive oil

Red wine vinegar

Freshly ground black pepper (optional)

Separate the romaine leaves and discard any that are bruised or yellowed. Wash under cold running water and dry well. Tear the leaves into bite-sized pieces and place in a salad bowl. Cut the tomato into small wedges or chunks. Cut the carrot into thin diagonal slices. Slice the fennel into julienne strips. Slice the radishes. Add the tomato, carrot, fennel, and radishes to the lettuce in the bowl. Season with salt. Drizzle with oil and vinegar, and if desired grind black pepper over the top. Toss salad and adjust the seasonings.

Insalata di Campo

Mixed "Wild" Greens

Serves 4

Insalata di Campo was once composed of field greens that grew wild in the Italian countryside. These greens were, in essence, weeds, which is what gave the salad its characteristic flavor. Nowadays it contains specially cultivated greens noted for assertive tastes. The shapes of the leaves are widely varied, the textures range from tender to resistant to the bite, and the flavors range from the peppery bite of arugula to the distinctive bitterness of radicchio and other chicories. The greens are picked when tender and young, and they are dressed with fine extra-virgin olive oil, imported red wine vinegar, salt, and sometimes black pepper. In this recipe, we use only a very rich fruity olive oil and good strong sea salt to dress the greens in order to savor their strong flavors. Select lettuces that have a good, peppery, oaky, slightly bitter, or other pronounced flavor. Many baby-lettuce mixes found in specialty produce markets contain an excellent choice of greens for this salad. Watercress, which is widely available, works well if you can't find other greens. You can serve Insalata di Campo before or after the main course. This recipe can be served with good wines, as it contains no acidic vinegar or lemon juice.

4 *large handfuls tender field lettuces*	*Sea salt*
	Extra-virgin olive oil

Carefully wash the lettuces and dry well. Place in a salad bowl. Dress with salt and olive oil. Toss lettuces and correct seasonings.

Insalata Verde con Prosciutto

Salad of Mixed Greens and Prosciutto

Serves 4

For this salad use an assortment of wild and domestic greens. The average market can yield a varied and interesting mix of greens. Try combining endive's tender white and pale yellow center leaves with romaine lettuce and watercress. If arugula can be found, use it in this salad. There are countless varieties of salad greens available in specialty produce markets as well as those that can be grown in your vegetable garden. When selecting the components for this salad, make sure you include at least one or two slightly bitter and assertive greens. With the addition of thin slivers of prosciutto, the salad becomes a good light first course or main dish.

2 *large handfuls mixed salad greens*

6 *thin slices prosciutto*

¼ *cup extra-virgin olive oil*

2 *tablespoons red wine vinegar*

Salt and freshly ground black pepper to taste

Tear the greens into bite-sized pieces. Slice the prosciutto into thin slivers. Combine greens and prosciutto in a salad bowl. Toss with the olive oil, vinegar, and salt and pepper to taste. Correct seasonings and serve immediately.

*Insalata di Rucola
e Radicchio Invernale*

Wintery Arugula
and Radicchio Salad

Serves 2 as a main-course salad or 4 as a first course

A country salad featuring two popular lettuces that have recently become widely available. The contrasting colors of deep green arugula, magenta radicchio, and white and bright yellow eggs make for a beautiful winter salad. Pancetta adds a savory touch.

2 *slices lean pancetta, ⅛ inch thick*

2–3 *small bunches arugula, cut into julienne, about 4 cups loosely packed*

1 *medium head radicchio, shredded, about 2 cups*

2 *hard-cooked eggs, very coarsely chopped*

¼ *cup extra-virgin olive oil*

¼ *cup red wine vinegar*

Salt and freshly ground black pepper to taste

Cut the pancetta into small strips and cook in a very small sauté pan over low heat until pancetta renders its fat. Place the arugula, radicchio, and eggs in a salad bowl. Add the pancetta and rendered fat to the salad bowl, along with the olive oil, vinegar, and salt and pepper to taste, and toss.

Insalata di Radicchio alla Vicentina

Radicchio Salad from Vicenza

Serves 4 to 6

A wonderful old regional dish with a very modern twist. This simple salad, documented by Anna Gosetti della Salda in *Le Ricette Regionali Italiane*, has its origins in a dish of radicchio dressed with a tepid dressing made of cooked salt pork. We substitute pancetta for the salt pork, and add shallots and a touch of balsamic vinegar.

3–4 *heads radicchio*

3 *ounces pancetta, thinly sliced, cut into rough dice*

⅓ *cup extra-virgin olive oil*

1 *shallot, peeled and minced*

1 *garlic clove, peeled and minced*

4 *tablespoons balsamic vinegar*

5 *fresh basil leaves, julienned*

2 *sprigs fresh thyme, chopped*

Salt and freshly ground black pepper to taste

1 *recipe Crostini (see page 45)*

Carefully wash and dry the radicchio and tear it into bite-sized pieces. Set aside in a serving bowl.

Fry the pancetta in a small skillet over high heat, until half cooked, or until it colors but before it crisps. Add the shallot and garlic, and sauté over high heat for 2–3 minutes. Add the vinegar and cook for 1 minute. Add the fresh herbs and salt and pepper to taste. Off the heat, toss the hot dressing with the radicchio. Serve immediately with Crostini.

Insalata Bianca

All-White Salad

Serves 4 to 6 as a side dish

This salad is a medley of subtle contrasts. Each vegetable has its own shade of white with small color accents—pale green celery, bits of bright red radish peel, fennel and endive in differing shades of white—and all these vegetables share texture, a wonderfully satisfying crunch. An elegant alternative to a lettuce salad. To make this salad a heartier part of a meal, simply add diced fresh Pecorino Romano cheese and/or cooked Arborio rice.

2 *fennel bulbs, tough outer leaves discarded, cut in half lengthwise and thinly sliced crosswise*

2 *celery stalks, thinly sliced crosswise*

2 *Belgian endives, stem ends trimmed, cut lengthwise into julienne*

12 *radishes, ends trimmed and thinly sliced crosswise*

⅓ *cup extra-virgin olive oil*

1-2 *garlic cloves, peeled and put through garlic press*

1 *tablespoon lemon juice*

2 *tablespoons white wine vinegar*

Salt and freshly ground black pepper to taste

½ *cup Parmesan cheese shavings*

Combine all ingredients except the Parmesan cheese in a large bowl and toss well. Serve on a large, brightly colored platter with Parmesan cheese shavings scattered over the salad.

Insalata di Pomodoro

Tomato Salad

Serves 4 to 6

The epitome of simple summer eating. Few vegetables are so strongly connected with a season as tomatoes and warm, languid summer days. If you can find low-acid yellow tomatoes, it's fun to alternate these rich yellow slices with those of deep red, ripe tomatoes. Combine two fresh herbs if possible. If you do not have a source for fresh herbs, you can use dried oregano but do so sparingly. To round out a summer supper, just add a plate of Mozzarella Saporita (see page 50) and simple Bruschetta (see page 39).

4 red, ripe, yet firm tomatoes

Handful coarsely chopped fresh herbs (Italian parsley, basil, oregano)

Coarse salt and freshly ground black pepper to taste

Extra-virgin olive oil to taste

Trim the stem ends of the tomatoes. Cut tomatoes into ½-inch-thick slices and arrange in a circular pattern on a serving dish. Sprinkle with the herbs and salt and pepper to taste. Drizzle with olive oil to taste. Serve immediately.

Insalata di Pomodoro
e Ricotta Salata

Salad of Tomatoes and
Ricotta Salata

Serves 4 to 6

This characteristic tomato salad of southern Italy adds a gutsy assertive note to a simple meal. The combination of strong black olives and salty aged sheep's milk ricotta salata accents the sweetness of the tomatoes.

4–5 *ripe tomatoes, cut into wedges*

¼ *cup Calamata or Moroccan olives*

¼ *pound ricotta salata, crumbled*

¼ *small red or white onion, peeled and thinly sliced (optional)*

Extra-virgin olive oil to taste

Salt and freshly ground black pepper to taste

Gently combine all ingredients in a simple serving bowl.

Insalata di Carciofi

Artichoke Salad

Serves 6

Italians love to eat artichokes raw. The distinctive bitterness of this vegetable is so prized that a few famous aperitifs, such as Campari and Cynar, use the artichoke as a flavoring agent. In our cooked version of the simplest of dishes, thinly sliced, raw artichoke heart salad, the hearts of the artichokes are lightly cooked, thinly sliced, quickly dressed with the finest extra-virgin oil, a bit of lemon juice, salt, pepper, and covered with Parmesan cheese shavings.

6 large artichokes

2 lemons

7 tablespoons extra-virgin olive oil, divided

Salt

Handful chopped Italian parsley

Salt and freshly ground black pepper to taste

½ cup Parmesan cheese shavings

Lemon slices

Trim the artichokes to the hearts, discarding all leaves and the hairy choke. Rub the artichoke hearts as you clean them with the cut side of a lemon to prevent discoloration. If you prepare the artichokes much in advance after rubbing them with lemon, soak them in water mixed with the juice of 1 lemon.

Bring a large saucepan of water to the boil. Add the juice of ½ lemon, 1 tablespoon olive oil, and salt. Cook the artichoke hearts in the boiling water until tender when pierced with a sharp paring knife. Remove the artichoke hearts from the water and let cool.

Slice the artichoke hearts thinly and arrange the slices on individual plates. Sprinkle with lemon juice, olive oil, parsley, and salt and pepper. Scatter Parmesan cheese shavings on top of the artichoke slices. Garnish with lemon slices.

Fagiolini Misti al Prosciutto e Pomodori Piccoli

Salad of Green and Yellow Beans, Prosciutto, and Cherry Tomatoes

Serves 4 to 6

Fresh green beans, wax beans, and tomatoes are a summery treat especially when slivers of prosciutto are tossed into the mix. Good olive oil, red wine vinegar, fresh garlic, and basil complement the flavors. This lovely salad is a great *contorno*, or side dish, for summer's grilled meats and fish.

¾ *pound young green beans*

¾ *pound young wax beans*

3 *slices prosciutto, cut into slivers*

12 *cherry tomatoes, cut in half*

8 *fresh basil leaves, cut into strips*

6 *tablespoons extra-virgin olive oil*

3 *tablespoons red wine vinegar*

1 *small garlic clove, cut into paper-thin slices*

Salt and freshly ground black pepper

Trim the green beans and wax beans. Cook separately in a generous amount of salted boiling water until tender but firm. Drain beans in a colander and refresh under cold running water to stop the cooking. Spread beans on a

(Continued)

clean dish towel to dry. Place in a shallow salad bowl along with the pro-sciutto, cherry tomatoes, and basil.

Drizzle the olive oil and vinegar over the salad. Distribute the garlic slices on top. Add salt and pepper to taste, and toss gently.

Insalata Siciliana

S i c i l i a n   S a l a d

Serves 4 to 6

This Sicilian salad of obvious Moroccan influence has extraordinary color and taste that contrast the sweet juiciness of navel oranges with pungent black olives and the sharp bite of red onion. Perfect and refreshing for a tired summer palate. If you can fine tarocchi, blood oranges, use them for this dish.

4 *navel or blood oranges, peeled, all pith removed, and sliced*

1 *very small or ½ large red onion, peeled and cut crosswise into paper-thin slices*

¼ *cup Moroccan oil-cured olives*

1–2 *fresh red chile peppers, seeded and finely minced, or 1 teaspoon red chile pepper flakes*

Salt to taste

Extra-virgin olive oil

Arrange the orange slices in a circular pattern on a flat serving platter. Scatter the onion slices, olives, and minced chile peppers over the oranges. Season with coarse salt to taste and drizzle olive oil over all.

Main Dish Salads

Main-dish salads are in a category all their own. More complex than the preceding small salads, they can contain such ingredients as seafood, meats, and cooked and raw vegetables. They are sometimes based on rice, pasta, or beans. Olives, anchovies, and capers are called upon to heighten flavors.

A few salads of this kind are bound with mayonnaise and are referred to as composed salads, since they are arranged on a plate rather than being tossed with dressing.

Main-dish salads serve as the focus of a light lunch or dinner, as part of an antipasto, as picnic food, or as part of a buffet, but they are never served in place of a lettuce salad. They are colorful, fresh, sometimes sophisticated, sometimes humble, and use a wide array of ingredients. Although more involved to assemble than small salads, main-dish salads reflect the Italian sense of restraint and simplicity and are never catch-alls for unrelated leftovers.

Insalata di Frize all'Uovo

Baby Frisée with Poached Egg and Pancetta

Serves 6

This delicious salad can be served as a light lunch or brunch dish. The Crostini are perfect for dipping into the warm egg yolk. There is something innately pleasurable when the rich yolk mixes with the vinegar of the salad dressing. We love how the tart dressing goes with the buttery rich egg yolk and the nutty bitter lettuce. We thank Marion Cunningham who, in *The Breakfast Book*, describes the easiest way we've found to poach eggs.

2 *tablespoons extra-virgin olive oil*

4 *thin slices pancetta, diced*

6 *eggs*

6 *bunches baby frisée, stems trimmed, well washed, and dried*

⅓ *cup extra-virgin olive oil*

2 *tablespoons balsamic vinegar*

1 *tablespoon red wine vinegar*

1 *garlic clove, peeled and minced*

1 *shallot, peeled and chopped fine*

Salt and freshly ground black pepper to taste

5 *cups water*

3 *teaspoons cider vinegar*

1 *recipe Crostini (see page 45)*

Place 2 tablespoons of olive oil and pancetta in a small skillet. Cook over medium heat until the pancetta is crisp. With a slotted spoon remove pancetta to paper towels to drain off fat. Set aside.

To make the salad dressing, combine the olive oil, vinegars, garlic, shallot, salt and pepper to taste in a small bowl. Set aside.

To poach the eggs, first bring enough water to cover the unshelled eggs to boil in a small saucepan. Gently lower the eggs into the boiling water. Let them boil only for 30 seconds, then carefully remove them. This preliminary cooking serves to set the whites a bit and makes the eggs much easier to handle.

Bring the 5 cups of water and cider vinegar to a simmer in a deep skillet. Gently crack each egg and open it directly over the simmering water. Let the egg gently slide into the water. Spoon simmering water over the eggs if they are not completely submerged. Remove the skillet from the heat and cover for 4 to 5 minutes. This will give you time to assemble the salad.

To make 6 individual servings, place 1 head of frisée on each plate and spoon the dressing on top. When poached eggs are ready, with a slotted spoon lift them out of the water and onto a kitchen towel to drain. Carefully place the drained eggs on the dressed frisées. Season to taste with additional salt and pepper to taste, and scatter pancetta over the eggs. Garnish each plate with freshly made Crostini. Serve immediately.

Insalata di Pollo e Verdura
al Maionese

Chicken and Vegetable Salad
in Mayonnaise

Serves 6

Similar in spirit to the classic Insalata Russa (see *Cucina Fresca*, page 66), the addition of chicken brings the salad center stage. The quality of the finished dish hinges on freshly made lemon mayonnaise. Serve small portions, as this salad is quite rich.

3 *boned chicken breasts, skin removed*	3 *tablespoons extra-virgin olive oil*
3 *medium boiling potatoes*	1 *tablespoon red wine vinegar*
½ *pound tender wax beans, trimmed*	*Salt to taste*
3 *medium carrots, peeled*	1 *recipe Maionese al Limone (see page 76)*
½ *cup peas, fresh or frozen*	3 *anchovy fillets, finely chopped*
3 *tablespoons capers*	*Assorted tender lettuce leaves*

Cook the chicken breasts in ¼ cup salted water over medium-low heat until they are springy to the touch. Remove chicken from the heat and let cool. Cut into ½-inch dice.

Cover the potatoes with cold water, bring to a boil, and cook until tender but firm. Do not pierce potatoes too much when you check them for doneness, as this causes them to become mushy and to fall apart. Drain potatoes and peel them when cool enough to handle. Cook the wax beans in abundant salted boiling water until tender but crisp. Drain beans and refresh them under cold running water. Drain well on paper towels. Repeat procedure for the carrots. Cut the cooked vegetables into small dice. Cook the peas in a small amount of salted water. (Fresh peas will take longer to cook than frozen, but the time will vary according to the size of the peas.) Drain well.

In a bowl combine the chicken, vegetables, and capers. Season with the olive oil, vinegar, and salt to taste. Mix together the mayonnaise and anchovies, and add to the chicken and vegetables. Toss gently. Serve garnished with lettuce leaves.

Insalata di Pollo ai Peperoni e Pinoli

Chicken Salad with Pepper and Pine Nuts

Serves 4 as a main-dish salad for lunch

A colorful, crunchy salad that is enhanced by the flavors and textures of toasted pine nuts and pickles.

4 *boned chicken breasts, skin removed*

1 *small red pepper*

1 *small yellow pepper*

1 *small green pepper*

⅓ *cup pine nuts*

1 *head romaine lettuce*

6–8 *cornichons*

¼ *cup extra-virgin olive oil*

¼ *cup freshly squeezed lemon juice*

Salt and freshly ground black pepper to taste

In a sauté pan cook the chicken breasts in ¼ cup salted water over medium-low heat until they are springy to the touch, about 10 minutes. Remove from the pan and let cool. Cut into thin slices.

With a vegetable peeler, peel the peppers. Cut peppers in half, remove the cores, seeds, and white membranes, and slice into slender julienne. Toast the pine nuts in a small sauté pan over medium-low heat, stirring frequently, until a light golden brown. Remove the pine nuts from the pan and cool on a plate. Cut the romaine lettuce into julienne strips. Cut the cornichons into julienne strips.

Place the lettuce strips in the bottom of a shallow salad bowl. Add the chicken, peppers, pine nuts, and cornichons. Drizzle with olive oil and lemon juice, add salt and pepper to taste, and toss. Correct seasonings, adding more olive oil or lemon juice if necessary.

Insalata di Pollo e Mozzarella

Chicken and Mozzarella Salad

Serves 4

This salad combines bright, crunchy vegetables with mild mozzarella and tender chicken. Extra-virgin olive oil, mellow red wine vinegar, and fresh basil compose the dressing. Try it without the chicken for a great vegetarian salad.

1 *whole chicken breast, split*

2 *sprigs fresh rosemary*

1 *garlic clove, thinly sliced*

5 *tablespoons extra-virgin olive oil, divided*

Salt and freshly ground black pepper to taste

1 *green pepper*

½ *hothouse cucumber*

1 *large, crisp tomato*

¼ *pound haricots verts or tender green beans*

3 *celery stalks from the heart*

1 *fresh mozzarella, about 8 ounces*

3 *tablespoons red wine vinegar*

5 *large fresh basil leaves*

Under the skin of each ½ chicken breast, insert a sprig of rosemary and a few slivers of garlic. Rub with 1 tablespoon of the olive oil. Season with salt and pepper to taste. Roast in a hot 450° oven for 12 to 15 minutes, or until the juices run clear. Let cool. Remove the skin and bones, and cut chicken into dice.

Peel the green pepper with a vegetable peeler. Remove the seeds and white membranes, and cut into thin strips. Peel the cucumber, cut in half lengthwise, and remove the seeds. Cut cucumber crosswise into slices. Dice

(Continued)

the tomato. Cook the haricots verts or tender green beans in salted boiling water to cover until tender but crisp. Refresh under cold water and drain on paper towels. Slice the celery stalks crosswise and coarsely chop the tender leaves. Cut the mozzarella into dice and drain on paper towels to remove excess moisture.

Assemble chicken, vegetables, and mozzarella in a shallow salad bowl. Add the remaining olive oil, vinegar, and salt and pepper to taste. Tear the basil leaves into fragments and sprinkle over the salad. Taste and correct seasonings.

Insalata d'Estate

Summer Salad

Serves 4 as a light lunch

Italians really enjoy boiled beef and have devised many ways of serving it. Leftover boiled beef often becomes transformed into a salad. In our recipe cubes of cooked beef are combined with tender, new romaine lettuce, green onions, crisp tomatoes, and fragrant basil. The salad is tossed with extra-virgin olive oil and good red wine vinegar and garnished with quartered hard-cooked eggs.

3 *thick green onions, ends trimmed with about 3 inches of green left*

1 *small head garden romaine*

1 *large, crisp tomato*

2 ½ *cups boiled beef, trimmed of all fat, cut into ¾-inch dice*

6–8 *fresh basil leaves*

3 *tablespoons extra-virgin olive oil*

5 *tablespoons red wine vinegar*

Salt and freshly ground black pepper to taste

3 *hard-cooked eggs*

Slice the green onions into rounds about ¾ inch thick. Wash and dry the lettuce well. Tear into bite-sized pieces. Cut the tomato into pieces to match the beef. Place the onions, lettuce, tomato, and beef in a salad bowl. Tear the basil leaves into fragments and sprinkle over the ingredients in the bowl. Add the olive oil, vinegar, and salt and pepper to taste. Toss well. Peel the eggs, cut them into quarters lengthwise, and use them to garnish the salad.

Insalata di Gamberi, Rucola, e Pomodoro

Shrimp, Arugula, and Tomato Salad

Serves 2

In this refreshing salad, sweet shrimp are combined with peppery arugula and crisp, tart tomato streaked with green. We saw this dish being served on the terrace of a Roman seafood restaurant on a warm night several summers ago, while we were feasting on grilled fish, fritto misto, and sweet roasted peppers. The sounds of talking and laughing filled the late night air, yet just beyond the lighted square of tables and the glowing white canopy, the quiet presence of the ancient darkened city could be felt all around us.

½ pound large shrimp

1 large tomato, slightly underripe

3 tablespoons extra-virgin olive oil

3 tablespoons lemon juice

Salt and freshly ground black pepper to taste

About 3 cups loosely packed arugula, cut into chiffonade

Lemon wedges (optional)

Devein the shrimp by making a shallow cut along the curved edge of the shell and removing the black vein. Cook the shrimp in boiling salted water until barely opaque at center, about 3 minutes. Drain and let cool. Remove the shells. Cut the shrimp in half lengthwise. Cut the tomato into coarse chunks measuring about 1 inch by 1 inch. Toss the shrimp and tomato in the olive oil, lemon juice, salt to taste, and plenty of freshly ground pepper. Arrange the arugula on a serving dish. Place the shrimp and tomato mixture and all its juices on the arugula, and garnish with lemon wedges, if desired.

Gamberi in Insalata con Verdura Cruda
Shrimp with Raw Vegetable Salad

Serves 4

Fresh, crisp vegetables and sweet shrimp flavor this simple yet chic summery salad from Venice's Gritti Hotel, whose spectacular setting forms a backdrop for elegant dining.

4 *white celery stalks from the heart, thinly sliced*

A *few crisp radishes, thinly sliced*

½ *green pepper, peeled with a vegetable peeler, thinly sliced*

1 *pound cooked, peeled shrimp*

¼ *cup extra-virgin olive oil*

Salt and freshly ground black pepper to taste

Lemon wedges

Combine the celery, radishes, and green pepper on a platter. Arrange the shrimp on top. Drizzle with the olive oil. Season with salt and pepper to taste. Serve with lemon wedges.

Insalata di Calamari

Squid Salad

Serves 2 to 4

This is a dazzling salad with its rings of white calamari, squares of butter yellow potato, bright strips of red pepper, and shiny black and earth green olives, pickles, and capers. We love the textural interplay of tender squid, creamy potatoes, crunchy slivers of piquant pickle, and crisp red pepper. This salad holds up well so it can be made many hours in advance, even the day before. The flavor actually improves as the salad marinates, which makes it a great addition to the buffet.

1 *pound cleaned squid (see directions for cleaning on page* 295)

Salt

¾ *pound new potatoes*

1 *tablespoon capers*

1 *large red bell pepper, roasted, peeled, and cut into strips, or* 1 *large red bell pepper preserved in vinegar, drained, rinsed, and cut into strips*

2 *small dill pickles, thinly sliced and cut into julienne*

1 *handful (about 10) oil-cured black olives, pitted and cut into quarters*

8 *fresh basil leaves*

¼ *cup extra-virgin olive oil*

6 *tablespoons lemon juice*

Salt and freshly ground black pepper to taste

Cut the squid into ½-inch rings. If the tentacles are large, cut them into smaller pieces. Boil the squid in salted water until tender. Test for tenderness after 15 minutes, and continue to cook until squid is meltingly tender. Drain.

In a separate pan boil the potatoes in water to cover until they are cooked through when pierced. Do not overcook. Potatoes should still be firm and hold their shape. Drain them when they are cool enough to handle, peel, and cut into ½-inch dice. In a serving dish combine squid and potatoes with the capers, red pepper, pickles, and olives. Tear the basil leaves into fragments and add. Dress with the olive oil, lemon juice, and salt and pepper. Marinate for at least 1 hour before serving. At serving time, check seasonings, adding more lemon juice or salt and pepper if needed. If dish is to be marinated longer than 1 hour, refrigerate it and return to room temperature before serving.

Insalata di Mare alla Moda Nostra

Seafood Salad "Our Way"

Serves 4

Italian seafood "salads" are almost a misnomer in that they contain seafood and little else. No lettuce or tomatoes extend this dish, a pure, extravagant expression of the Italian love of seafood. A simple and refreshing salad that tastes of the sea. Make it for a picnic at the beach, or as a prelude to an elaborate seafood dinner. Shrimp and scallops continue to cook as they cool, so remove them from the heat and drain them a few seconds before you anticipate they are done.

1 *pound cleaned squid (see directions for cleaning on page 295)*	¼ *cup small oil-cured black olives*
½ *pound bay scallops*	1 *garlic clove, peeled and crushed*
½ *pound medium shrimp*	6 *small fresh basil leaves*
7 *tablespoons extra-virgin olive oil*	*Salt and freshly ground black pepper to taste*
6 *tablespoons lemon juice*	

Cut the squid sac into rings. Trim the tentacles, and if they are very large cut them in half. Cook the rings and tentacles in a pot of boiling salted water until tender. Check for tenderness after 15 minutes, although it may take as long as 30 minutes. Transfer squid to a colander, then to a medium-sized serving bowl.

Meanwhile, cook the scallops in another pot of boiling salted water for about 2 minutes. Transfer to a colander. When cool, cut the scallops in half horizontally and add to the bowl containing the squid. Devein the shrimp by making a shallow cut along the curved edge of the shell and rinsing away the black vein. Cook in boiling salted water for 2 minutes. Transfer to a colander. When cool, remove the shells and cut each shrimp into 3 pieces. Add to the bowl. Toss the seafood in the olive oil, lemon juice, olives, garlic, and basil, and season with salt and pepper to taste. Best eaten after 1 to 2 hours of marination.

Insalata Tagliata con Tonno

C h o p p e d   G r e e n s   w i t h   T u n a   a n d   G a r l i c

Serves 4

The combination of tart escarole, crunchy romaine, and rich tuna makes a refreshing and tasty salad. Chopping the greens reduces their volume and makes the escarole more tender. If you desire, garnish the salad with garlicky Crostini.

½ head escarole with a creamy white and pale yellow center

½ head romaine

2 6½-ounce cans solid tuna, packed in oil or water

6 tablespoons extra-virgin olive oil

1 clove garlic, finely minced

¼ cup red wine vinegar

Salt and freshly ground black pepper to taste

1 recipe Crostini (see page 45)

Wash the escarole and romaine and dry them well. Cut lettuces into thin strips. Drain the tuna. In the bottom of a salad bowl combine the oil, garlic, and vinegar. Stir to blend. Add the chopped greens, tuna, and salt and freshly ground pepper to taste. Toss well. Serve with Crostini, if desired.

Insalata di Tonno Fresco e Ceci

F r e s h   T u n a   a n d   C h i c k - p e a   S a l a d

Serves 2 as a main-dish salad

This satisfying, fresh-tasting dish features tuna, crisp red bell pepper, celery, and creamy-fleshed, pale gold chick-peas. If fresh tuna is not available, substitute canned tuna, which is often used in salads in Italy.

¾ *pound fresh tuna, sliced 1 inch thick*

Salt

5 *tablespoons extra-virgin olive oil, divided*

1 *red bell pepper*

1 *small onion*

3 *tender celery stalks with leaves*

Salt and freshly ground black pepper to taste

1½ *cups cooked chick-peas, drained*

3 *tablespoons red wine vinegar*

Handful fresh basil leaves, chopped

Cook the tuna in a sauté pan in ¼ cup salted water over medium heat for about 4 to 5 minutes, or until cooked but still slightly pink at the center. Remove the tuna from the pan, drizzle with 1 tablespoon of olive oil, and let cool.

Peel the red bell pepper with a vegetable peeler and cut into julienne. Thinly slice the onion. Cut the celery stalk crosswise and coarsely chop the leaves.

Break up the tuna into chunks, adding salt and pepper to taste. Place in a shallow salad bowl along with the red bell pepper, onion, celery and leaves, and chick-peas. Add the remaining olive oil, the vinegar, and more freshly ground pepper to taste. Gently toss. Correct seasonings, adding more oil and vinegar if necessary. Add the basil leaves and toss again. If making the dish in advance, do not add the basil until immediately before you serve the salad.

Insalata di Riso Festiva

Festive Rice Salad

Serves 4 as a main-dish salad or 6 as a first course

Savory diced ham, sweet vegetables, and piquant pickled onions and capers make a lively, wildly colorful rice salad that is perfect for a summer light lunch or first course.

1½ cups raw rice, Arborio or long grain

6 tablespoons extra-virgin olive oil, divided

1 small yellow pepper

1 small red pepper

1 medium carrot

¼ pound Black Forest ham, sliced ¼ inch thick

6 pickled onions

Small handful fresh basil leaves

2 tablespoons capers

¼ cup red wine vinegar

Salt and freshly ground black pepper to taste

Cook the rice in abundant salted boiling water until al dente. Drain well and place on a platter. Drizzle with 2 tablespoons of the olive oil and toss.

Using a vegetable peeler, peel the yellow and red peppers. Seed peppers, remove white membranes, and cut into small dice. Peel the carrot and cut

(Continued)

into small dice. Blanch carrot very briefly in salted boiling water, just enough to slightly soften its texture. Refresh under cold running water to stop the cooking. Drain well. Trim any fat from the ham and cut ham into small dice. Chop the pickled onions very coarsely. Slice the basil into julienne strips.

Add the vegetables, ham, pickled onions, and basil to the rice along with the remaining 4 tablespoons of olive oil, capers, and vinegar. Season with salt, grind pepper over the top, and gently toss. Correct seasonings.

Insalata di Riso con Gamberi

Rice Salad with Shrimp

Serves 4

This is a simple rice salad made with summer vegetables and sweet shrimp. The Italians make ingenious use of rice in salads whose ingredients vary from simple to baroque depending on what the pantry and refrigerator yield. There are many variations on the theme of rice salad—meats, seafood, beans, or fresh herbs, or tangy olives, capers, or anchovies. When you assemble a rice salad, make sure all the components are fresh, and do not go overboard on the number of ingredients, as they may conflict with one another and blur the flavors. We recommend Arborio rice, but long-grain rice works well, too. The rice itself must be cooked al dente—mushiness is the death of a good rice salad.

1 *cup raw rice, Arborio or long grain*

½ *pound cooked, peeled shrimp, diced*

1 *yellow bell pepper, peeled, cut in half, seeds and membranes removed, and diced*

1 *cucumber, peeled, seeded, and diced*

4 *Roma tomatoes, seeded and diced*

2 *tablespoons capers*

6 *tablespoons extra-virgin olive oil*

Juice of 1 *large lemon*

1 *small garlic clove, peeled and minced*

Handful fresh basil leaves, torn

1 *sprig fresh oregano, leaves only, chopped*

Salt and freshly ground black pepper to taste

Cook the rice in abundant boiling salted water until al dente. Drain well. Place rice in a bowl and combine with the other ingredients. Toss and add salt and pepper to taste.

Zuppe e Minestre

Soups

Italian soups derive from the peasant tradition of one-pot dishes. These simple, country meals were based on whatever was on hand, sometimes utilizing broth, but more often water, and vegetables that could be stored in the cellar, such as onions, potatoes, and cabbage. These basics were supplemented by available seasonal produce and/or small amounts of cured meats. The soups were thickened and made more substantial by the addition of pasta, rice, or stale bread. This chapter follows in this tradition. We present a variety of soups that are similar in their humble, inexpensive ingredients and savory, filling character. The majority of these soups are meant to be the main focus of informal meals for family and close friends. However, we also include a few lighter, more elegant broth-based soups, which can properly serve as *primi*, or first courses.

Brodo di Pollo

Chicken Broth

Makes approximately 1½ quarts

Asimple, versatile, and flavorful broth that can be used as a base for soups, risotti, and, from time to time, for moistening braised dishes or pasta sauces. If you want the broth to be richly colored, leave the peel on the onion. It will add a deep burnished-gold color to the broth.

1 *medium stewing chicken*

1 *pound chicken backs and necks*

Water

2 *carrots, trimmed and peeled*

3 *celery stalks, washed and trimmed*

3 *sprigs Italian parsley with stems*

2 *garlic cloves, peeled*

1 *small onion*

1 *bay leaf*

5–10 *peppercorns*

Wash the chicken carefully, rinsing out any blood that remains in the cavity, and gently pull off any extra fat attached to the breast or tail area. Place the whole chicken and backs and necks in a large, heavy soup pot. Cover chicken completely with water. Bring to a boil, and skim off the scum that rises to the top. When there is no more scum, add the remaining ingredients and lower the heat.

Barely simmer the broth, uncovered or partly covered, for 2 hours. Strain the broth and either use it immediately or refrigerate it for later use. When broth is well chilled, carefully lift off the congealed chicken fat and discard it.

Brodo di Manzo

Beef Broth

Makes approximately 4 quarts

In classic French cooking, a very rich-flavored beef stock that is suitable for soups is created by roasting the bones. If you want a beef broth as a base for risotti or other dishes that call for a more delicate flavor, do not brown the bones first, omit the mushrooms, and add 1 or 2 tomatoes. This recipe produces a lighter, more traditionally Italian beef broth.

7 *pounds beef bones, such as shank or flanken*

Olive oil for coating bones

1 *large onion, unpeeled, coarsely chopped*

1 *large carrot, coarsely chopped*

1 *celery stalk with tops, coarsely chopped*

Handful mushrooms

Whole head garlic

5 *sprigs Italian parsley*

5 *sprigs fresh thyme*

2 *bay leaves*

10 *whole peppercorns*

6–7 *quarts water*

Preheat the oven to 450°. Lightly rub the beef bones with the olive oil and place in a heavy roasting pan. Roast bones for about 20 minutes. Add the chopped onion and continue to roast for about 30 minutes, or until bones brown. Remove the bones and onion from the oven and carefully place in a large stockpot with the vegetables, herbs, and spices. Add water to cover by 4 inches and bring to a simmer. Skim off scum and fat until broth is clear. Simmer broth gently at least 4 hours. Strain the broth, use it immediately or refrigerate for later use. When broth is well chilled, carefully lift off any remaining congealed fat and discard it.

Pollo in Brodo Aromatico

Spiced Broth with Chicken Breast

Serves 4

Cinnamon, cloves, and nutmeg are the spices called for in this aromatic chicken soup. Marsala, too, lends its fruity, faintly caramel bouquet. Egg yolk is carefully incorporated into the soup, making the broth lightly creamy, and slivers of poached chicken breast are added at the last moment.

Ingredients for Brodo di Pollo
  (see page 118)

½ *stick cinnamon*

2 *cloves*

½ *chicken breast, boned*

Salt

4 *egg yolks*

½ *cup dry Marsala*

Freshly grated nutmeg

Make Brodo di Pollo according to the directions on page 118. Add the cinnamon and cloves during the last hour of cooking. Simmer until you have 4 cups of strong broth. Strain, cool, and remove all fat from the surface.

Cook the chicken breast in a little salted boiling water until springy to the touch. Remove the skin and any traces of fat. Cut the chicken breast into thin, 2-inch slivers. Put chicken in a small bowl, cover, and place in a warm spot on the stove.

Lightly beat together the egg yolks and the Marsala. Add to the chicken broth and stir well. Strain the mixture through cheesecloth into a soup pot. Slowly heat broth, stirring constantly, until mixture is hot but not boiling. Do not let broth boil or the eggs will curdle.

To serve, place a few slivers of chicken breast in the bottoms of shallow soup bowls. Ladle the soup over the chicken and sprinkle with a touch of freshly grated nutmeg.

Mariola

Clear Beef Broth with Thin Frittata Strips

Serves 4

The food of Calabria is very often flavored with fiery hot red chile peppers, and this soup is no exception. Very thin frittate spiced with ground red chili peppers are cut to resemble fettuccine. The strips of frittata are warmed in a clear beef broth for a light but nourishing soup perfumed with a touch of marjoram.

4 *eggs, lightly beaten*

2 *teaspoons chopped fresh marjoram leaves*

2 *tablespoons chopped Italian parsley leaves*

1 *tablespoon toasted bread crumbs*

2 *tablespoons grated Pecorino Romano cheese*

Ground red chile pepper to taste

1 *tablespoon extra-virgin olive oil*

5 *cups homemade Brodo di Manzo (see page 119)*

Combine the beaten eggs with the marjoram, parsley, bread crumbs, cheese, and red chile peppers. Beat lightly with a fork. Lightly oil the bottom of a medium-sized nonstick skillet. Turn up the heat to medium. Pour enough of the egg mixture into the pan to form a thin pancake. Cook just until the bottom of the frittata is firm. Gently flip it over and cook the other side. Remove and set aside. Repeat until you have used up all the egg mixture. When the frittate are cool, cut into strips about ½ inch wide. Bring the broth to a boil. Add the strips of frittata and simmer for a few minutes.

Zuppa dei Funghi

Mushroom Soup

Serves 4 to 6

A delicious, woodsy-flavored broth filled with the delicate texture of mushrooms. Ladle the soup over large Crostini (see page 45) for a rich beginning to a simple winter supper. Follow with Insalata di Radicchio alla Vicentina (see page 90).

¼ *cup extra-virgin olive oil*

1 *onion, peeled and finely chopped*

1 *pound white mushrooms, trimmed and sliced*

1 *pound shiitake mushrooms, stems removed, sliced*

1 *ounce dried porcini mushrooms, soaked in warm water for 20 minutes, drained and cleaned of any grit*

2 *garlic cloves, peeled and minced*

¼ *cup dry Marsala*

1 *tablespoon tomato paste*

Handful coarsely chopped Italian parsley

5 *cups hot Brodo di Manzo (see page 119)*

1 *recipe Crostini (see page 45)*

Grated Parmesan cheese for table use

Salt and freshly ground black pepper to taste

Heat the olive oil in a soup pot. Add the onion and cook until soft. Add the garlic and mushrooms, and sauté until mushrooms are nearly tender. If the pot is too small, sauté the mushrooms in batches. Add the Marsala and deglaze the pan over high heat. Add the tomato paste and parsley. Stir to mix tomato paste into the mushrooms and cook 1 to 2 minutes. Add the beef broth and bring to a simmer. Cook for 30 minutes. Taste and season with salt and pepper. Place large Crostini in individual bowls and pour broth over them. Serve sprinkled with Parmesan cheese.

Zuppa Verde

Green Soup

Serves 4

Escarole and endive are cooked in a small amount of water that becomes intensely flavorful with a slightly bitter edge. The greens and their broth are then ladled over toasted country bread, which absorbs the juices and makes the soup more substantial. Soups of this kind, consisting of field greens, or wild mushrooms, or potatoes from the pantry, were often the mainstay of many Italian peasant families. Since bread was an intrinsic part of every Italian meal and nothing was ever wasted, pieces of leftover dried bread would be used to thicken and enrich the soups. Remember that the bread must have good flavor and texture, a crucial factor in simple soups like this.

(Continued)

1 small head escarole

1 small head curly endive

3 tablespoons extra-virgin olive oil, plus additional for drizzling over soup

2 large garlic cloves, peeled and lightly crushed

1 small fresh red chile pepper, chopped, or ½ teaspoon crushed dried red chile pepper

4 cups water

Salt to taste

1 recipe Bruschetta (see page 39), using 4 slices of bread

Freshly ground black pepper to taste

6 tablespoons grated Parmesan cheese

2 tablespoons grated Pecorino Romano cheese

Trim and wash the escarole and endive, and coarsely chop. In a large pot heat the olive oil, garlic, and fresh or dried red chile pepper Sauté over low heat until garlic is light golden brown. Add the chopped greens and any water that clings to them, cover, and cook over medium heat until the greens wilt, tossing them occasionally in the oil. Add the water and salt to taste, and bring to a boil. Adjust to a simmer and cook for 20 minutes. Prepare the Bruschetta and place a slice in the bottom of individual shallow soup bowls. Ladle the soup over the bread. Drizzle olive oil and grind some peppers over the top. Combine the cheeses in a small bowl, and serve on the side.

Minestra di Finocchio

Fennel and Tomato Soup

Serves 6 to 8

An unusual soup that combines the sweet licorice flavor of fennel with the rich acidity of tomatoes. Serve this striking red soup in simple white bowls.

1 *medium onion, chopped*

4 *tablespoons extra-virgin olive oil*

5 *garlic cloves, minced*

3 *fennel bulbs, sliced very thin*

10–12 *fresh basil leaves, julienned*

10–12 *Roma tomatoes, peeled, seeded, and chopped*

6 *cups Brodo di Pollo (see page 118)*

Salt and freshly ground black pepper to taste

Sauté the onion in the olive oil until soft. Add the garlic and sauté until it turns opaque and releases its aroma. Add the fennel and cook for a few minutes until slightly tender. Add the basil and tomatoes, and cook over medium-high heat until the mixture has reduced and thickened. Add the chicken stock and simmer for about ½ hour. Add salt and pepper to taste.

Minestrone alle Fave

Vegetable Soup with Fava Beans

Serves 4 to 6

There is an almost infinite variety in minestrone recipes. This is a light soup filled with the fresh clean taste of fennel and escarole. The favas add an earthy undertone.

½ cup extra-virgin olive oil

1 small onion, peeled and diced

1 fennel bulb, ends trimmed, thinly sliced

2 garlic cloves, peeled and minced

3 medium tomatoes, peeled, seeded, and coarsely chopped

2 carrots, peeled, ends trimmed, cut into ¼-inch dice

2 celery stalks, diced

2 small, firm zucchini, ends trimmed, cut into ¼-inch dice

8–10 fresh basil leaves

5 cups water

½ head escarole, washed, bruised leaves removed, and shredded

1 cup shelled fava beans, skins of beans removed

½ cup imported tubetti (optional)

Salt and freshly ground black pepper to taste

Heat the olive oil in a heavy soup pot. Add the onion and cook over moderate heat until it begins to wilt. Add the fennel and sauté until it is just tender but not completely soft. Add the garlic and cook until it gives off its characteristic aroma. Add the chopped tomatoes and cook about 5 minutes, or until tomatoes begin to break down and give off their juices. Add the carrots and celery, and gently sauté for 5 minutes. Add the zucchini and basil, and sauté for about 5 minutes. Add the water and bring to a boil. Add the escarole and fava beans. Turn down heat and simmer for approximately 20 minutes, or until all vegetables are very tender. Season to taste with salt and pepper. If you wish to add pasta to the soup, add the tubetti approximately 10 minutes before the end of the cooking time.

Minestrone Leggera

Light Minestrone

Serves 8 to 10

This flavorful yet delicate minestrone, perfect for a light lunch, goes well with good sturdy bread. The recipe can easily be adapted to the availability of seasonal produce to create a variety of soups all year round.

2 *medium onions, peeled and chopped*

¼ *cup extra-virgin olive oil*

2 *carrots, trimmed, peeled, and diced*

2 *celery stalks, trimmed and diced*

5 *garlic cloves, peeled and minced*

Large handful chopped Italian parsley

10 *fresh basil leaves, cut into julienne*

6–8 *Roma tomatoes, stem ends removed, coarsely chopped*

2 *zucchini, ends trimmed, cut into dice*

½ *head cauliflower, broken into flowerets*

2 *medium russet potatoes, peeled and diced*

1 *16-ounce can white beans with liquid*

2 *quarts water*

Salt and freshly ground black pepper to taste

4 *ounces imported dried pasta; if pasta is long, break into short pieces, or use short pasta like little shells or elbows*

Sauté the onion in olive oil in a large soup pot until it begins to wilt. Add the carrots, celery, and garlic. Continue to sauté vegetables over moderate heat until they are half cooked, approximately 15 minutes. Add the parsley, basil, and tomatoes, and continue sautéing. When tomatoes begin to break down and release their juice, add the zucchini, cauliflower, potatoes, beans with their liquid, water, and salt and pepper to taste. Bring the soup to a simmer and cook until all the vegetables are tender and the broth is flavorful, approximately 40 minutes. Just before ready to serve add the pasta and cook until tender.

Zuppa del Ortolano

Soup from the Greengrocer

Serves 4 to 6

This soup features a wealth of garden vegetables. A small amount of pancetta imparts richness, and Pecorino Romano cheese lends its salty tang as contrast to the sweetness of the vegetables.

¼ *cup extra-virgin olive oil*

2 *slices pancetta, about 2 ounces, cut into small strips*

1 *onion, peeled and chopped*

1 *celery stalk, strings removed, finely diced*

½ cup *tablespoons chopped Italian parsley*

2 *large ripe tomatoes, peeled, seeded, and diced*

3 *medium zucchini, ends trimmed, diced*

6 *small carrots, peeled and diced*

½ *pound green beans, ends trimmed, cut into short lengths*

1 *pound boiling potatoes, peeled and diced*

6 *cups light chicken broth or water*

Salt to taste

½ *cup grated Pecorino Romano cheese*

Small handful fresh basil leaves, coarsely chopped

Freshly ground black pepper to taste

1 *recipe Bruschetta (see page 39), using 4–6 slices of bread*

Place the olive oil, pancetta, onion, celery, and parsley in a large soup pot. Sauté over low heat for about 10 minutes, or until onion and celery soften. Add the rest of the vegetables, broth or water, and salt to taste. Bring to a boil, adjust to a gentle simmer, cover, and cook for 30 to 45 minutes, or until the vegetables are tender and the broth is flavorful. Stir in the grated cheese, basil, and pepper to taste. Cover and let rest for a couple of minutes. For each serving, place a piece of Bruschetta in the bottom of a soup bowl. Ladle soup over the top.

Passato di Verdura con Pane Fritto

Puree of Vegetable Soup
Served with Crostini

Serves 6 to 8

This recipe makes great use of leftover minestrone. The soup is equally delicious served at room temperature and drizzled with a fine extra-virgin olive oil as it is served hot, and makes a lovely, light luncheon dish.

FOR THE SOUP:

1 *medium onion, peeled and chopped*

4 *tablespoons extra-virgin olive oil*

4 *garlic cloves, peeled and minced*

2 *leeks, cleaned and chopped*

1 *fennel bulb, chopped*

8 *fresh basil leaves, julienned*

2 *sprigs fresh oregano, chopped*

8 *Italian tomatoes, chopped*

1 *carrot, trimmed, peeled, and chopped*

2 *stalks celery, chopped*

2 *zucchini, ends trimmed, and cubed*

½ *bunch broccoli, cut into small pieces*

3 *medium potatoes, peeled and cubed*

6 *cups water*

Salt and freshly ground black pepper to taste

FOR THE CROSTINI:

¼ *cup extra-virgin olive oil*

4 *garlic cloves, peeled and minced*

½ *cup Italian parsley, chopped fine*

4–6 *slices Tuscan bread*

Sauté the onion in the olive oil until soft. Add the garlic, leeks, and fennel, and sauté over medium-high heat until just slightly tender. Add the fresh herbs and then the tomatoes, and cook until the tomatoes break down and the mixture is quite saucey. Add the remaining vegetables and cook over high heat for about 2 minutes. Add the water, bring to a boil, lower heat, and simmer until the soup has reduced and vegetables are very tender. Add salt and pepper to taste. Puree the soup using a food mill, blender, or food processor with steel blade.

To make the Crostini, heat the oil in a sauté pan. Add the garlic and parsley, and sauté until the garlic releases its aroma. Add the slices of bread and fry until golden; then turn each piece over and cook the other side. Place 1 slice of bread in the bottom of each bowl and pour the soup over the top. Serve immediately.

Minestra di Pomodoro Fresco e Riso

Fresh Tomato and Rice Soup

Serves 4 to 6

A very fresh-tasting tomato soup with the added creamy touch of Arborio rice. This is a great way to put tomatoes to good use if you are blessed with a prolific summer garden.

2 tablespoons extra-virgin olive oil

1 onion, peeled and diced medium fine

2 garlic cloves, peeled and chopped

3 slices pancetta, cut into small strips

2 pounds ripe tomatoes, peeled, seeded, and coarsely pureed

Salt to taste

8 cups light chicken broth or water

1 cup Arborio rice

Handful fresh basil leaves, cut into julienne

Grated Parmesan cheese

Place the olive oil, onion, garlic, and pancetta in a medium-sized stockpot and sauté over low heat for 10 minutes, or until onion is tender and the pancetta renders its fat. Add the tomatoes and salt to taste. Cook over medium heat for 10 minutes. Add the chicken broth or water and bring to a boil. Add the rice and stir well. Adjust the heat to medium and cook until rice is tender but still a little al dente, about 15 minutes. Stir often to prevent sticking. Sprinkle with the basil and Parmesan cheese to taste.

Minestra di Zucca e Riso

Red Squash and Rice Soup

Serves 4

This soup is very thick, almost like a risotto. Mild sweet squash and creamy rice are its two main ingredients. The squash is cooked until it breaks down and resembles a coarse puree; then it is combined with the rice, turning the soup a lovely shade of golden orange. An ideal soup to serve in cold weather.

1 *pound butternut squash*

2 *tablespoons extra-virgin olive oil*

4 *slices pancetta, finely diced*

1 *medium onion, peeled and finely diced*

5 *cups beef broth or water*

1 *cup Arborio rice*

½ *cup grated Parmesan cheese, plus additional cheese for the table*

Freshly ground black pepper to taste

Cut the squash in half. Scoop out the seeds, scrape squash clean, and cut into large chunks to facilitate peeling. Peel squash with a vegetable peeler and cut into ½-inch dice. Heat the oil in a medium-sized soup pot. Add the pancetta and sauté over low heat for several minutes. Add the onion and cook until it is pale gold. Add the diced squash and sauté for 1 to 2 minutes. Add the broth or water and bring to a boil. Adjust the heat to a slow simmer, cover, and cook for about 40 minutes, or until the squash is completely soft. Add the rice and cook until rice is tender but slightly al dente at the center, about 15 minutes. Transfer the soup to a tureen, stir in the Parmesan cheese, and grind pepper over the top. Pass Parmesan cheese.

Riso con Piselli

Rice Soup with Peas

Serves 6 to 8

A lighter broth-filled version of risi e bisi, the Venetian dish of rice and peas. Peas and rice have a natural affinity for one another. This is a real comfort soup for when you're feeling low.

1 *small onion, peeled and chopped*

4 *tablespoons extra-virgin olive oil*

3 *ounces pancetta, sliced very thin*

4 *garlic cloves, peeled and minced*

2 *celery stalks, chopped*

10 *ounces homemade tomato sauce or canned crushed tomatoes with tomato paste*

Handful Italian parsley, chopped

10-ounce package frozen peas, thawed

5 *cups chicken stock*

Salt and freshly ground black pepper to taste

½ *cup Arborio or long-grain rice*

Grated Parmesan cheese for table use

Sauté the onion in the olive oil until soft in a soup pot. Add the pancetta and cook over low heat for several minutes, or until the pancetta renders its fat. Add the garlic and cook for 1 minute. Add the celery and cook until tender. Add the tomato sauce and parsley, and cook until the tomatoes thicken. Add the peas and chicken stock and simmer for about ½ hour. Add salt and pepper to taste. About ½ hour before serving bring the soup to a lively boil and add the rice. Cook over high heat until the rice is tender, about 15 minutes. Serve immediately. Pass grated Parmesan cheese.

Minestra di Verza e Riso

Cabbage and Rice Soup

Serves 6 to 8

Simple, healthful ingredients that are always available create this delicious, savory soup.

1 *head Savoy or green cabbage*

¼ *cup extra-virgin olive oil*

6 *ounces prosciutto, roughly chopped*

2 *quarts water*

Salt and freshly ground black pepper to taste

½ *cup long-grain rice*

Grated Parmesan cheese for table use

Core the cabbage and shred as for cole slaw. Heat the oil in a soup pot with a heavy bottom. Add the prosciutto and sauté over low heat until it renders its fat. Add the shredded cabbage and stir until it is well coated with oil. Add the water to cover the cabbage. Bring to a boil, then turn down the heat and simmer the soup gently. If you wish, place the cover slightly askew on the soup pot. Cook until cabbage is very tender, approximately 1½ hours. Add salt and pepper to taste. About ½ hour before serving, remove the cover, bring the soup to a lively boil, and add the rice. Cook over high heat until the rice is tender, about 15 minutes. Serve immediately, passing grated Parmesan cheese to sprinkle on the soup.

Riso e Preboggion

Rice · Soup with Greens and Pesto

Serves 4 to 6

Preboggion is a word from the Ligurian dialect that refers to a mixture of wild greens, including dandelion, chard, beet greens, chicory, and borage used in cooking on the Italian Riviera. The pungent scent of green herbs such as basil and marjoram is often one's first introduction to any restaurant in this celebrated coastal zone. This traditional soup unites two important aspects of the Ligurian kitchen.

¼ *cup extra-virgin olive oil*

½ *medium onion, peeled and diced*

½ *head escarole, core removed, washed, and finely sliced*

1 *bunch Swiss chard, ends trimmed, coarsely chopped*

2 *quarts water*

Salt and freshly ground black pepper to taste

½ *cup long-grain rice*

3 *tablespoons pesto (see page 200)*

Heat the olive oil in a soup pot. Add the onion and cook over medium heat, stirring frequently, until onion begins to wilt. Add the escarole and Swiss chard, and lightly fry for 1 to 2 minutes. Add the water and bring the soup to a boil. Cook over medium heat until escarole and Swiss chard are tender. Add salt and pepper to taste. The soup can be made ahead to this point.

Add the rice to the soup approximately 10 to 15 minutes before serving. Stirring frequently, cook the rice at a low simmer until it is tender. Serve soup in individual bowls, garnishing each with a large teaspoon of pesto to swirl into the soup.

Pappa al Pomodoro

B r e a d - T h i c k e n e d   T o m a t o   S o u p

Serves 6 to 8

Another traditional Tuscan soup, a favorite of anyone who likes to dunk bread into tomato sauce. The consistency should be thick, but not as thick as Ribollita (see page 140).

1 *cup extra-virgin olive oil*

2 *garlic cloves, peeled and minced*

1 *bunch fresh sage leaves, roughly chopped, or 2 teaspoons dried sage*

1 *28-ounce can imported Italian tomatoes*

6 *cups Brodo di Pollo (see page 118) or water*

Salt and freshly ground black pepper to taste

1 *2-pound loaf stale unsalted Tuscan bread or other rough country loaf, sliced*

Heat the olive oil in a heavy soup pot. Add the garlic and sage. Cook until garlic gives off its characteristic aroma. Add the tomatoes, passing them through the coarsest disk of a food mill right into the pot. Cook the tomato mixture for 5 to 8 minutes. Add the chicken broth or water to the tomato mixture and bring to a boil. Add salt and pepper to taste. Add the bread. Cook for approximately 5 minutes, cover, and remove from heat. Let the soup stand for at least 1 hour. Stir thoroughly before serving. Serve hot or tepid (the latter is our preference), topped with a drizzle of very fine extra-virgin olive oil.

Ribollita

Bread-Thickened Minestrone

Serves 6 to 8

This most traditional of all Tuscan soups is found in nearly every trattoria in Florence, where it is served more like a *pappa*, or mush, than a liquid. The term *ribollita* means reboiled and refers to the fact that the prepared minestrone is brought back to the simmer with the bread. The thickness of the soup is determined by how much bread is added. Our recipe makes a thick but less dense soup than the traditional version.

½ cup extra-virgin olive oil

2 garlic cloves, peeled and minced

2 medium onions, peeled and diced fine

2 celery stalks, washed, trimmed, and diced

4 carrots, peeled and roughly chopped

3 large, ripe tomatoes, stem ends removed, roughly chopped

1 bunch green Swiss chard, washed, trimmed, and chopped

1 bunch kale, washed, tough ribs discarded, and chopped

½ head Savoy cabbage, shredded

2 potatoes, peeled and diced

2 cups cooked white beans with liquid

Salt and freshly ground black pepper to taste

Pinch of red chile pepper flakes

Water

1 loaf stale Tuscan bread or other sturdy country bread, sliced thickly

Additional extra-virgin olive oil for drizzling

Heat the olive oil in a large soup pot. Add the garlic, onions, celery, and carrots. Cook until the onions begin to soften and turn translucent. Add the chopped tomatoes and cook another 5 minutes, or until they begin to break down and become saucey. Add the remaining vegetables, including the beans with their liquid, salt and pepper to taste, and a pinch of red chile pepper flakes. Add water to just cover the vegetables. Bring to a boil, reduce the heat, cover, and simmer for approximately 2 hours, or until all the vegetables are very tender and the resultant broth is rich with flavor. Serve the soup immediately as a minestrone, or reboil it with the bread to create the Ribollita.

To reboil the soup with bread, in the pot layer the stale bread slices alternately with ladlefuls of soup. Bring the soup to a boil slowly, and cook carefully so that the bottom does not burn. Stir frequently to mix bread evenly through the soup. The soup is done when the bread dissolves completely and is absorbed into the liquid. Allow the soup to cool slightly so that it is not steaming hot. Pour into individual bowls and garnish with a drizzle of olive oil.

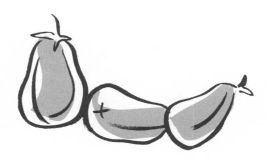

Minestra di Lenticchie e Scarola

Lentil and Escarole Soup

Serves 4 to 6

A hearty version of lentil soup that will please vegetarians. For a light meal all you need is coarse, flavorful bread and fruit for dessert.

¼ *cup extra-virgin olive oil*

1 *small onion, peeled and cut into ¼-inch dice*

2–3 *garlic cloves, peeled and minced*

2 *carrots, peeled and cut into small dice*

3 *medium tomatoes, stem ends removed, cut into small dice*

8–10 *fresh basil leaves, cut into thin shreds*

⅔ *cup lentils*

5 *cups water*

1 *small head escarole, washed, bruised leaves discarded, and roughly chopped*

Salt and freshly ground black pepper to taste

Heat the olive oil in a heavy soup pot. Add the onion and sauté until very soft. Add the garlic and sauté until it gives off its characteristic aroma. Add the carrots, tomatoes, and basil, and cook, stirring frequently, until the tomatoes begin to break down and give off their juice. Add the lentils to the tomato mixture and stir. Allow lentils to absorb the juices of the vegetables for 1 to 2 minutes, then add the water. Bring the soup to a boil, turn down heat to an active simmer, and cook approximately 20 minutes. Add the escarole and continue cooking at a simmer until the lentils are soft and the escarole is tender, approximately 30 minutes more. Add salt and pepper to taste.

Zuppa di Ceci

Chick-pea Soup with Croutons

Serves 6 to 8

The word *zuppa* usually refers to a soup served over bread, and is probably derived from the verb *inzuppare*, to dip—presumably one's bread in the soup. Zuppa di Ceci is hearty and nutty-tasting, and is colored a beautiful deep golden red. A great recipe for when you want a filling soup that can be made quickly.

¼ cup extra-virgin olive oil

1 medium onion, peeled and minced

3 garlic cloves, peeled and minced

8 Roma or 4 round tomatoes, peeled, seeded, and chopped

1 can chick-peas with liquid

5 cups water

12 fresh basil leaves, divided

Salt and freshly ground black pepper to taste

6 slices country bread, cut ½ inch thick, for crostini

Extra-virgin olive oil for drizzling

Heat the olive oil in a heavy soup pot. Add the onion and garlic, and cook over moderate heat until onion is soft and translucent. Add the tomatoes and cook until they begin to break down and give off their juice. Add the chick-peas, water, and half the basil leaves. Bring to a boil, then reduce the heat to a simmer. Cook approximately 45 minutes, or until the chick-peas begin to break down. Add salt and pepper to taste. Remove the mixture from the heat and pass through a food mill, using the large-holed disk, into a tureen or serving bowl. Correct seasonings and set aside. The soup should have the consistency of heavy cream. If it is too thick, add a little

(Continued)

hot water. While the soup is cooking, make the crostini. Brush the bread slices with olive oil and place on a baking sheet. Bake in a preheated 400° oven until light golden brown.

To serve, place a crostino in individual soup bowls, then ladle soup over it. Garnish each serving with a healthy drizzle of olive oil and a whole basil leaf.

Pasta e Fagioli

White Bean Soup

Serves 6

One can never have too many bean soup recipes. Smooth, creamy white beans complement a seemingly unending number of flavor combinations. If you wish, you can start from scratch, using dried white beans. Our version shows a quicker way to arrive at a traditional soup using imported canned Italian beans.

1 *small onion, peeled and chopped fine*

4 *tablespoons extra-virgin olive oil*

4 *garlic cloves, peeled and minced*

3 *cups canned Italian tomatoes*

8–10 *fresh basil leaves, cut into julienne*

Handful chopped Italian parsley

3 15-*ounce cans Italian cannellini beans, undrained,*

or 6 cups cooked dried white beans with their cooking liquid

5 *cups water*

Salt and freshly ground black pepper to taste

4 *ounces imported dried pasta, such as elbows, broken spaghetti, or tiny shells*

Extra-virgin olive oil for drizzling

Sauté the onion in the olive oil in a medium-sized soup pot until soft. Add the garlic and sauté until it turns opaque and releases its aroma. Add the tomatoes, basil, and parsley, and cook over moderately high heat until tomatoes become saucey. Add the beans with their liquid and the water. Cook over medium heat at least 15 minutes, or until beans begin to break down and soup thickens. Just before serving, add the pasta to the simmering soup and cook until al dente. Serve immediately. Pass additional extra-virgin olive oil for drizzling over the soup.

Scarola e Fagioli

Escarole and White Bean Soup

Serves 6

The delicately bitter flavor of the green escarole cuts the richness of the white beans in this recipe.

1 *large onion, peeled and chopped*

¼ *cup extra-virgin olive oil*

4 *garlic cloves, peeled and minced*

3 *celery stalks, thinly sliced*

Handful chopped Italian parsley

10 *fresh basil leaves, cut into julienne*

8 *Roma tomatoes, peeled, seeded, and roughly chopped*

2 *15-ounce cans Italian cannellini beans, undrained,*

or 4 cup cooked dried white beans with their cooking liquid

5 *cups water*

1 *head escarole, tough outer leaves removed, roughly chopped*

Salt and freshly ground black pepper to taste

Grated Parmesan cheese for table use

Sauté the onion in the olive oil in a medium-sized soup pot until it is just wilted. Add the garlic and celery, and lightly sauté until the garlic releases its aroma. Add the parsley, basil, and tomatoes, and cook over moderately high heat until the tomatoes become saucey. Add the beans with their liquid and the water, and bring to a boil. Add the escarole and salt and pepper to taste. Turn down the heat and simmer the soup until the escarole is tender. Serve, and pass Parmesan cheese.

Minestra della Fattoria

Broccoli, Bean, and Pasta Soup

Serves 6 to 8

A savory, rich, and healthy soup brimming with the deep flavor of broccoli.

1 *red onion, peeled and chopped*

4 *tablespoons extra-virgin olive oil*

6 *garlic cloves, peeled and minced*

1 *sprig fresh oregano, chopped*

2 *sprigs fresh thyme, chopped*

1 *bunch broccoli, chopped very fine*

2 *15-ounce cans Italian cannellini beans, undrained,* or 3 *cups cooked dried white beans with their cooking liquid*

6 *cups chicken stock*

4 *ounces imported dried pasta, such as elbows, broken spaghetti, or tiny shells*

Salt and freshly ground black pepper to taste

Parmesan cheese for grating at the table

Sauté the onion in the olive oil in a soup pot until it is soft. Add the garlic and sauté until it turns opaque and releases its aroma, about 2 to 3 minutes. Add the herbs and the broccoli, and cook over moderate heat until the broccoli is quite soft. Add the beans with all their liquid and the chicken stock. Cook at least 15 minutes, or until the soup thickens. Just before serving add the pasta and cook it in the simmering soup until al dente. Add salt and pepper to taste. Serve immediately and pass Parmesan cheese to grate into the soup.

Pasta

Variations on pasta are as inexhaustible as the human appetite, and fresh inspiration is as close at hand as the next meal. This chapter contains discoveries and inventions—from spontaneous raw summer sauces to savory, rich-tasting ones for winter days. An illustrated guide to the pasta shapes called for in this chapter (see pages 150–151) will help you through a bewildering array of names and shapes. Pasta, more than any other food, reflects the character of the Italian people and their cooking—direct, eloquent, and resourceful. Yet it has transcended its ethnic status and is loved by everyone.

When buying dried pasta, look for imported Italian brands. The resulting taste and texture will be infinitely more satisfying. Cook dried pasta al dente, until it is slightly resistant to the bite. When cooked, the pasta should have body and resilience and not collapse on itself. Never rinse pasta after it has been drained. The bit of starch that clings to the pasta helps the sauce adhere.

Fresh pasta, made with egg in the dough, is entirely different in texture and taste. Tenderness is its hallmark. Cook fresh pasta until it is tender to the bite but not soft. In *Pasta Fresca*, we provide detailed instructions for making fresh pasta, as well as an extensive guide to pasta shapes, both dried and fresh.

It is important to remember that good-quality dried pasta and fresh egg pasta have equal merit. The difference between them lies in their use. The stronger texture and more assertive wheat flavor of dried pasta need sauces with greater character. Egg pasta is at its best when served with the more subdued flavors of dairy products like butter, cream, and rich cheeses, or where its special delicate flavor and texture are the focus of the dish.

Illustrated Guide to Pasta Shapes

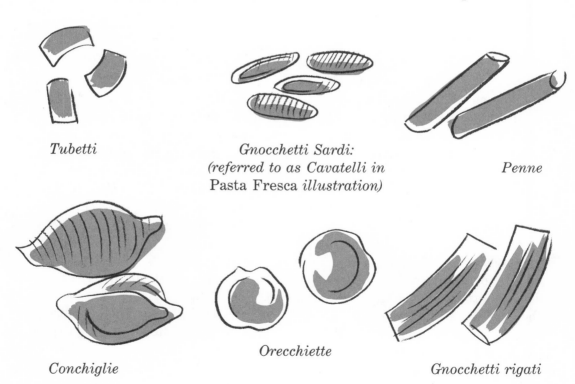

Tubetti

Gnocchetti Sardi:
(referred to as Cavatelli in
Pasta Fresca *illustration)*

Penne

Conchiglie

Orecchiette

Gnocchetti rigati

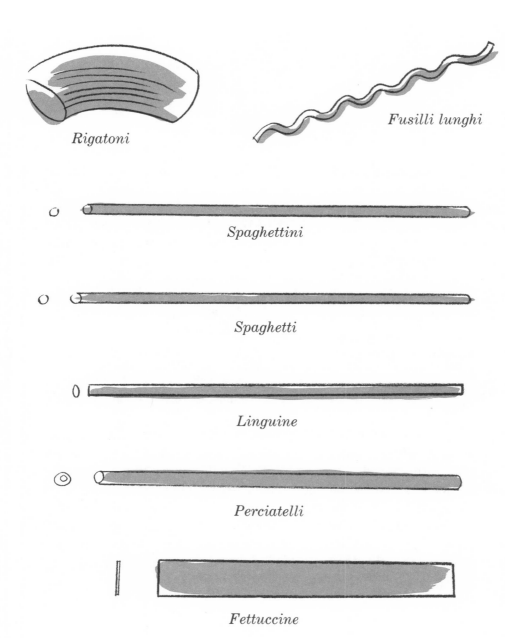

Rigatoni

Fusilli lunghi

Spaghettini

Spaghetti

Linguine

Perciatelli

Fettuccine

Spaghetti "Picchi Pacchi"

Fast Spaghetti

Serves 4 to 6

The ease of preparation of this Sicilian dish is expressed in its title. *Picchi pacchi* is a phrase in Sicilian dialect, which loosely translates as "quick" or "fast." The cheese required is a spicy aged provolone called provolone piccante. Auricchio, the long-established Italian cheesemaking company, now produces this cheese along with others in Wisconsin, so this delicious provolone is now available at a reasonable price. In southern Italian cooking it is common to substitute aged provolone for grated Parmesan cheese.

5 red, ripe tomatoes

10 fresh basil leaves, cut into julienne, or 1 teaspoon dried basil

Red chile pepper flakes to taste

2 garlic cloves, peeled and minced

¼–½ cup extra-virgin olive oil

¼ pound aged provolone, grated

1 pound imported spaghetti

Remove stem ends from the tomatoes and cut tomatoes into ½-inch dice. In a small bowl mix together the diced tomatoes, basil, red chile pepper flakes to taste, garlic, and olive oil. Stir well, and set aside, covered, in a shady place at room temperature for at least 1 hour.

When ready to serve, cook the spaghetti in abundant boiling salted water until al dente. Quickly drain the pasta in a colander. In a large, shallow serving dish toss the tomato mixture, including the accumulated juices, with the spaghetti. Sprinkle the provolone over the pasta. Serve immediately.

Spaghetti al Pomodoro Arrostito

Spaghetti with Roasted-Tomato Sauce

Serves 4 to 6

Roasting tomatoes to remove the skins adds a smoky flavor in this simple, uncooked sauce. Experiment with adding herbs or even other grilled vegetables, such as zucchini or eggplant.

8 *medium red, ripe tomatoes*

4 *garlic cloves, peeled and minced*

10 *fresh basil leaves, coarsely chopped*

3 *sprigs fresh oregano, leaves only, chopped*

¼–½ *cup extra-virgin olive oil*

Salt and freshly ground black pepper to taste

1 *pound imported spaghetti*

Grated Parmesan or Pecorino Romano cheese for table use

Impale the tomatoes through the blossom end on a fork and roast them over a gas flame until their skins char lightly. Peel, seed, and coarsely chop the tomatoes, and place them in a small stainless-steel bowl. Using a fork, mash the tomatoes a bit, allowing their juices to emerge. Add the garlic, basil, oregano, olive oil, and salt and pepper to taste. Mix well and let marinate at room temperature for at least 1 hour before serving.

Cook the spaghetti in abundant boiling salted water until al dente. Drain the pasta well in a colander and toss with the tomato mixture in a shallow serving bowl. Serve immediately. Pass Parmesan or Pecorino Romano cheese.

Spaghetti con Pomodoro e Pinoli

Spaghetti with Tomato and Pine Nuts

Serves 4 to 6

Two popular Italian ingredients, tomatoes and pine nuts, combine to create a simple, unusual dish. The pine nuts enrich the tomatoes and make a more elegant presentation in this easy uncooked sauce.

1/4 *cup extra-virgin olive oil*

3 *garlic cloves, peeled and thinly sliced*

1/2 *cup pine nuts*

6 *large red, ripe tomatoes, stem ends removed, cut into small dice*

Handful chopped Italian parsley

Salt and freshly ground black pepper to taste

1/2 *cup extra-virgin olive oil*

1 *pound imported spaghetti*

Grated Parmesan cheese for table use

Heat the olive oil in a skillet and lightly fry the garlic over moderate heat. Add the pine nuts and sauté until they are golden. Be careful not to burn them. Remove skillet from the heat and let the oil cool. Mix the tomatoes, parsley, salt and pepper to taste, and 1/2 cup olive oil together in a small bowl. Add the cooled garlic and pine nuts and all their cooking oil. Mix the tomato mixture well and set aside to marinate in a cool spot out of the refrigerator for at least 1 hour.

Cook the spaghetti in abundant boiling salted water until al dente. Drain the pasta well in a colander. In a shallow serving bowl mix the hot pasta together with the tomato mixture. Serve with Parmesan cheese.

Spaghettini al Pesto di Prezzemolo Infiammato

Thin Pasta with Inflamed Italian Parsley Pesto

Serves 4 to 6

This uncooked herb sauce is tossed with hot pasta just before serving. An assertive-tasting dish that packs the triple punch of raw garlic, fresh red chile pepper, and spicy salame. The flavor is refreshed by a generous amount of Italian parsley and grated lemon rind, which adds its fragrant and flowery note. Serve this summer pasta with a cool white wine, and bowls of assorted fruit in ice water for dessert.

½ cup extra-virgin olive oil

2 garlic cloves, peeled and finely chopped

1 small, fresh red chile pepper, finely chopped

1 bunch Italian parsley, chopped

Grated rind of 1 small lemon

6 slices spicy salame, ⅛ inch thick, cut into small dice

Salt to taste

1 pound imported spaghettini

Grated Parmesan cheese (optional)

(Continued)

In a small bowl combine all the ingredients except the spaghettini, adding salt to taste. It should be a fairly dense mixture.

Cook the spaghettini in abundant boiling salted water until al dente. Drain the pasta, allowing plenty of the cooking water to cling to the strands of pasta and reserve a little to thin the sauce if necessary. Add the parsley pesto to the hot spaghettini and toss. Serve immediately and pass Parmesan cheese at the table, if desired.

Spaghetti Aglio e Olio

Spaghetti with Oil and Garlic

Serves 4 to 6

The pasta to eat when nothing seems to taste good anymore. The simplest ingredients combine to create a completely satisfying meal. We add a bit of lemon juice to brighten the flavor of the garlic but, strictly speaking, it isn't necessary. This is one of those recipes where amounts should be considered as a guide. Make the dish according to your personal taste. Some like the pasta to have a very strong flavor of garlic and red chile; others prefer just to lightly brown whole cloves of garlic in oil, which are then discarded for a more subtle, nutty taste. Experiment. The balance of flavor is up to you.

½–¾ *cup extra-virgin olive oil,*
plus more for drizzling

12 *garlic cloves, or more*
according to taste, peeled and
thinly sliced

½ *teaspoon red chile pepper*
flakes or 2 whole cayenne
peppers, or more according to
taste

½ *teaspoon salt*

½ *lemon*

Large handful chopped Italian
parsley

1 *pound imported spaghetti*

Heat the olive oil gently with the garlic in a small skillet. When the garlic turns opaque, add the red chile pepper flakes or whole cayenne peppers, the salt, and squeeze the lemon into the hot oil. Turn off the heat and let the garlic turn light golden at the edges. The garlic will continue to cook in the hot oil. When the oil has cooled somewhat, add the parsley.

Meanwhile, cook the spaghetti in abundant boiling salted water until al dente. Drain the pasta well in a colander and place in a shallow serving bowl. Pour the warm olive oil with the garlic, chile, and parsley over the pasta and mix well. If desired, drizzle more extra-virgin olive oil on top. Serve immediately.

Pasta Forte

Strong Pasta

Serves 4 to 6

This dish's strong flavors and simple preparation result in a flash of memory. There was a small trattoria at the end of a hot, dusty country road. A simple, spare menu revealed this intensely flavored pasta made of black olives, capers, anchovies, and garlic. The robust pasta hit the spot served with a huge chilled beer.

½ cup black olives, either in brine or oil cured, pitted

3 anchovy fillets

2 tablespoons capers

4 garlic cloves, peeled

3 tablespoons extra-virgin olive oil

Generous pinch of red chile pepper flakes

Small amount of freshly ground black pepper

Salt to taste

1 pound imported spaghetti

Finely chop the olives with a knife or in a food processor with a steel blade. Set aside. Finely chop together the anchovy fillets, capers, and garlic. Heat the olive oil in a medium-sized skillet. Add all the finely chopped ingredients and sauté over medium heat, adding the red and black peppers and salt to taste.

Cook the spaghetti in abundant boiling salted water until al dente. Drain the pasta and place it in a skillet with the sauce, adding 2 to 3 tablespoons of the pasta cooking water to moisten the sauce. Heat briefly over moderate heat, stirring well. Serve immediately in individual pasta bowls.

Pasta Festiva

Festive Pasta

Serves 4 to 6

This dish is a dressed-up version of Spaghetti Aglio e Olio (see page 156). A simple fresh tomato sauce rings the edge of the plate, and a couple of handfuls of coarse, crunchy bread crumbs top the center of the pasta to create a beautifully colorful dish. This pasta is easy to assemble if all the elements are ready beforehand. Make the breadcrumbs first, maybe even the day before. The tomato sauce can also be made in advance. Then you merely need to cook the pasta and dress it with the hot garlicky oil and arrange the other elements on top.

1 *recipe Spaghetti Aglio e Olio (see page 156)*

FOR THE BREAD CRUMBS:

4 *tablespoons extra-virgin olive oil*

3 *cloves garlic, peeled and minced*

3 *cups fresh, coarse bread crumbs*

3 *sprigs fresh thyme, leaves only, chopped (optional)*

Freshly ground black pepper to taste

Grated Parmesan cheese (optional)

Heat the olive oil in a skillet. Add the garlic and cook just until it turns opaque. Add the bread crumbs, thyme, and pepper to taste. Cook until bread crumbs are golden brown. Remove from the skillet to a small bowl and let cool.

(Continued)

FOR THE TOMATO SAUCE:

¼ cup extra-virgin olive oil

4 garlic cloves, peeled and minced

16 Roma tomatoes, stem ends removed and diced, or 8 large red, ripe tomatoes, stem ends removed and chopped

Pinch of red chile pepper flakes

Heat the olive oil in a skillet, then add the garlic. Cook over moderate heat until the garlic gives off its characteristic aroma, then add the tomatoes and red chile pepper flakes. Cook the tomatoes over high heat, stirring frequently, until they break down, become saucey, then begin to thicken. When the sauce is thick enough to serve, set it aside while you prepare the pasta.

TO ASSEMBLE DISH:

Make Spaghetti Aglio e Olio according to the recipe on page 156. Place the spaghetti in a shallow serving dish. Pour the piping-hot tomato sauce in a ring around the edge of the pasta so the spaghetti is visible in the center. Sprinkle the bread crumbs over the spaghetti in the center of the dish, completely covering it. Present the dish at the table, then toss pasta before serving. Pass Parmesan cheese, if desired.

Penne al Pomodoro Arrichito

Penne with Enriched Tomato Sauce

Serves 4 to 6

Tomatoes, butter, and wine seem an unusual combination for the Italian kitchen, which usually pairs olive oil with tomatoes. However, this sauce is strong on flavor and extremely simple to make. A welcome, if only occasional, break from olive-oil–based tomato sauces.

4 *tablespoons unsalted butter*

1 *medium onion, peeled and finely chopped*

16 *Roma tomatoes, peeled, seeded, and chopped, or 8 large red, ripe tomatoes, peeled, seeded, and chopped*

¾ *cup dry white wine*

10 *fresh basil leaves, roughly chopped*

Salt and freshly ground black pepper to taste

1 *pound imported penne*

Grated Parmesan cheese for the table

Melt the butter in a skillet. Add the onion and fry over low heat until soft and translucent. Add the tomatoes to the skillet and cook until they begin

(Continued)

to give up their juice and become saucey. Add the wine, basil, and salt and pepper to taste, and continue cooking until the sauce thickens.

Meanwhile, cook the penne in abundant boiling salted water until al dente. Drain the pasta very well in a colander. If the skillet is not big enough to accommodate all the pasta and sauce, place both in the pot used to boil the pasta water. Heat the penne and sauce together over high heat just until the pasta absorbs some of the sauce. Serve immediately in a shallow serving bowl. Pass Parmesan cheese.

Conchiglie ai Funghi

Shells with Mushroom Sauce

Serves 4 to 6

A simple sauce, rich with the distinctive flavor of mushrooms and rosemary. The shell shape of the pasta works perfectly with this sauce, trapping bits of mushroom and fresh tomato.

1 *pound white mushrooms*

¼ *cup extra-virgin olive oil*

1 *small onion, peeled and finely diced*

2 *garlic cloves, peeled and lightly smashed*

4 *red, ripe tomatoes, peeled, seeded, and chopped*

1 *sprig fresh rosemary, leaves only, finely minced*

2 *anchovy fillets, very finely minced*

Freshly ground black pepper to taste

1 *pound imported medium-sized pasta shells*

Grated Parmesan cheese for table use

Carefully wipe the mushrooms clean with a damp kitchen towel. Trim stems and cut the mushrooms into vertical slices. Set aside.

Heat the olive oil in a large, heavy skillet. Add the onion and garlic, and cook slowly over low heat for approximately 10 minutes, or until onion wilts and softens. Add the mushrooms and cook over high heat until they are tender and the liquid they throw off nearly completely evaporates. Add the tomatoes and rosemary, and cook until tomatoes begin to break down and release their juices, about 5 minutes. Add the anchovy fillets and pepper to taste, mixing well. Cook just until anchovies melt into the sauce.

Cook the pasta shells in abundant boiling salted water until al dente. Drain the shells in a colander. Transfer the drained pasta and the hot mushroom sauce to a large, shallow bowl. Toss to mix well. Serve immediately, passing Parmesan cheese at the table.

Fusilli Lunghi con Verdure alla Griglia

Long Fusilli with Grilled Vegetables

Serves 4 to 6

The ingredients in this dish can be varied according to the season and the amount of time you wish to spend at the kitchen stove or backyard grill. This recipe uses vegetables that require little effort in preparation. The unique smoky taste of the grill is imparted to the vegetables while fresh thyme and sun-dried tomatoes add strong flavor notes.

4 *small, firm zucchini, ends trimmed, cut into thin slices lengthwise*

4 *Japanese eggplants, stem ends trimmed, cut in half lengthwise*

2 *red onions, peeled and cut into medium crosswise slices*

3 *heads Belgian endive, trimmed and cut in half lengthwise*

Extra-virgin olive oil for grilling plus ¾ cup extra-virgin olive oil

½ *cup lemon juice*

6 *garlic cloves, peeled and minced*

10 *fresh basil leaves, cut into julienne*

½ *cup roughly chopped Italian parsley leaves*

1 *tablespoon fresh thyme leaves*

12 *sun-dried tomatoes, packed in oil, cut into julienne*

Salt and freshly ground black pepper to taste

1 *pound imported long fusilli or spaghetti*

Grated imported Parmesan cheese for use at the table

Heat a gas or charcoal grill or ridged stovetop griddle until medium hot. If a grill or griddle is unavailable, use a preheated broiler. Lightly brush the prepared vegetables with olive oil. Grill the zucchini approximately 1 minute per side, or just until grill marks are apparent. Do not overcook. Transfer from grill to a bowl. Grill the eggplant, cut side down, for approximately 2 minutes. Eggplant should be dark brown with very apparent grill marks. Turn and grill on other side just until eggplant softens. When cooked, place in the bowl with the zucchini. Grill the onion slices until translucent and very soft, turning once. Add to the other vegetables. Grill the Belgian endive approximately 2 minutes per side, or just until it begins to wilt. Transfer to the bowl with the other vegetables.

When the grilled vegetables are cool enough to handle, cut them into rough julienne as follows: Slice the zucchini, eggplant, and endive crosswise into thin strips. Cut the onion slices in half. Mix the vegetables together in a medium-sized stainless-steel, glass, enamel, or pottery bowl.

In a small bowl mix together ¾ cup of olive oil, lemon juice, and garlic. Add the dressing to the grilled vegetables and toss gently to mix. Add the basil, parsley, thyme, sun-dried tomatoes, and salt and pepper, and toss again gently to mix. Set vegetables aside to marinate at least 1 hour. Then correct the seasonings, adding additional olive oil or lemon juice if desired.

When ready to serve, cook the fusilli or spaghetti in abundant boiling salted water until al dente. Drain the pasta in a colander. Place drained pasta immediately in a large, shallow serving bowl. Add the marinated grilled vegetables and toss gently to mix. Pass grated Parmesan cheese.

Gnocchetti Sardi con Verdura

Gnocchetti Sardi with Greens

Serves 4 to 6

A country-style pasta from Sardinia that traditionally features greens and fresh cream baked with eggs broken over the top. In our version the eggs and cream are lightly beaten together, which when cooked results in a custardy texture.

Salt

2 *bunches Swiss chard, leafy green parts only*

2 *bunches tender spinach, tough stems removed*

1 *pound imported gnocchetti sardi*

3 *tablespoons butter*

3 *cloves garlic, peeled and finely chopped*

¾ *cup grated Pecorino Romano cheese, plus additional for sprinkling on top*

Salt to taste

2 *cups cream*

2 *eggs, lightly beaten*

Bring a big pot of water to a boil. Add salt and the Swiss chard and stir. When the chard is almost cooked, after about 4 minutes, add the spinach and finish cooking until the greens are tender. Lift the greens out of the pot and reserve the cooking water. Finely chop the greens. Cook the gnocchetti sardi in the reserved cooking water until slightly more firm than al dente. Meanwhile, place the butter and garlic in a small sauté pan and cook over low heat for 2 to 3 minutes, or until the garlic is opaque. Drain the pasta well and toss with the butter and garlic, the chopped greens, Pecorino Romano cheese, and salt to taste. Select a gratin dish large enough to contain the pasta mixture. Distribute pasta evenly in gratin dish. Lightly beat together the cream and eggs, and pour over the pasta. Sprinkle with more grated cheese. Bake in a preheated 350° oven for about 10 to 15 minutes, or until very hot. Remove from the oven and let settle for a few minutes before serving.

Spaghetti con Peperoni Fritti

S p a g h e t t i   w i t h   F r i e d   P e p p e r s

Serves 4 to 6

We combine a favorite antipasto of peppers, garlic, capers, and olives with pasta to create a flavorful dish bright with color. Frying peppers brings out their lush sweetness.

¼ *cup extra-virgin olive oil*

2 *green bell peppers, stems removed, seeded, cut into julienne*

2 *yellow bell peppers, stems removed, seeded, cut into julienne*

2 *red bell peppers, stems removed, seeded, cut into julienne*

4–5 *garlic cloves, peeled and minced*

1 *tablespoon capers*

20 *Calamata olives, pitted and cut in quarters lengthwise*

3 *anchovy fillets, soaked in milk 10 minutes, rinsed, and finely chopped*

Salt and freshly ground black pepper to taste

1 *pound imported spaghetti*

Handful chopped Italian parsley

Grated Parmesan cheese for the table

Heat the olive oil in a skillet and gently fry the peppers over moderate heat until they are half cooked, approximately 10 to 15 minutes. Add the

(Continued)

garlic, capers, olives, and anchovies, and continue to cook until the peppers are tender with a bit of golden brown around the edges.

Meanwhile, cook the spaghetti in abundant boiling salted water until al dente. Drain the pasta well in a colander, then place in the skillet with the pepper mixture. Toss briefly over high heat so the pasta can absorb some of the sauce. Place the pasta and peppers in a shallow serving dish, and serve immediately. Pass Parmesan cheese.

Conchiglie ai Carciofi alla Panna

Pasta with Artichoke and Cream Sauce

Serves 4 to 6

This pasta dish in muted shades of green and gold is pleasing to the eye as well as the palate. Just the edible trimmed portion of the artichoke heart is used, so that nothing interferes with the smooth texture. Moist, golden Parmesan cheese provides a perfect finishing touch to the rich flavor.

3 *artichokes*

2 *lemons, cut in half*

¼ *cup extra-virgin olive oil*

1 *medium onion, peeled and cut into small dice*

1 *garlic clove, peeled and minced*

3 *tablespoons chopped Italian parsley*

Salt and freshly ground black pepper to taste

1 *cup heavy cream*

1 *pound imported conchiglie rigate*

¼ *cup grated Parmesan cheese, plus additional for use at the table*

Clean the artichokes as directed on page 94. Cut the cleaned artichokes into small ¼-inch slivers. Fill a medium-sized bowl with water and squeeze the lemons into it, adding the lemon halves to the water, too. Immerse the slivered artichokes in the lemon water to prevent them from darkening. Place the olive oil, onion, garlic, and parsley in a medium-sized sauté pan. Sauté over low heat until the onion is tender, about 10 minutes. Drain the artichoke slivers and add to the sauté pan. Toss them in the oil, season to taste with salt and pepper, cover and cook over moderate heat until artichokes are tender, about 10 minutes. It adds to their flavor if they brown a little. Add the cream and boil for a few minutes until the mixture thickens slightly. Meanwhile, cook the conchiglie rigate in abundant boiling salted water until al dente. Drain the pasta and put in a shallow serving dish. Toss with the sauce and a ¼ cup of Parmesan cheese. Serve immediately and pass extra cheese at the table.

Linguine al Tutti Colori

Linguine with Colorful Sauce

Serves 4 to 6

This easy, light summer pasta is alive with the bright colors of red and yellow peppers. The flavors of leeks, herbs, olives, and sun-dried tomatoes are complemented by the pungent goat cheese, which adds a special touch to the dish.

¼ cup extra-virgin olive oil

4 leeks, thoroughly cleaned, sliced thinly

2 yellow bell peppers, stems removed, seeded, cut into julienne

3 red bell peppers, stems removed, seeded, cut into julienne

½ cup dry white wine

10 fresh basil leaves, cut into julienne

2 sprigs fresh thyme, leaves only, chopped

6 sun-dried tomatoes, cut into julienne

20 Calamata olives, pitted and coarsely chopped

Salt and freshly ground black pepper to taste

4 ounces goat cheese, crumbled

1 pound imported linguine

Grated Parmesan cheese for the table

Heat the olive oil in a skillet. Add the leeks and sauté just until they begin to go limp. Add the peppers and gently fry over moderate heat until they soften. Add the white wine and cook over high heat until wine evaporates. Turn down the heat and add the herbs, sun-dried tomatoes, olives, and salt and pepper to taste. Continue cooking approximately 5 minutes, so the flavors of the herbs and olives blend with the peppers. Place the goat cheese in a shallow serving bowl.

Meanwhile, cook the linguine in abundant boiling salted water until al dente. Drain the pasta well in a colander, then place it in the serving bowl with the goat cheese. Quickly toss to mix the goat cheese well with the pasta. Add the pepper mixture, toss briefly, and serve. Pass Parmesan cheese.

Linguine all'Algheresa

Sardinian Clam Sauce

Serves 4 to 6

Nothing is quite as enticing as a bowl of pasta and fresh clams. In this highly flavorful clam sauce from Alghero, Sardinia, the use of green olives in cooking reflects a Spanish and Catalan influence.

2 *pounds fresh clams*

½ *cup extra-virgin olive oil*

4 *garlic cloves, peeled and minced*

½ *teaspoon dried red chile pepper flakes*

3 *large red, ripe tomatoes, approximately 1 pound, peeled, seeded, and coarsely chopped*

1 *level tablespoon small capers*

¼ *cup pitted green olives, cut into quarters lengthwise*

2 *tablespoons coarsely chopped fresh oregano or 1 teaspoon dried oregano*

2 *tablespoons coarsely chopped Italian parsley, divided*

Salt to taste

1 *cup dry white wine or 1 cup pasta cooking water*

1 *pound imported linguine*

To clean clams, place them in abundant cold salted water to soak. (The kitchen sink is more convenient for this than a bowl.) Soak the clams for

(Continued)

about ½ hour. Lift them out of the water, a few at a time, rinse under cold running water, and place in a bowl. Clean the sink thoroughly of all sand and fill again with cold water and salt. Gently add the clams to the water and let soak for another ½ hour. Lift the clams out and rinse under fresh cold water. Place the cleansed clams in a bowl, discarding those that are open and do not close at a touch, any with cracked shells, and any that seem too heavy (they are probably filled with mud). Set clams aside in the refrigerator until needed.

Heat the olive oil over low heat in a large skillet or casserole with a wide base. Add the garlic and red chile pepper flakes, and gently sauté just until the garlic gives off its characteristic aroma. Add the chopped tomatoes, capers, olives, oregano, 1 tablespoon parsley, and a pinch of salt. Stir to mix, cover the skillet, and cook over moderate heat just until tomatoes begin to break down, approximately 3 to 5 minutes. Remove the cover.

Add the clams to the tomato sauce. Add the wine or pasta cooking water. Cover the skillet and turn up heat to high. Cook clams quickly, just until they open up, shaking skillet occasionally to make sure each clam has contact with the high heat. When all the shells are open, remove the cover, take the skillet off the heat, and discard any clams that refuse to open. Quickly transfer all the clams from the skillet to a bowl. Cover with a towel to keep warm while cooking the pasta.

Meanwhile, cook the linguine in abundant boiling salted water until just barely al dente. Drain the pasta in a colander. Add the drained pasta to the skillet with the tomato-clam sauce. Toss the linguine with the sauce over high heat so that the pasta begins to absorb some of the sauce. Place the pasta immediately in a large shallow serving bowl, and put the cooked clams in the shell on top. Pour any juices remaining in the skillet over the clams. Sprinkle the remaining tablespoon of chopped parsley over all.

Gnocchetti Rigati alla Ciociara

Farmwoman's Pasta with Ricotta

Serves 4 to 6

Adding a touch of pasta water to ricotta creates a creamy-textured sauce that is less rich than cream yet clings wonderfully to the pasta. Just a bit of bacon lends extra flavor. The onion intensifies the naturally sweet taste of the ricotta, along with the pungent bite of green onion.

¼ *cup extra-virgin olive oil*

1 *onion, peeled and diced*

2 *slices bacon, coarsely chopped*

1 *pound ricotta*

¼ *cup coarsely chopped Italian parsley leaves*

15 *fresh basil leaves, coarsely chopped*

1 *tablespoon finely chopped green onion tops*

¼ *cup grated Parmesan cheese, plus additional for table use*

Salt and freshly ground black pepper to taste

1 *pound imported gnocchetti rigati or rigatoni*

Heat the olive oil in a medium-sized heavy skillet. Add the onion and bacon, and cook over low heat until the onion is soft and translucent and the bacon renders its fat but is not yet crisp. Remove from the heat and set aside.

In a small mixing bowl beat with a wooden spoon the ricotta with the parsley, basil, green-onion tops, and Parmesan cheese. Add the cooked onion, the bacon and its fat, and salt and pepper to taste. Mix well.

Cook the gnocchetti rigati or rigatoni pasta in abundant boiling salted water until al dente. While the pasta is cooking, add ¼ to ½ cup of the cooking water to the ricotta mixture. Mix well. Drain the pasta in a colander, immediately placing it in a shallow serving bowl. Add the ricotta mixture and toss. Serve immediately, passing additional Parmesan cheese.

Linguine ai Gamberi

Linguine with Shrimp

Serves 4 to 6

A simple tasty dish of shrimp, fresh tomatoes, and herbs that takes about 10 minutes to make. Shrimp is at its best when it is just cooked through, so take care not to keep it on the stove any longer than necessary.

¼ cup extra-virgin olive oil

4 garlic cloves, peeled and minced

½ teaspoon dried red chile pepper flakes (or to taste)

3 pounds red, ripe tomatoes, peeled, seeded, and chopped, approximately 4½ cups

1 cup dry white wine

15 fresh medium basil leaves, roughly chopped

½ cup chopped Italian parsley, leaves only

1 pound medium shrimp, peeled and deveined

1 pound imported linguine

Heat the olive oil in a 10- to 12-inch skillet over low heat. Add the garlic and red chile pepper flakes to the oil and stir. Lightly sauté the garlic until it gives off its characteristic aroma, approximately 1 minute.

Add the tomatoes and white wine to the skillet. Cover and cook the tomatoes over medium heat for 2 to 3 minutes, or until they begin to break down and release their juice. Add the basil and parsley. Stir frequently and continue cooking over moderate heat, cover removed, until the tomatoes and wine form a sauce, approximately 10 to 15 minutes.

Add the shrimp to the sauce and cook over high heat just until the shrimp are tender. They will continue to cook when they are removed from the heat, so be careful not to overcook them.

Meanwhile, cook the linguine in abundant boiling salted water until al dente. Drain the pasta in a colander. Add the drained pasta to the skillet with the shrimp-tomato sauce. Toss the linguine with the sauce over high heat so that the pasta begins to absorb some of the sauce. Serve immediately in individual pasta dishes or in a large, shallow serving bowl.

Pasta con Tonno alla Siciliana

Pasta with Fresh Tuna and Mint

Serves 4 to 6

A variation on a Sicilian dish in which a chunk of fresh tuna is stuffed with mint and garlic and braised in tomato sauce. In our recipe the tuna is diced and quickly sautéed, then added to the sauce to finish cooking. Paper-thin slices of garlic and chopped fresh mint are added at the last moment and cooked very briefly so that their flavors stay strong and bright.

(Continued)

Pasta
175

6 tablespoons extra-virgin olive oil, divided

1 large onion, peeled and cut into medium dice

2½ pounds tomatoes, peeled, seeded, and coarsely chopped

1 pound fresh tuna, cut into ½-inch-thick steaks

Salt and freshly ground black pepper to taste

½ cup chopped fresh mint

3 garlic cloves, thinly sliced

1 pound imported conchiglie rigate

Place 4 tablespoons of the olive oil and the onion in a large sauté pan. Cook over low heat until the onion is tender, about 10 to 12 minutes. Add the tomatoes and salt and pepper to taste. Cook over medium heat, partly covered, until juices thicken and a sauce forms, about 15 minutes.

Cut the tuna into ½-inch dice. Season with salt and pepper to taste. Place the remaining 2 tablespoons of olive oil in a separate medium-sized skillet. Turn up heat to medium, add tuna, and toss until tuna is cooked on the surface but still pink at the center.

When the sauce has thickened, add the tuna, mint, and garlic, and cook for an additional 2 to 3 minutes, or until tuna is just cooked.

Cook the conchiglie rigate in abundant salted boiling water until al dente. Drain the pasta well. Place in a serving bowl. Add the sauce and toss gently. Serve immediately.

Linguine al Tonno alla Puttanesca

Linguine with Fresh Tuna
Puttanesca Style

Serves 4 to 6

Fresh tuna has an affinity for the piquant and strong flavors of the traditional Roman puttanesca sauce. It seems a natural—to combine the meaty fish with capers, black olives, garlic, plenty of hot red pepper, and tomatoes.

¼ cup extra-virgin olive oil

4–5 garlic cloves, peeled and minced

½–1 teaspoon red chile pepper flakes

12 Roma tomatoes, peeled, seeded, chopped, or 6 ripe, round tomatoes, peeled, seeded, and chopped

1 tablespoon capers

¼ cup pitted Moroccan or Calamata olives, cut into quarters lengthwise

3 anchovy fillets, soaked in milk for 10 minutes, rinsed in cold water, and finely chopped

1 pound fresh tuna, roughly cut into 1-inch dice

1 pound imported linguine

Heat the olive oil in a skillet over moderate heat. Add the garlic and red chile pepper flakes and let cook just until the garlic begins to give off its characteristic fragrance. Add the tomatoes and cook over high heat, stirring frequently until tomatoes begin to break down and give off their juice. Add the capers and olives, turn down heat, and continue to cook until the sauce begins to thicken. Add the anchovies and tuna. Simmer until the tuna is cooked through and the sauce thickens.

(Continued)

Meanwhile, cook the linguine in abundant boiling salted water until just barely al dente. Drain the pasta in a colander, then add the drained pasta to the skillet with the tomato-tuna sauce. Toss the linguine with the sauce over high heat so that the pasta begins to absorb some of the sauce. Place the pasta immediately in a large shallow serving bowl.

Sugo Sciue Sciue

Fast Ragù

Serves 4 to 6

This is it. Spaghetti sauce. The Neapolitan fast, fast version of ragù. Simple and satisfying with no pretensions. Serve it with plenty of real Parmigiano-Reggiano or Pecorino Romano cheese. Many of our Napoletani friends do not use any garlic in this dish (although we prefer it). Try preparing it without garlic for a change.

¼ cup extra-virgin olive oil

1 large onion, peeled and minced

2 garlic cloves, peeled and minced (optional)

1 pound ground chuck

Small handful coarsely chopped Italian parsley

8 fresh basil leaves, coarsely chopped, or 1 teaspoon dried basil

1 28-ounce can imported Italian tomatoes, pureed with juice

Salt and freshly ground black pepper to taste

1 pound imported spaghetti or rigatoni

Grated Pecorino Romano or Parmesan cheese for table use

Heat the olive oil in a medium sized, heavy skillet. Add the onion (and garlic, if desired), and cook slowly over low heat until the onion becomes very soft. Add the ground chuck and sauté over high heat, stirring frequently to break up any large lumps. Add the parsley and basil. When the meat has lost all pinkness, add the pureed tomatoes and salt and pepper to taste, and cook over medium-low heat until the tomato puree has mixed with the meat and become thick. This should take approximately ½ hour. Do not overcook this sauce!

Cook the spaghetti or rigatoni in abundant boiling salted water until al dente. Drain the pasta in a colander. Place the drained pasta in the skillet with the sauce, and mix together over low heat so that the pasta absorbs some of the sauce. Place the pasta in a shallow serving bowl. Serve immediately, passing plenty of imported grated Pecorino Romano or Parmigiano-Reggiano cheese.

Orecchiette al Pomodoro Fresco
e Carne Magro
Little Ears with Fresh Tomato
and Lean Beef Sauce

Serves 4 to 6

This sauce is even faster than Sugo Sciue Sciue (see page 178). It is the opposite of traditional long-simmered meat sauces. Lean ground beef is lightly cooked in extra-virgin olive oil. Chopped fresh tomatoes are added and cooked quickly over high heat, and fresh basil is stirred into the sauce just before serving. The small, cupped orecchiette serve as perfect containers for the bits of meat and tomato. Make this sauce in the summer when ripe tomatoes are plentiful.

6 tablespoons extra-virgin olive oil, divided	*2½ pounds ripe Roma tomatoes, peeled, seeded, and chopped*
¾ pound lean ground beef	*1 pound imported orecchiette*
Salt to taste	*Handful fresh basil leaves, chopped*
2 garlic cloves, peeled and finely chopped	*Grated Pecorino Romano cheese*

Place 2 tablespoons of the olive oil in a large sauté pan. Add the ground beef and cook over low heat until the meat loses its raw color, stirring often to break up the lumps. Drain off excess fat and season with salt to taste.

Put the remaining 4 tablespoons of olive oil in the sauté pan. Add the garlic, and cook over low heat for a few minutes until garlic turns opaque. Add the tomatoes, season with salt to taste, raise the heat to medium high, and cook until the tomatoes lose their excess juice and break down into a sauce, about 15 minutes.

Cook the orecchiette in salted boiling water until al dente, and drain well. Place the pasta in a serving bowl, toss with the sauce, chopped basil, and about ¼ cup of the grated Pecorino Romano cheese. Serve immediately, passing additional grated cheese at the table.

Genovese Finto

Rich Sauce of Onions and Prosciutto

Serves 4 to 6

Genovese, a famous Neapolitan sauce, demonstrates the ingenuity of the poor in providing a full meal from meager rations. In most traditional Genovese recipes, a not-so-tender cut of meat is stewed for hours with an enormous quantity of onions; the cook may add some wine, tomatoes, or carrots. The resultant flavorful cooking juices, along with a few bits of meat, are used to sauce pasta while the rest of the meat, by now tender, is reserved for the second course or to create an entirely new dish. Our recipe duplicates the rich flavor of the more traditional recipe in the long, slow cooking of the onions and prosciutto. Do not hurry the process. The longer the onions cook, the more flavorful and rich the sauce. The trick is to let them cook in just enough liquid and olive oil that they caramelize to a very deep dark brown but do not burn. When the dish is finished, you should have approximately 2 cups of dark brown onions in a small amount of reduced, richly flavored broth.

(Continued)

½ cup extra-virgin olive oil

3 onions, peeled and cut into small dice

6 thin slices prosciutto, cut crosswise into thin slivers

½ cup red wine

2 cups (approximately) water or broth

Freshly ground black pepper to taste

1 pound imported penne

Large handful grated Parmesan cheese

Heat the olive oil in a large, heavy skillet. Add the onions and stir well so they are completely coated with oil. Cover the skillet and cook onions over medium-low heat for approximately 3 hours. Lift the cover frequently and stir. Add the red wine to the skillet during the first 15 minutes of cooking when the onions have wilted a bit. Add the prosciutto after the onions have cooked about 1½ hours. When the wine has been absorbed into the onions and the liquid begins to evaporate, add a small amount of water or broth from time to time, and stir well to deglaze the pan and reincorporate any dark brown or burned bits that may stick to the bottom or sides of the skillet. Add freshly ground black pepper to taste toward the end of the cooking time.

Cook the penne in abundant boiling salted water until al dente. Drain the pasta and place in the skillet containing the onions. Heat briefly over moderately high heat just until the pasta absorbs the flavor of the sauce. Place the pasta in a shallow serving bowl and serve immediately, topped with grated Parmesan cheese.

Fettuccine al Prosciutto e Pomodoro

Fettuccine with Prosciutto and Tomato

Serves 4

In this quickly cooked sauce, the heat lightly touches the sweet butter, salty prosciutto, and fresh tomatoes, warming them just enough to release their flavor. Fettuccine is the pasta of choice, its porous surface greedily absorbing all the buttery juices.

6 *slices prosciutto, sliced slightly thicker than paper thin*

1½ *pounds Roma tomatoes*

8 *tablespoons unsalted butter, at room temperature, divided*

Salt

1 *pound fresh fettuccine*

Freshly ground black pepper to taste

Grated Parmesan cheese

Slice the prosciutto crosswise into julienne. If the prosciutto sticks together, separate the strips and let them dry for a few minutes on a plate.

Peel, seed, and cut the tomatoes into small dice. Let drain in a colander to remove the excess liquid.

Place 4 tablespoons of the butter in a medium-sized sauté pan, and melt over low heat. Add the prosciutto strips and toss in the butter for a few minutes until the meat turns a dark shade of pink. Add the tomatoes, and cook for 1 to 2 minutes, or just long enough to gently warm them.

Cook the fettuccine in abundant salted boiling water until just tender. Drain well. Place the remaining butter in the bottom of a shallow serving dish. Add the fettuccine, the sauce from the sauté pan, and a generous amount of freshly ground black pepper to taste. Toss quickly. Taste for and add more salt, if needed. Serve with Parmesan cheese on the side.

Perciatelli con Pancetta e Vino Rosso

Perciatelli with Pancetta and Red Wine

Serves 4 to 6

This sauce derives its savory flavor from a small touch of pancetta and robust red wine. The sharp tang of Pecorino Romano cheese is a must.

3 tablespoons extra-virgin olive oil	2½ pounds ripe tomatoes, peeled, seeded, and coarsely pureed
1 small onion, peeled and finely diced	Salt and freshly ground black pepper to taste
2 tender celery stalks, finely diced	⅓ cup rich red wine
2 small carrots, peeled and finely diced	1 pound imported perciatelli, broken into short lengths
¼ cup chopped Italian parsley	6 tablespoons grated Pecorino Romano cheese, plus additional for the table
3 slices lean pancetta (about 3 ounces), cut into strips	

Place the olive oil in a medium-sized sauté pan. Add the onion, celery, carrots, and parsley. Cook over medium-low heat for a few minutes, then add the pancetta and continue to cook until the onion is tender, approximately 10 minutes. Add the tomatoes and salt and pepper to taste, raise the heat to medium, and cook for about 10 minutes. Add the red wine and continue to cook the sauce over medium-low heat until it thickens, about 15 minutes.

Cook the perciatelli in abundant salted boiling water. When the pasta is al dente, drain it well. Place the pasta in a serving bowl. Add the sauce and 6 tablespoons of grated Pecorino Romano cheese. Toss well and serve with additional cheese on the side.

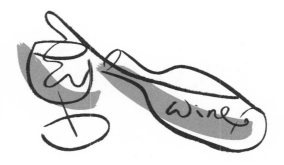

Pasta Fresca con Fagioli e Pancetta

Fettuccine with Borlotti Beans and Pancetta

Serves 4

A great example of how simplicity and sophistication can go hand in hand. The faintly sweet and nutty flavor and rich, creamy texture of borlotti beans contrasted with tender egg pasta are what distinguishes this very special dish.

(Continued)

¼ cup extra-virgin olive oil

3–4 garlic cloves, peeled and finely chopped

1 teaspoon red chile pepper flakes

2 slices lean pancetta, about ⅛ inch thick, cut into strips

1½ cups cooked borlotti beans, drained

Salt and freshly ground black pepper to taste

1 pound fresh fettuccine

Small handful fresh basil leaves, chopped

Grated Parmesan cheese, optional

Cruet of extra-virgin olive oil for table use

Place the olive oil, garlic, red chile pepper flakes, and pancetta in a large sauté pan. Cook over low heat until the pancetta renders its fat, about 5 minutes. Keep the heat low so that the garlic does not burn. Add the borlotti beans and salt and pepper to taste, and stir well to coat the beans in the oil. Continue to cook gently over low heat for about 10 minutes, or until the beans are hot and have absorbed the flavor of the garlic, red chile, and pancetta. Add a few tablespoons of warm water to keep the mixture moist. Cook the fettuccine in abundant salted boiling water until just tender, and drain, but leave some water clinging to the pasta strands. Place the pasta in the sauté pan with the beans, sprinkle with basil, toss, and gently warm over low heat for 1 to 2 minutes to let the pasta absorb the flavor. Taste for salt, place in a serving bowl, and grind a little fresh black pepper over the top. Serve, with grated cheese, if desired. Place the cruet of extra-virgin olive oil on the table so each person can drizzle a little oil over the pasta.

Fettuccine con Salame

Fresh Pasta with Salame

Serves 4 to 6

The smooth flavor of pasta all'uovo, or egg pasta, is an unusual contrast to the strong bite of the salame. This is a very light dish that nonetheless satisfies because of the salame and prosciutto it contains. It is a good example of a pasta dish that is not "saucey." The sauce is a simple reduction of white wine and chicken broth which lightly moistens the pasta. Do not drain the fettuccine completely; adding a little pasta cooking water to the dish will help keep it moist.

3 *tablespoons extra-virgin olive oil*

1 *medium red onion, peeled and minced*

2 *celery stalks, trimmed and minced*

4 *garlic cloves, peeled and minced*

3 *ounces thinly sliced prosciutto, cut into julienne*

3 *ounces Italian dry salame, thinly sliced, cut into julienne*

1 *cup fresh or frozen peas*

½ *cup dry white wine*

½ *cup chicken broth*

Handful chopped Italian parsley

Salt and freshly ground black pepper to taste

1½ *pounds fresh egg fettuccine or 1 pound dried egg fettuccine*

Grated Parmesan cheese for table use

Heat the olive oil in a skillet and sauté the onion until it is wilted. Add the celery and garlic, and cook until the vegetables are soft. Add the prosciutto

(Continued)

and salame, and cook just until the prosciutto changes color. Add the peas and white wine. Let the wine come to the boil and cook until the alcohol evaporates. Add the chicken broth and cook until it reduces slightly. Add the parsley and salt and pepper to taste just before tossing sauce with the pasta.

Meanwhile, cook the fettuccine in abundant boiling salted water until just tender. Drain carefully and add the pasta to the skillet with the sauce. Toss over high heat briefly to let the fettuccine absorb the sauce. Serve in a shallow serving bowl. Pass Parmesan cheese.

Orecchiette con Salsicce e Finocchio

Little Ears with Sausage and Fennel

Serves 4 to 6

In this savory dish the light anise flavor of the fennel seed in the sausage is echoed by the fresh fennel. The optional cream serves to smooth out the sauce and help it cling to the pasta.

¼ *cup extra-virgin olive oil*

½ *medium onion, peeled and minced*

2 *fennel bulbs, trimmed and thinly sliced*

2 *garlic cloves, peeled and minced*

10 *ounces sweet Italian sausage, casings removed, crumbled*

10 *fresh basil leaves, cut into julienne*

5 *sprigs fresh oregano, leaves only*

½ *cup chicken broth*

½ *cup young red wine*

Salt and freshly ground black pepper to taste

½ *cup cream (optional)*

1 *pound imported orecchiette*

Grated Parmesan or Pecorino Romano cheese for the table

Heat the olive oil in a medium-sized skillet. Add the onion and gently sauté over low heat until it wilts. Add the fennel and continue cooking until both fennel and onion are soft. Turn up the heat and add the garlic to the skillet. Sauté garlic briefly just until it turns opaque and releases its characteristic aroma. Add the sausage and brown over high heat. When no trace of pink remains in the sausage, add the basil, oregano, chicken broth, red wine, and salt and pepper to taste. Turn down the heat to medium and cook sauce until the liquids reduce and the flavors are well blended. Add the cream, if desired, and cook just until it reduces slightly, about 5 minutes.

Cook the orecchiette in abundant boiling salted water until al dente. Drain the pasta thoroughly and transfer to the skillet with the sauce. Cook briefly over moderate heat, stirring well. Serve immediately in a large shallow serving bowl topped with plenty of grated cheese of your choice.

Fettuccine al Sugo Invernale

Fettuccine with Winter Sauce

Serves 4

This pasta for a winter day has all the comforting flavor and richness that cold weather requires. Pancetta, sausage, and porcini mushrooms are cooked with tomatoes, tossed with golden fettuccine, and dusted with freshly grated Parmigiano-Reggiano cheese.

1 *ounce dried porcini mushrooms*

3 *tablespoons unsalted butter, divided*

½ *medium onion, peeled and cut into small dice*

2 *slices pancetta, coarsely chopped*

1 *sprig fresh rosemary, leaves chopped*

2 *sweet Italian sausages, casings removed*

¼ *cup dry white wine*

1 *28-ounce can imported Italian tomatoes*

Salt and freshly ground black pepper to taste

1 *pound fresh fettuccine*

¼ *cup freshly grated Parmigiano-Reggiano cheese, plus additional for the table*

Place the porcini mushrooms in a small bowl and cover with hot water. After 20 minutes, lift the mushrooms out of the soaking liquid, rinse gently, and coarsely chop. Strain the soaking liquid and reserve.

Place 2 tablespoons of the butter, onion, pancetta, and rosemary in a large sauté pan. Cook over medium-low heat until the onion is tender and the pancetta has rendered its fat, about 10 minutes. Stir frequently to prevent sticking. Add the sausage and cook over medium heat, breaking up the meat with a wooden spoon. After 5 minutes add the white wine and cook until the alcohol evaporates. Lift the tomatoes out of the can, scoop out seeds with your fingers, and crush the tomatoes into the sauce, adding salt and pepper to taste. After 10 minutes add the chopped mushrooms and 3 table-spoons of the reserved porcini soaking liquid. Continue cooking the sauce for another 20 minutes, adding more porcini soaking liquid if sauce becomes dry.

Cook the fettuccine in abundant boiling salted water until just tender. Drain the pasta and place in a shallow serving bowl. Add the remaining tablespoon of butter, the sauce, and 4 tablespoons of grated cheese. Toss quickly and serve. Pass additional grated cheese at the table.

Orecchiette con Broccoli e Salsicce

Orecchiette with Broccoli and Sausage

Serves 4 to 6

A great full-flavored pasta. After a preliminary blanching, the broccoli is cooked slowly with the sausages to create a deep, rich blend of flavors. Grated Pecorino Romano cheese melts into the finished dish, giving the sauce a creamy finish. Orecchiette—small, round cup-shaped pasta whose name, literally translated, means little ears—catch bits of sausage and broccoli. A very savory sauce, one of our favorites.

(Continued)

1 *bunch tender broccoli*

Salt

3 *tablespoons extra-virgin olive oil, plus extra for drizzling*

3 *garlic cloves, peeled and minced*

½ *pound sweet sausage*

½ *cup water*

Salt and freshly ground black pepper to taste

1 *pound imported orecchiette*

½ *cup grated Pecorino Romano cheese*

Trim and peel the broccoli stalks, and cut broccoli into quarters lengthwise. Bring a large pot of water to the boil. Add the salt and broccoli pieces, and cook until broccoli is tender but crisp. Drain and chop medium-fine. Combine the olive oil and garlic in a medium-sized sauté pan. Cook over low heat for several minutes, or until garlic releases its aroma. Remove the sausage from its casings and crumble it into the pan. Cook sausage over low heat until it loses its raw color. Add the broccoli and toss. Add about ½ cup water and season with salt and pepper to taste. Cook until the broccoli breaks down and forms a coarse puree. Use the back of a wooden spoon to break down the broccoli as it cooks. Add more water if mixture becomes dry.

Cook the orecchiette in abundant boiling salted water until al dente. Drain the pasta and place in a serving bowl. Drizzle with a little olive oil and toss. Add the sauce and ½ cup grated Pecorino Romano cheese and toss until the cheese melts into the sauce.

Spaghetti alla Carbonara

Serves 4 to 6

Thereare probably as many versions of Spaghetti alla Carbonara as there are Roman cooks. One evening we watched a friend, a beautiful young Roman dancer, prepare this version at home. We find that the touch of wine and fresh parsley lightens this famous sauce.

¼ *cup extra-virgin olive oil*

1 *small onion, peeled and finely diced*

3 *thin slices pancetta or prosciutto, cut into thin slivers*

½ *cup dry white wine*

1 *pound imported spaghetti*

4 *egg yolks*

Small handful chopped Italian parsley

½ *cup grated Parmesan cheese*

½ *cup grated Pecorino Romano cheese*

Freshly ground black pepper to taste

Grated Parmesan cheese for the table

Heat the olive oil over moderate heat. Add the onion and the pancetta or prosciutto, and cook over moderate heat until the onion is translucent and the pancetta is cooked but not crisp. Add the white wine, turn up the heat, and deglaze the pan. Let the mixture cool.

When ready to serve, cook the spaghetti in abundant boiling salted water until al dente. Quickly drain the pasta in a colander, being careful to reserve some of the cooking water. Meanwhile, in a large, shallow serving bowl beat together the egg yolks, parsley, cheeses, and pepper. Add the pancetta-onion or prosciutto-onion mixture to the eggs and stir well. Add about ¼ cup of pasta cooking water to the egg-onion mixture and stir well.

(Continued)

Add the drained pasta to the serving bowl and mix well. Work rapidly, as the heat of the pasta helps to cook the egg yolks. Pass additional Parmesan cheese at the table.

Carbonara con Salsiccia

Sausage, Eggs, and White Wine Sauce with Gnocchetti Rigati

Serves 4 to 6

This sauce is similar to a carbonara sauce except that sausage is used instead of bacon or pancetta. It makes a smooth, spicy, and satisfying dish. The hot red chile pepper in the sausage and dry white wine relieve some of the richness. Serve with a fresh, palate-cleansing green salad.

2 tablespoons unsalted butter

1 tablespoon extra-virgin
olive oil

1 small onion, peeled and finely
diced

2 garlic cloves, peeled and
lightly crushed

2 bay leaves

3 fresh spicy sausages

½ cup dry white wine

4 eggs, lightly beaten

Salt and freshly ground black
pepper to taste

3 tablespoons chopped Italian
parsley

¼ cup grated Pecorino Romano
cheese, plus additional for the
table

1 pound imported gnocchetti
rigati

Place the butter and olive oil in a medium-sized sauté pan. Add the onion, garlic, and bay leaves. Sauté over low heat until the onion is tender, about 10 minutes. Remove the sausages from their casings and add to the sauté pan. Raise the heat to medium and cook until the sausages lose their raw color. As they cook, break them up into small chunks with a wooden spoon. Add the white wine and simmer for 15 minutes or until the juices thicken a little. In a small bowl combine the beaten eggs, salt and pepper to taste, parsley, and ¼ cup of the cheese.

Cook the gnocchetti rigati in abundant boiling salted water until al dente. Drain pasta and return to the pot. With the heat off, add the mixture from the sauté pan, removing the garlic and bay leaves if desired. Toss to coat the pasta. Add the beaten egg mixture and toss again until a creamy coating forms and the eggs lose their raw taste. If necessary, turn on the heat to low and toss pasta quickly to lightly cook the eggs. (Cook just long enough to gently warm the egg mixture.) Turn off the heat as soon as the eggs start to lose their runny quality. Otherwise the eggs will scramble, which is not the desired effect. Serve immediately and pass extra cheese at the table.

Risotto

There is an idea, a mystique, about risotto, that to produce this creamy dish requires a special talent. Nothing could be further from the truth. Risotto simply requires Arborio rice, a good broth, and concentration. And that's all. The rice itself is the most crucial ingredient of any true risotto. Arborio, Arborio Superfino, Vialone, and Carnaroli rice all have a fat roundish grain that has the ability to absorb a large quantity of liquid without becoming mushy. It is this noted porridge-like texture that sets a traditional risotto apart from every other rice dish.

Risotti are among the few recipes in this book that cannot be prepared without your full, uninterrupted attention. We don't recommend that you intermittently leave the kitchen to catch up on some reading. Risotto needs you in the kitchen to watch the pot from beginning to end. But since magic happens in the pot, it isn't such an onerous task. A typical risotto requires about 25 minutes to prepare from start to finish. It requires gentle heat and almost constant stirring. At around 18 minutes of cooking, the magic appears—the rice gives up its starch, which merges with the other ingredients, the *condimenti*, to create a unique dish. As you leaf through the chapter, you will notice that the recipes are very similarly structured. Almost all use butter and/or extra-virgin olive oil, onion, rice, and wine. The difference among them lies in the *condimenti* that are added to create the individual risotto. Once you try two or three recipes you will see that risotto is a genuinely versatile dish of which there are as many variations as there are raw materials and imagination.

As a special treat we've added recipes for two traditional deep-fried Italian street foods—Arancini and Supplì.

Risotto all'Estate

Summertime Risotto

Serves 4 to 6

This risotto is ideal with a salad of fresh tomatoes (see page 92).

¼ cup extra-virgin olive oil plus 2 tablespoons, divided

½ onion, peeled and diced

2 medium zucchini, diced

2 garlic cloves, peeled and minced

6 cups chicken broth

2 cups Arborio rice

8 fresh basil leaves, cut into thin strips

Salt and freshly ground black pepper to taste

4 ounces fresh mozzarella, drained and diced

½ cup grated Parmesan cheese

Heat ¼ cup olive oil in a heavy 2-quart saucepan over low heat. Add the onion and sauté slowly until soft. Add the zucchini and garlic, and briefly sauté over moderate heat until the garlic gives off its characteristic aroma. Heat the broth until it is very hot. Turn off the heat but keep the broth hot. Add the rice to the zucchini mixture and, stirring constantly, sauté until the rice is opaque and makes a clicking sound against the metal of the saucepan, approximately 1 to 2 minutes. Add hot broth to the rice one ladleful at a time, stirring frequently. The rice should cook very slowly over low heat. Wait until all the liquid is absorbed before adding the next ladleful of broth. Midway in the cooking time add the basil and salt and pepper to taste.

When the risotto is al dente, add the mozzarella, the remaining 2 tablespoons of olive oil, and the Parmesan cheese. Turn off the heat and stir vigorously until all the oil and cheese are absorbed. Serve immediately.

Risotto con Pomodoro e Pesto

Risotto with Tomatoes and Pesto

Serves 4 to 6

As fragrant as summertime, this risotto features plump, sweet tomatoes and aromatic basil at their best. Tomatoes and olive oil have a special affinity for each other, so we think it makes sense to start and finish the dish with olive oil rather than the more traditional butter.

FOR THE PESTO:

1 *cup fresh basil leaves, firmly packed*

2 *garlic cloves, peeled*

½ *cup extra-virgin olive oil*

¼ *cup grated Parmesan cheese*

Salt and freshly ground black pepper to taste

2 *tablespoons pine nuts*

FOR THE RISOTTO:

¼ *cup extra-virgin olive oil*

½ *onion, peeled and diced*

1 *garlic clove, peeled and minced*

8 *Roma or 4 round tomatoes, peeled, seeded, and chopped*

2 *cups Arborio rice*

6 *cups water, or 4 cups water and 2 cups chicken broth*

Salt and freshly ground black pepper to taste

2 *tablespoons extra-virgin olive oil*

½ *cup grated Parmesan cheese*

TO MAKE THE PESTO:

Place the basil and garlic in the bowl of a food processor with a steel blade or in a blender. Process until the basil is minced very fine. With the food processor or blender running, add the olive oil very slowly. Stop the machine when all the oil is absorbed. Add the Parmesan cheese and salt and pepper to taste. Process just until the cheese is absorbed. Add the pine nuts and process so that they are coarsely chopped. Using a rubber spatula, remove the pesto from the processor or blender and place it in a small bowl. Pour a thin layer of olive oil on top to prevent the pesto from darkening. When making pesto in advance, store it in a tightly closed container in the refrigerator. Bring the pesto back to room temperature before using it.

TO MAKE THE RISOTTO:

Heat the olive oil in a small, heavy 2-quart saucepan. Add the onion and cook over low heat until it is tender. Add the garlic, and when it gives off its characteristic aroma, add the tomatoes. Cook over moderate heat until the tomatoes break down and form a sauce. Add the rice, turn down the heat to low, and cook slowly until the rice absorbs all the tomato sauce.

Meanwhile, heat the water or broth until it is very hot. Turn off the heat, but keep the liquid hot on a warm burner. Add the hot liquid to the rice one ladleful at a time, stirring frequently. The rice should cook very slowly over low heat. Wait until all the liquid is absorbed before adding the next ladleful of broth. Midway in the cooking time add salt and pepper to taste.

When the risotto is just tender, add the 2 tablespoons of olive oil and the Parmesan cheese. Turn off the heat and stir risotto vigorously until all the oil and cheese are absorbed. Distribute the risotto in individual bowls and add a generous teaspoon of pesto to each dish. Swirl the pesto into the rice so that it makes a spiral pattern. Serve immediately.

Risotto al Pomodoro

Fresh Tomato Risotto with Mozzarella

Serves 4 to 6

If you enjoy ripe summer tomatoes and fresh mozzarella, this risotto will fast become a staple. The mozzarella is quickly tossed into the hot risotto at the end of the cooking time. Its milky melted strands give additional creaminess to the dish.

4 *tablespoons unsalted butter, divided*

3 *tablespoons extra-virgin olive oil*

1 *medium onion, peeled and finely chopped*

4 *garlic cloves, peeled and minced*

10 *Roma tomatoes, peeled, seeded, and chopped*

2 *cups Arborio rice*

¼ *cup red wine*

¼ *cup dry white wine*

6 *cups water or chicken broth, or a mixture of both*

Salt and freshly ground black pepper to taste

¾ *cup fresh mozzarella in water, drained and diced*

10–12 *fresh basil leaves, coarsely chopped*

¾ *cup grated Parmesan cheese, plus additional for the table*

Melt 2 tablespoons of the butter with the olive oil in a heavy 2-quart saucepan. Add the onion and cook over low heat until it is tender. Add the garlic, and when it gives off its characteristic aroma, add the tomatoes. Cook over moderate heat until the tomatoes break down and form a sauce. Add the rice, turn down the heat to low, and cook slowly until the rice absorbs all the tomato sauce. Add the red and white wines and cook until they are completely absorbed.

Meanwhile, heat the water or broth until it is very hot. Turn off the heat, but keep the liquid hot on a warm burner. Add the hot liquid to the rice, one ladleful at a time, stirring frequently. The rice should cook very slowly over low heat. Wait until all the liquid is absorbed before adding the next ladleful of broth. Midway in the cooking time add salt and pepper to taste.

When the risotto is just tender, add the mozzarella, basil, the remaining 2 tablespoons of butter, and the Parmesan cheese. Turn off the heat and stir vigorously until all the butter and cheese are absorbed. Serve immediately.

Risotto al Ortolano

R i s o t t o   f r o m   t h e   P r o d u c e   S t a n d

Serves 4 to 6

This dish is just one of an almost infinite variety of mixed-vegetable risotti. Cooking the onion slowly until its sweetness develops is what sets this risotto apart from the crowd. Do not hurry the process of cooking the onions.

(Continued)

¼ cup extra-virgin olive oil

4 tablespoons unsalted butter, divided

1 onion, peeled and diced

1 leek, washed and thinly sliced

4 medium tomatoes, peeled, seeded, and chopped

6 cups chicken broth

2 cups Arborio rice

½ cup dry white wine

½ pound medium asparagus, stalks trimmed, cut into 2-inch pieces

½ pound freshly shelled peas or 1 cup frozen peas

8–10 fresh basil leaves

Salt and freshly ground black pepper to taste

½ cup grated Parmesan cheese

Heat the olive oil and 2 tablespoons of the butter in a heavy 2-quart saucepan over moderate heat until the butter melts. Add the onion and sauté over very low heat until it is very soft and golden in color. Add the leek and continue cooking another 5 minutes or so, or until the leek becomes limp. Add the tomatoes and cook over moderate heat until the tomatoes break down and become saucey.

Meanwhile, heat the broth until it is very hot. Turn off the heat but keep the broth hot on a warm burner. Add the rice to the tomato mixture and cook over low heat until it absorbs all the juice of the tomatoes. Add the white wine and cook slowly, stirring frequently until the wine is completely absorbed. Begin to add hot broth to the rice one ladleful at a time, stirring frequently. The rice should cook very slowly over low heat. Wait until all the liquid is absorbed before adding the next ladleful of broth. Midway in the cooking time add the asparagus, peas, basil, and salt and pepper to taste.

When the risotto is al dente, add 2 tablespoons of butter and the remaining Parmesan cheese. Turn off the heat and stir vigorously until all the butter and cheese are absorbed. Serve immediately.

Risotto agli Spinaci

Risotto with Spinach

Serves 4 to 6

The structure of this recipe is a guide for any risotto made with greens or tender vegetables, like zucchini, asparagus, or peas. Simply substitute a different vegetable for the spinach.

½ *stick unsalted butter*

1 *medium onion, peeled and finely chopped*

2 *large carrots, peeled and finely chopped*

2 *celery stalks, finely chopped*

2 *cups Arborio rice*

6 *cups chicken broth*

½ *cup dry white wine*

1 *bunch spinach, well washed, leaves only, coarsely chopped*

Salt and freshly ground black pepper to taste

2 *tablespoons unsalted butter*

3/4 *cup grated Parmesan cheese, plus additional for the table*

(Continued)

Melt the butter in a heavy 2-quart saucepan. Add the onion, carrots, and celery, and cook slowly over low heat until the vegetables are wilted and nearly tender. Add the rice and, stirring constantly, sauté until the grains of rice are opaque and make a clicking sound against the metal of the saucepan, about 1 to 2 minutes. Meanwhile, heat the broth until it is very hot. Turn off the heat, but keep the broth hot on a warm burner. Add the white wine to the rice and cook slowly, stirring constantly, until it is completely absorbed. Add the spinach and stir to mix well into the rice. Add the hot broth to the rice-spinach mixture one ladleful at a time, stirring frequently. The rice should cook very slowly over low heat. Wait until all the liquid is absorbed before adding the next ladleful of broth. Midway in the cooking time add salt and pepper to taste.

When the rice is just barely tender, add the 2 tablespoons of butter and Parmesan cheese. Turn off the heat and stir vigorously until all the butter and cheese are absorbed. Pass additional Parmesan cheese at the table.

Risotto ai Peperoni

Rissotto with Red Pepper Puree

Serves 4 to 6

The vibrant red-orange of the summer sun comes alive in this dish. We puree half the roasted peppers to give the risotto its incredible color.

4 *large, meaty red bell peppers*

1 *tablespoon plus ¼ cup extra-virgin olive oil, divided*

1 *medium onion, peeled and finely diced, divided*

2 *garlic cloves, peeled and minced*

16 *fresh basil leaves, cut into thin shreds*

½ *cup dry white wine, divided*

6 *cups unsalted chicken broth*

¼ *cup unsalted butter, or ¼ cup extra-virgin olive oil*

2 *cups Arborio rice*

Salt and freshly ground black pepper to taste

2 *tablespoons unsalted butter (optional)*

½ *cup grated Parmesan cheese*

To roast the bell peppers, place them on a cookie sheet or in a low-sided roasting pan. Lightly brush 1 tablespoon of olive oil over the entire surface of the peppers. Roast the oiled peppers in a preheated 450° oven for approximately 20 minutes, turning them frequently. They should look blistered, with the skin beginning to come away from the meaty insides. Do not let the peppers char too much. Remove the peppers from the oven, and immediately put them into a plastic or paper bag. Close the bag and let the peppers sweat for 5 minutes. Remove them one by one from the bag and peel them. Cut open the peppers carefully and remove the seeds, ribs, and stems. Cut the peppers lengthwise into thin ¼-inch strips. Set aside ¼ of the sliced peppers for later use.

(Continued)

Heat ¼ cup of olive oil in a heavy skillet, and gently fry the thinly sliced peppers with half the onion, garlic, and basil until the onion and peppers are very soft. Add ¼ cup of the white wine and deglaze the pan, to scrape up all the bits of onion and pepper that have stuck to the pan. In a blender or a food processor with a steel blade, puree the red pepper–onion mixture until smooth. Set aside.

Heat the broth until it is very hot. Turn off the heat, but keep the broth hot on a warm burner. Melt the butter (or olive oil) in a heavy 2-quart saucepan. Add the remaining onion and sauté until soft. Add the rice and sauté, stirring constantly, for approximately 1 to 2 minutes. The grains should still be opaque and make a clicking sound against the metal of the saucepan. Add the remaining white wine to the rice and cook over low heat, stirring very frequently, until the rice absorbs all the wine. Add the red pepper puree to the rice and stir. Begin to add hot broth to the rice one ladleful at a time, stirring frequently. The rice should cook very slowly over low heat. Wait until all the liquid is absorbed before adding the next ladleful of broth. Midway in the cooking time add salt and pepper to taste.

When the risotto is al dente, add the reserved slices of roasted pepper, butter or olive oil, and Parmesan cheese. Turn off the heat and stir vigorously until all the butter and cheese are absorbed. Serve immediately.

Risotto con i Finocchi

RISOTTO WITH FENNEL

Serves 4 to 6

The sweet, light licorice taste of fennel is enhanced by the onion. The use of milk to finish this risotto makes the texture especially comforting.

4 *tablespoons unsalted butter*

1 *small onion, peeled and finely diced*

2 *fennel bulbs, diced*

2 *cups Arborio rice*

5 *cups water, or 2½ cups water and 2½ cups chicken broth*

½ *cup dry white wine*

Salt and freshly ground black pepper to taste

1 *cup milk*

10 *fresh basil leaves, cut into thin strips*

2 *tablespoons unsalted butter*

1 *cup grated Parmesan cheese, plus additional for the table*

Melt the butter in a heavy 2-quart saucepan. Add the onion and cook it slowly over low heat until it begins to wilt. Add the fennel and continue cooking over low heat until it is nearly tender. Add the rice and, stirring constantly, sauté until the grains of rice are opaque and make a clicking sound against the metal of the saucepan, approximately 1 to 2 minutes.

Meanwhile, heat the water and/or broth until it is very hot. Turn off the heat, but keep the liquid hot on a warm burner. Add the white wine to the rice and cook slowly, stirring constantly, until it is completely absorbed. Add the hot liquid to the rice one ladleful at a time, stirring frequently. The rice should cook very slowly over low heat. Wait until all the liquid is absorbed before adding the next ladleful of broth. Midway in the cooking time add salt and pepper to taste. Heat the milk in a small saucepan to very warm. When all the broth is absorbed by the rice, add the warm milk.

When the rice is just barely tender, add the basil, 2 tablespoons of butter, and Parmesan cheese. Turn off the heat and stir vigorously until all the butter and cheese are absorbed. Pass additional Parmesan cheese at the table.

Risotto con Carciofi

Risotto with Artichokes

Serves 4 to 6

A subtle, deep-flavored risotto that is a good accompaniment to simple roast meats.

4 tablespoons unsalted butter, divided

3 tablespoons extra-virgin olive oil

1 medium onion, peeled and finely chopped

1 10-ounce package frozen artichoke hearts, defrosted and sliced thin lengthwise

4 garlic cloves, peeled and minced

Small handful chopped Italian parsley, divided

2 cups Arborio rice

½ cup dry white wine

3 cups beef broth mixed with 3 cups water

Salt and freshly ground black pepper to taste

Grated Parmesan cheese

Melt 2 tablespoons of the butter with the olive oil in a heavy 2-quart saucepan. Add the onion and cook over low heat until it wilts and begins to soften. Add the sliced artichoke hearts and garlic, and sauté over low heat until the onion and artichokes are tender. Add half the parsley. Add the rice and turning the heat to low, sauté rice with the onion and artichokes until it turns opaque and begins to make a clicking sound against the metal of the saucepan. Add the white wine and cook slowly until it is completely absorbed.

Meanwhile, heat the beef broth and water until the liquid is very hot.

(Continued)

Turn off the heat, but keep the broth hot on a warm burner. Add the hot broth to the rice one ladleful at a time, stirring frequently. The rice should cook very slowly over low heat. Wait until all the liquid is absorbed before adding the next ladleful of broth. Midway in the cooking time add salt and pepper to taste.

When the risotto is just tender, add the rest of the parsley, the remaining 2 tablespoons of butter, and the Parmesan cheese. Turn off the heat and stir vigorously until all the butter and cheese are absorbed. Serve immediately.

Risotto al Cavolfiore

R i s o t t o   w i t h   C a u l i f l o w e r

Serves 4 to 6

Although at first glance this recipe may seem less than exciting, it is well to remember what full flavor the vegetables in the *Brassica* family have. A risotto containing cauliflower, broccoli, or cabbage is simple to make, the ingredients are readily available, and the taste is hard to beat.

4 tablespoons unsalted butter, divided

3 tablespoons extra-virgin olive oil

1 medium onion, peeled and chopped

2 cloves garlic, peeled and minced

½ head cauliflower, core trimmed, leaves removed, and broken into flowerets

2 bay leaves

½ cup dry white wine

1½ cups water

2 cups Arborio rice

5–6 cups chicken broth and/or water

Salt and freshly ground black pepper to taste

1 cup grated Parmesan cheese

Melt 2 tablespoons of the butter with the olive oil in a heavy 2-quart saucepan. Add the onion and cook over low heat until it wilts and begins to soften. Add the garlic and sauté over low heat until it gives off its characteristic aroma. Add the cauliflower, bay leaves, white wine, and water. Bring to a boil, cover, and turn down the heat. Cook the cauliflower until it is tender when pierced with a fork, approximately 10 to 15 minutes. Add the rice and, turning the heat to low, sauté the rice with the onion and cauliflower until all the cooking liquid is absorbed.

Meanwhile, heat the water and/or broth until it is very hot. Turn off the heat but keep the liquid hot on a warm burner. Add the hot liquid to the rice one ladleful at a time, stirring frequently. The rice should cook very slowly over low heat. Wait until all the liquid is absorbed before adding the next ladleful of broth. Midway in the cooking time add salt and pepper to taste.

When the risotto is just tender, add the remaining 2 tablespoons of butter and the Parmesan cheese. Turn off the heat and stir vigorously until all the butter and cheese are absorbed. Serve immediately.

Risotto al Cavolo

Risotto with Savoy Cabbage

Serves 4 to 6

This wintery dish is perfect accompanied by spicy grilled sausages and Insalata di Campo (see page 87) dressed with extra-virgin olive oil, red wine vinegar, and a touch of minced garlic.

4 *tablespoons unsalted butter*	4 *fresh sage leaves, chopped*
1 *medium onion, peeled and finely chopped*	2 *cups Arborio rice*
3 *thin slices pancetta, cut into small dice*	½ *cup dry white wine*
	6 *cups chicken broth*
1 *small to medium head Savoy cabbage, core removed, shredded*	*Salt and freshly ground black pepper to taste*
	2 *tablespoons unsalted butter*
	¾ *cup grated Parmesan cheese*

Melt the butter in a heavy 2-quart saucepan. Add the onion and cook over low heat until it begins to wilt. Add the pancetta and cook until it gives up its fat and the onion is soft. Add the cabbage and sage. Continue cooking over moderate heat until the cabbage wilts. Add the rice and stir until the grains are coated with butter. Add the white wine and cook until the wine is completely absorbed.

Meanwhile, heat the broth until it is very hot. Turn off the heat, but keep the broth hot on a warm burner. Add the hot broth to the rice one ladleful at a time, stirring frequently. The rice should cook very slowly over low heat. Wait until all the liquid is absorbed before adding the next ladleful of broth. Midway in the cooking time add salt and pepper to taste.

When the risotto is just tender, add the remaining 2 tablespoons of butter and the Parmesan cheese. Turn off the heat and stir vigorously until all the butter and cheese are absorbed. Serve immediately.

Risotto alla Campagnola

R i s o t t o   C o u n t r y   S t y l e

Serves 4 to 6

This simple country-style risotto featuring aromatic vegetables and fresh ricotta is well suited to an informal evening at home. Virtually every Italian housewife makes a version of this dish.

½ stick unsalted butter

½ onion, peeled and finely chopped

2 carrots, trimmed and finely chopped

2 celery stalks, trimmed and finely chopped

Handful coarsely chopped Italian parsley, divided

2 cups Arborio rice

⅓ cup dry white wine

6 cups chicken broth

Salt and freshly ground black pepper to taste

6 ounces ricotta

2 tablespoons unsalted butter

½ cup grated Parmesan cheese, plus additional for the table

Melt the butter in a heavy 2-quart saucepan. Add to the pan the onion, carrots, celery, and half the parsley, and cook slowly over low heat until the vegetables are wilted and nearly tender. Add the rice and, stirring

(Continued)

constantly, sauté until the grains of rice are opaque and make a clicking sound against the metal of the saucepan, approximately 1 to 2 minutes.

Meanwhile, heat the broth until it is very hot. Turn off the heat, but keep the broth hot on a warm burner. Add the white wine to the rice and cook slowly, stirring constantly, until it is completely absorbed. Add the hot broth to the rice one ladleful at a time, stirring frequently. The rice should cook very slowly over low heat. Wait until all the liquid is absorbed before adding the next ladleful of broth. Midway in the cooking time add salt and pepper to taste.

When the risotto is just tender, add the ricotta, 2 tablespoons of butter, Parmesan cheese, and the remaining parsley. Turn off the heat and stir vigorously until all the butter and cheese are absorbed and the ricotta is well mixed into the risotto. Serve immediately. Pass additional Parmesan cheese at the table.

Risotto con la Zucca Gialla

Risotto with Summer Squash and Fontina

Serves 4 to 6

Yellow summer squash are often sweeter and smoother tasting than the green varieties, and in this dish their deep yellow color brightens the white rice. Fontina cheese, melted to a silky smoothness, adds a pleasing nutty flavor.

4 tablespoons unsalted butter

1 small onion, peeled and finely diced

3 medium yellow zucchini, crookneck, or pattypan squash, diced

2 cups Arborio rice

6 cups chicken broth

½ cup dry white wine

Handful coarsely chopped Italian parsley

Salt and freshly ground black pepper to taste

½ cup imported Italian fontina, diced

10 fresh basil leaves, cut into thin strips

2 tablespoons unsalted butter

½ cup grated Parmesan cheese, plus additional for the table

Melt the butter in a heavy 2-quart saucepan. Add the onion and cook slowly over low heat until it is very soft and just beginning to take on color. Add the squash and continue cooking over low heat until squash is nearly tender. Add the rice and, stirring constantly, sauté until the grains of rice are opaque and make a clicking sound against the metal of the saucepan, about 1 to 2 minutes.

(Continued)

Meanwhile, heat the broth until it is very hot. Turn off the heat, but keep the broth hot on a warm burner. Add the white wine to the rice and cook slowly, stirring constantly, until it is completely absorbed. Add the hot broth to the rice one ladleful at a time, stirring frequently. The rice should cook very slowly over low heat. Wait until all the liquid is absorbed before adding the next ladleful of broth. Midway in the cooking time add salt and pepper.

When the rice is just barely tender, add the fontina and gently cook, stirring continuously, until the cheese begins to soften. Add the basil, 2 tablespoons of butter, and the Parmesan cheese. Turn off the heat and stir vigorously until all the butter and cheese are absorbed. Pass additional Parmesan cheese at the table.

Risotto con Gorgonzola e Spinaci

Risotto with Gorgonzola and Spinach

Serves 4 to 6

Cheeses are natural additions to risotto, reinforcing the characteristic creamy texture of the dish, and few cheeses are better suited than Gorgonzola. It's luscious yet sharp flavor balances the mildness of the rice. Spinach gives the dish color interest as well as additional flavor.

3 tablespoons unsalted butter

1 medium onion, peeled and finely diced

2 cups Arborio rice

6 cups water

½ cup dry white wine

1 bunch spinach, well washed, leaves only, coarsely chopped

Salt and freshly ground black pepper to taste

½ cup dolce latte Gorgonzola

¼ cup cream

¾ cup grated Parmesan cheese, plus additional for the table

Melt the butter in a heavy 2-quart saucepan. Add the onion and cook slowly over low heat until it is wilted and tender. Add the rice and, stirring constantly, sauté until the grains of rice are opaque and make a clicking sound against the metal of the saucepan, about 1 to 2 minutes.

Meanwhile, heat the water until it is very hot. Turn off the heat, but keep the water hot on a warm burner. Add the white wine to the rice and cook slowly, stirring constantly, until it is completely absorbed. Add the spinach into the rice and stir so that it is well mixed. Add the hot water to the rice-spinach mixture one ladleful at a time, stirring frequently. The rice should cook very slowly over low heat. Wait until all the liquid is absorbed before adding the next ladleful of water. Midway in the cooking time add salt and pepper to taste.

When the rice is just barely tender, add the Gorgonzola cheese and cream, and cook just until the cheese begins to soften. Add the Parmesan cheese, turn off the heat, and stir vigorously until the cheese and cream are absorbed. Pass additional Parmesan cheese at the table.

Risotto ai Frutti di Mare

MIXED SEAFOOD RISOTTO

Serves 4 to 6

This dish is well worth the time it takes to make. All the seafood can be prepared early in the day, after which this risotto is no more difficult to make than any other. We recommend serving it as a main course with a simple lettuce salad dressed with tart vinegar.

FOR THE SEAFOOD
MIXTURE:

4 *tablespoons extra-virgin olive oil*

2 *garlic cloves, peeled and finely chopped*

12 *medium shrimp, peeled and deveined*

½ *pound squid*

12 *mussels*

12 *clams*

¼ *cup dry white wine*

Juice of ½ lemon

2 *sprigs fresh thyme*

2 *sprigs fresh oregano*

FOR THE RISOTTO:

2 *tablespoons unsalted butter*

3 *tablespoons extra-virgin olive oil*

1 *small onion, peeled and chopped*

4 *garlic cloves, peeled and minced*

10 *Roma tomatoes, peeled, seeded, and chopped*

2 *cups Arborio rice*

½ *cup dry white wine*

Small handful chopped Italian parsley

10 *fresh basil leaves, coarsely chopped*

4 *cups Brodo di Pesce (see page 304), or 2 cups chicken broth and 2 cups fish stock*

Salt and freshly ground black pepper to taste

TO CLEAN THE SEAFOOD:

To clean fresh squid, carefully pull the head and tentacles from the body sac. Cut the tentacles above the eyes. Pop out the little ball or beak in the center of the tentacles. Discard it and the innards. Pull out the glasslike bone in the body sac and discard. Peel off the skin. Thoroughly rinse the interior of the body sac and the tentacles. Drain. Cut the body sac crosswise into ¼-inch-thick rings. Set the cleaned squid aside in a small bowl until needed.

Scrub the mussels well under cold running water, making sure the shells are completely free of sand and grit. Remove the beards that protrude from the shells by firmly moving them up and down the shell until they pull free. Discard any mussels that are broken or not completely closed.

Soak the clams in heavily salted cold water (preferably in the sink) for 15 minutes. Lift clams from the soaking water, rinsing briefly under cold running water. Discard the dirty water and clean the sink or bowl of any sand or grit. Soak the clams again in the salted cold water another 15 minutes. Rinse again under cold running water.

(Continued)

TO COOK THE SEAFOOD MIXTURE:

Heat the olive oil in a medium-sized skillet. Add the garlic and cook briefly until it gives off its aroma. Add the shrimp and sauté just until shrimp begins to stiffen. Remove the shrimp from the skillet and place them in a small bowl. Return skillet to stove, add the squid, and cook over moderate heat quickly, approximately 1 to 2 minutes. Do not overcook! Remove the squid from the skillet to the bowl with the shrimp.

Place the mussels and clams in the skillet with the white wine, lemon juice, and herbs. Cover the skillet and cook over high heat until all the shells open. Remove the clams and mussels from the pan and reserve the cooking juices for finishing the risotto. Discard the herb sprigs. As soon as the clams and mussels are cool enough to handle, remove the meat, discard the shells, and place them in the same bowl as the shrimp and squid.

TO MAKE THE RISOTTO:

Melt the butter together with the olive oil in a heavy 2-quart saucepan. Add the onion and cook slowly over low heat until it is wilted and tender. Add the garlic and cook briefly until it gives off its characteristic aroma. Add the tomatoes and cook over moderate heat until they give off their juice and begin to become saucey. Add the rice and, stirring constantly, cook slowly until the rice has absorbed all the juice of the tomatoes. Add the white wine to the rice and cook slowly, stirring constantly, until it is completely absorbed. Add the parsley.

Meanwhile, heat the fish broth until it is very hot. Turn off the heat, but keep the broth hot on a warm burner. Add the hot broth to the rice one ladleful at a time, stirring frequently. The rice should cook very slowly over low heat. Wait until all the liquid is absorbed before adding the next ladleful. Midway in the cooking time, after approximately 15 minutes, add the cooked seafood and salt and pepper. Continue cooking, adding as much fish broth as is necessary, one ladleful at a time.

Add the reserved clam and mussel juices, and cook rice just until it is barely tender.

Risotto Rosso

Tomato-Sausage Risotto

Serves 4 to 6

This dish has many of the classic flavors associated with Italian food. Rich and hearty sausage, tomato, and garlic combine with the comforting, creamy risotto to create an especially satisfying meal.

2 tablespoons unsalted butter

3 tablespoons extra-virgin olive oil

1 medium onion, peeled and finely chopped

½ pound sweet Italian sausage, removed from its casings and crumbled

4 garlic cloves, peeled and minced

2 cups imported Italian tomatoes, crushed

15 fresh basil leaves, coarsely chopped

2 cups Arborio rice

½ cup red wine

5–6 cups beef or chicken broth

Salt and freshly ground black pepper to taste

1 cup grated Parmesan cheese, plus additional for the table

Melt the butter with the olive oil in a heavy 2-quart saucepan. Add the onion to the pan and cook slowly over low heat until it is very soft and just begins to take on color. Add the crumbled sausage meat and garlic, and cook over moderate heat until the meat no longer shows any pink. Add the tomatoes with their juice and the basil. Cook for approximately 10 minutes, or until the tomatoes and meat form a slightly thickened sauce. Add the rice and, stirring constantly, cook until it absorbs all of the sauce. Add the

(Continued)

red wine to the rice and cook slowly, stirring constantly, until it is completely absorbed.

Meanwhile, heat the beef or chicken broth until it is very hot. Turn the heat off, but keep the broth hot on a warm burner. Add the hot broth to the rice one ladleful at a time, stirring frequently. The rice should cook very slowly over low heat. Wait until all the liquid is absorbed before adding the next ladleful of broth. Midway in the cooking time add salt and pepper.

When the rice is just barely tender, add the Parmesan cheese. Turn off the heat and stir vigorously until all the butter and cheese are absorbed. Pass additional Parmesan cheese at the table.

Risotto all'Amatriciana

Risotto with Tomato, Pancetta, and Hot Pepper

Serves 4

This risotto is based on the famous pasta dish from the town of Amatrice near Rome that features tomato, pancetta, and hot pepper.

¼ cup unsalted butter

1 small onion, peeled and finely chopped

3 slices pancetta, cut into short strips

½ teaspoon crushed dried red chile peppers, or to taste

1½ pounds Roma tomatoes, peeled, seeded, and chopped

Salt and freshly ground black pepper to taste

2 cups Arborio rice

6 cups light meat broth

6 tablespoons grated Pecorino Romano cheese, plus additional for the table

Place the butter in a heavy 2-quart saucepan. Add the onion and cook over low heat until the onion starts to wilt. Add the pancetta and red chile peppers, and sauté until the pancetta renders its fat and the onion is completely tender. Add the tomatoes and salt and pepper. Raise the heat to medium and cook until the tomatoes thicken and turn into a sauce, about 10 minutes. Add the rice, stir, and reduce the heat to low.

Heat the broth to boiling. Turn off the heat, but keep the broth hot on a warm burner. Begin adding the broth to the rice mixture a ladleful at a time, stirring constantly to prevent sticking. As the rice absorbs the broth, add another cup of warm broth. Continue adding broth until the rice is al dente, tender outside but with a little bite at its center, and the mixture is quite moist. Turn off the heat and stir in the remaining butter and the 6 tablespoons of grated Pecorino Romano cheese. Serve extra grated cheese at the table.

Arancini and Supplì

Arancini and Supplì are popular street snacks in southern Italy, Sicily, and Sardinia. They are rice balls, stuffed with meat, cheese, or vegetables, rolled in bread crumbs, and fried in olive oil. They are never better than when made with leftover risotto or with a risotto made especially for stuffing and deep-frying these snacks. Arancini and Supplì are equally good eaten finger-burning hot or at room temperature. We love them on a sultry summer day when appetites wane, or as an appetizer to a special meal. Here are two recipes that use the risotti in this chapter: one for Arancini (traditionally meat filled) and the other Supplì (usually stuffed with cheese). Experiment! We've even made elegant antipasti Supplì using risotto made with radicchio.

Arancini

Makes approximately 8 orange-sized rice balls

The name arancini comes from *arancia,* the Italian word for orange. It refers both to the size and shape of the rice ball and to the orange color derived from the tomato in the risotto.

1 *recipe Risotto Rosso (see page 223)*

1 *cup mozzarella in water, drained and diced*

1 *cup frozen tiny peas, cooked and cooled to room temperature*

4 *eggs, beaten*

3 *cups fine bread crumbs*

Oil for deep-frying, preferably olive or peanut oil

Scoop up a bit of cooled risotto, about the size of a small orange, and spread it in your left hand so that it forms a thick "cake." Place 1 piece of mozzarella and 1 teaspoonful of peas in the center. Gently place more risotto over the filling, then carefully enclose the filling by rolling the cake into a ball. Set aside and repeat until all ingredients are used. Dip the stuffed Arancini in beaten egg and roll in the bread crumbs. Pour the olive oil in a heavy saucepan to a depth of 3 inches. Heat oil until very hot but not smoking. Fry a few Arancini at a time, being careful not to crowd the pan. As they color a deep golden brown, remove them with a slotted spoon and place on paper towels to drain. Serve either immediately or at room temperature.

Supplì al Battuto

Makes approximately 18 large walnut-sized pieces

The full name for Supplì is Supplì al Telefono. *Telefono* means telephone lines. This description refers to the thin strings of mozzarella that form when you bite into a Supplì then pull it away from your mouth. In Rome, these snacks are traditionally stuffed only with mozzarella. However, here we have included not only the mozzarella in the risotto recipe, but also an untraditional *soffritto*, or sauté, of a battuto, a mix of finely chopped aromatic vegetables, to use as a stuffing.

1 *recipe Risotto al Pomodoro (see page 202)*

2 *tablespoons extra-virgin olive oil*

1 *carrot, trimmed, peeled, and finely chopped in food processor*

1 *fennel bulb, trimmed of tough leaves, finely chopped in food processor*

1 *celery stalk, trimmed, and finely chopped*

3 *garlic cloves, peeled and minced*

2 *sprigs fresh thyme, chopped*

5 *Roma tomatoes, peeled, seeded, and finely chopped*

4 *eggs, beaten*

3 *cups fine bread crumbs*

Oil for deep-frying, preferably olive or peanut oil

Heat 2 tablespoons of olive oil in a skillet. Add the carrot, fennel, celery, garlic, and thyme. Fry lightly until vegetables are tender. Add the tomatoes and cook until they give up their juice and thicken to form a sturdy sauce. Remove tomatoes from heat and cool to room temperature. Scoop up a large walnut-sized piece of cooled risotto and spread it in your left hand so that it forms a thick "cake." Place ½ teaspoonful of the vegetable-tomato filling in the center. Gently place more risotto over the filling, then carefully roll the cake into a small ball. Set aside and repeat until all the ingredients are used.

Dip all the Supplì in beaten egg and roll in the bread crumbs. Pour the frying oil in a heavy saucepan to a depth of 2 inches. Heat oil until very hot but not smoking. Fry a few Supplì at a time, being careful not to crowd the pan. As they color a deep golden brown, remove them with a slotted spoon and place on paper towels to drain. Serve either immediately or at room temperature.

Polenta

In his *Il Libro della Polenta*, Vincenzo Buonassisi, a famous Italian gastronome, describes the society of polenta. It was made up of poverty, daily struggle, cold winter winds, and long winter nights. At its center was always a huge copper pot, set over a red-hot wood fire, that the women of the household stirred interminably. The result was a beautiful, comforting disk of sunny, yellow cooked cornmeal to soften the hard edges of life and to give the body sustenance. Polenta is a food that is hard to separate from its cultural setting; it seems old-fashioned. However, you will find it has the same addictive quality as a perfect plate of mashed potatoes or country bread. Because of its versatility it is suited to many different preparations. Its simple nobility can be experienced as a bowl of soft, buttery polenta enriched with creamy Italian cheese or as a simple grilled "crouton" on which to spoon a wild mushroom sauté. Here we present a cross-section of typical polenta dishes.

We urge you to try them for, once hooked, you will make polenta an integral part of your culinary repertory. The only obstacle in preparing it is the time that you must put in at the stove. A good 30 to 40 minutes are required to achieve the correct texture, during which time you must stir the polenta constantly. However, stirring polenta has a ritualistic aspect that can be gratifying when you have the time and energy. Nothing is more satisfying than when, muscles aching and face flushed, you see the polenta is ready. It is a reminder of when tremendous energy and strength were required for cooking, and this leads us to the topic of instant polenta. Since making polenta the traditional way is so time-consuming, and because this dish is so good, more often than not we use imported instant polenta to satisfy our cravings. It has excellent flavor and texture and can be made in about 5 minutes: You can use it in all the recipes that call for polenta.

Polenta Tradizionale
Traditional Polenta

Serves 4 to 6

6½ *cups water*

2 *teaspoons salt*

1½ *cups imported polenta or coarse yellow cornmeal*

Bring the water to a boil and add the salt. When the water returns to the boil, whisk in the polenta, adding it in a slow, steady stream. Reduce the heat to medium and, with a wooden spoon, stir continuously for 30 to 40 minutes, or until the polenta is thick and soft. Serve immediately or let cool and slice.

Polenta Istantanea
Instant Polenta

Serves 4 to 6

6½ *cups water*

2 *teaspoons salt*

1 *package (13 ounces) imported instant polenta*

Bring the water to a boil. Add salt. When water returns to a boil, quickly add all the instant polenta, stirring it with a wooden spoon. Continue stirring for 5 minutes, or until the polenta is thick and soft. Serve immediately, or let cool and slice.

Polenta ai Tre Formaggi

Soft Cornmeal Mush with Three Cheeses

Serves 4 to 6

One of our favorite recipes for soft polenta; this dish is great for a cold winter evening meal with close friends. Serve with red wine, followed by Insalata di Radicchio alla Vicentina (see page 90).

1 *recipe Polenta (see page 232 or page 233)*

4 *tablespoons unsalted butter*

¼ *pound dolce latte Gorgonzola, cut into chunks*

½ *pound imported fontina, diced*

½ *cup grated Parmesan cheese, plus additional for the table*

Freshly ground black pepper to taste

Cook Polenta according to the traditional or instant recipe. When the polenta is thick and nearly ready, add the butter and stir until it is completely absorbed. Add the cheeses and stir until they begin to melt into the polenta. Add pepper to taste. Stir. Immediately pour the polenta into individual serving bowls. Pass grated Parmesan.

Polenta con Pancetta e Salvia

Polenta with Pancetta and Sage

Serves 4 to 6

Here the polenta is cooked until tender, then butter and Parmesan cheese are added to create a creamy texture. Then the mixture is poured into a mold, immediately turned out onto a serving platter, and garnished with slices of pancetta and whole sage leaves sautéed in butter.

1 *recipe Polenta (see page 232 or page 233)*

½ *cup unsalted butter, divided*

¼ *pound pancetta, cut into 3-inch lengths*

1 *bunch fresh sage, leaves only*

6 *tablespoons grated Parmesan cheese*

Cook Polenta according to the traditional or instant recipe.

Place 4 tablespoons of the butter in a medium-sized sauté pan. Add the pancetta and sage, and sauté over low heat until the pancetta colors, about 10 minutes.

When the polenta is tender, stir in the remaining butter and the Parmesan cheese. Pour polenta into a wet bowl and immediately invert it onto a serving platter. Pour the juices from the sauté pan over the polenta, and garnish with the pancetta slices and sage leaves.

Polenta ai Ferri

Grilled Polenta with Wild Mushroom Sauté

Serves 6 to 8

This autumnal dish of lightly charred polenta slices smothered with rosemary and thyme-scented mushrooms can be served as a nonmeat entrée, as an appetizer, or to accompany simple roast meat.

1 *ounce dried porcini mushrooms*

1 *recipe Polenta (see page 232 or page 233)*

¼ *cup extra-virgin olive oil*

2 *garlic cloves, peeled and minced*

1 *sprig fresh rosemary*

2 *sprigs fresh thyme, leaves only*

¼ *cup coarsely chopped Italian parsley*

½ *pound mixed wild mushrooms, such as shiitake and chanterelles, trimmed and sliced*

½ *pound white mushrooms, trimmed and sliced*

Salt and freshly ground black pepper to taste

¼ *cup grated Pecorino Romano cheese (optional)*

Soak the porcini mushrooms in warm water to cover for about 20 minutes. Oil a small loaf pan. Set aside.

Cook Polenta according to the traditional or instant recipe. When polenta becomes thick, pour it into the oiled pan. Set the pan aside to cool at room temperature, then place it in the refrigerator until cold.

To prepare the mushrooms, drain the porcini of their soaking liquid and carefully wash away any remaining sand or grit. Roughly chop the porcini. Heat the olive oil, rosemary, and garlic together in a skillet. Add the mushrooms and sauté over high heat. Add the thyme, parsley, salt, and pepper. Cook the mushrooms until they are tender. Set aside.

Heat a charcoal or gas grill or cast-iron ridged griddle over high heat. Unmold the polenta and slice into ½-inch-thick pieces. Lightly brush the polenta slices with olive oil. Grill the polenta for about 2 to 3 minutes on each side, or until grill marks are evident.

Line a large serving platter with the grilled polenta and top with hot sautéed mushrooms. Sprinkle with Pecorino Romano cheese, if desired.

Polenta con Salsa Piccante

Layered Polenta with Spicy Fresh Tomato Sauce

Serves 6

This is a glorious-looking dish with its layers of golden polenta alternating with bright red bands of tomato sauce. The fresh tomatoes, a minimal amount of sausage, and the quick cooking keep the traditional pairing of tomato and sausage from becoming heavy. An ideal dish for a rustic buffet, it can be assembled in advance and cut into neat squares for serving.

FOR THE POLENTA:

1 *recipe Polenta (see page 232 or page 233)*

FOR THE SAUCE:

¼ *cup extra-virgin olive oil*

1 *onion, peeled and diced*

1 *clove garlic, peeled and finely chopped*

Handful fresh basil leaves, chopped

½ *pound sweet sausage, removed from its casing*

½ *teaspoon ground cayenne pepper*

2 *pounds ripe tomatoes, peeled, seeded, and coarsely pureed*

Salt and freshly ground black pepper to taste

TO ASSEMBLE THE DISH:

3 *tablespoons unsalted butter*

¾ *cup grated Parmesan cheese*

¾ *cup grated Pecorino Romano cheese*

Cook Polenta according to the traditional or instant recipe. Pour into an oiled loaf pan. When cool, cut polenta into ¼-inch-thick slices. Set aside.

To make the sauce, combine the olive oil, onion, garlic, and basil in a sauté pan. Sauté over low heat until the onion softens. Add the sausage meat, crumbled, and the ground cayenne pepper. Cook over gentle heat for several minutes or until meat loses its raw color. Add the tomatoes and season with salt and pepper to taste. Cook for 15 to 20 minutes, or until sauce thickens. Tip the pan and spoon off any excess fat on the surface of the sauce.

To assemble, lightly butter a rustic baking dish that is large enough to contain all the polenta to a depth of 3 inches. Arrange a layer of polenta slices on the bottom of the dish. Cover with some sauce, sprinkle with some grated cheese, and dot with a little of the butter. Continue layering, ending with a layer of polenta. Sprinkle the surface with the remaining grated cheese and dot with butter. Bake at 375° for about 30 minutes, or until the polenta is bubbling hot and the top is golden brown. Let settle for a few moments before serving.

Polenta al Forno con Melanzane

Polenta "Lasagna"

Serves 6 to 8

This recipe has its roots in many variations on polenta pasticciata, a traditional recipe in which polenta is layered with tomato and béchamel sauces. This is a great way to use up leftovers. Experiment with different sauces, vegetables, and cheeses.

1 *recipe Polenta (see page 232 or page 233)*

½ *stick unsalted butter*

3 *tablespoons all-purpose flour*

2 *cups hot milk*

Salt and freshly ground black pepper to taste

1 *eggplant, trimmed and cut lengthwise into ¼-inch slices*

Extra-virgin olive oil

1 *recipe tomato sauce for Spaghetti al Pomodoro e Pinoli (see page 154)*

Handful coarsely chopped Italian parsley

2 *bunches fresh basil, leaves only, roughly chopped*

2 *cups grated imported Parmesan cheese*

Prepare Polenta according to the traditional or instant recipe. When it is thick, pour it into a baking dish so that it makes a ½-inch layer. If necessary, smooth the polenta with a rubber spatula. Set aside.

To make the béchamel sauce, melt the butter in a small saucepan over low heat. Add the flour and stir to form a smooth paste. Heat the milk in a separate saucepan. When it is hot but not boiling, pour it into the butter-flour mixture, stirring constantly with a whisk or wooden spoon. Cook over low heat until the sauce thickens and the floury taste is gone. Add salt and pepper to taste. Set aside.

Cook the eggplant by either brushing it lightly with oil and grilling it, or by frying it in hot oil. Place on paper towels to drain the excess oil.

To assemble the "lasagna," spoon half the tomato–pine-nut sauce onto the polenta, then make layers of eggplant, béchamel, the remaining tomato sauce, and Parmesan cheese.

Place baking dish, uncovered, in a preheated 375° oven and bake for approximately 35 minutes, or until "lasagna" is bubbling hot. Serve immediately.

Contorni

Vegetables

Vegetables play a central role in Italian cooking and Italian eating habits. Because of Italy's rich agricultural tradition, the variety and quality of vegetables are astonishing and go hand in hand with the special attention they are accorded. Rather than obscure their unique properties in the shadow of a veal chop or a roast chicken, vegetables are served separately, a sign of respect. Produce stands line the streets of small towns and sprawling metropolitan centers, bearing witness to the worship of the vegetable. Beautifully displayed, lovingly handled, vegetables appear in markets piled in towering pyramids or in small, careful groupings. They are cultivated in vast fields, or they are coaxed from small family plots—a few lettuces, some herbs, a bunch of onions. Whatever the source, their colors and fragrance are a part of life. Italians look to vegetables for their health-giving properties, to purify themselves body and soul. They look to vegetables for celebration, to mark the changing seasons.

This chapter is more than just a collection of side dishes. Many of these recipes would serve well as the focus of a dinner, or as a first course in place of pasta or rice. As eating habits change in America, we are looking more and more to vegetables as a mainstay of our diet, for their beauty and ability to sustain and refresh us. Through them we feel a strong connection to the earth.

Verdure Miste alla Griglia

Mixed Grill of Seasonal Vegetables

Grilled vegetables are a natural accompaniment to any grilled meat or fish dish. They are also a delicious and healthful main course, served either plain from the grill, or scattered with herbs, drizzled with olive oil, and served with a wedge of lemon. Almost any vegetable can be grilled, but some like fennel and asparagus benefit from a quick blanching in salted boiling water. Serve this dish all year round, varying the components according to the season. We present a selection of seasonal suggestions.

SPRING:

Baby artichokes, trimmed, cut in half lengthwise, and blanched

Asparagus

Garlic bulbs, cut in half crosswise

Green onions or baby leeks

Sliced yellow and/or green pattypan squash

FALL:

Whole large cultivated white or brown mushrooms

Whole shiitake mushrooms

Onion slices

Blanched turnip slices

Potato slices

Banana or butternut squash slices

SUMMER:

Tomato halves

Green and/or golden zucchini, cut into lengthwise slices

Red, yellow, and green bell peppers, cut into quarters

Eggplant slices or halved Japanese eggplants

Red onion slices

FOR GRILLING VEGETABLES:

Extra-virgin olive oil

WINTER:

Belgian endive, cut in half lengthwise

Radicchio, cut into halves or quarters lengthwise

Blanched fennel slices

Blanched sliced beets

Salt to taste

Fresh seasonal herbs

Lemon wedges

Heat a gas or charcoal grill, or a ridged stovetop griddle until medium hot. If a grill or griddle is unavailable, use a preheated broiler. Lightly brush the prepared vegetables with olive oil. Cook until grill marks are apparent, being careful not to overcook each individual vegetable. As vegetables cook, season with salt and pepper, then transfer them to a large platter. Serve drizzled with extra-virgin olive oil, with herbs of your choice scattered over the vegetables, or simply serve with lemon wedges.

Tortino di Carciofi

Baked Artichoke Frittata

Serves 4 to 6

A classic egg and artichoke dish. The Tortino is baked in the oven rather than being cooked on top of the stove like a frittata. This dish is best served warm. If it sits too long, the artichoke discolors the eggs.

1 *lemon, cut in half*	*Salt and freshly ground black pepper to taste*
4 *medium artichokes*	
3 *tablespoons unbleached flour*	6–8 *eggs*
7 *tablespoons extra-virgin olive oil, divided*	¼ *cup milk*
	¼ *cup grated Parmesan cheese*

Fill a large bowl with water. Squeeze the juice of ½ lemon into the water and add the squeezed lemon half. Use the other ½ lemon to rub the cut areas of the artichokes to prevent them from discoloring. Trim the artichokes by snapping off all the tough outer leaves until only the pale yellow leaves remain. Cut off the tops of the leaves, leaving an inch or so of tender leaf. With a paring knife, carefully cut away dark green areas around the base of the artichokes. Trim the stems and cut away dark green areas around the stems. Cut the artichokes in half. Remove the chokes by cutting along the edge of the artichoke heart. Slice the artichokes ¼ inch thick and place them in the acidulated water until needed.

Drain the artichokes and dry them on a clean dish towel. Lightly dust them with flour. Place 6 tablespoons of the olive oil in a large sauté pan. Over medium heat, cook the artichoke slices on both sides, seasoning them with salt and pepper to taste, until tender and golden. Drain on paper towels. Let cool.

In a bowl beat together the eggs, milk, Parmesan cheese, and salt and pepper to taste. With the remaining olive oil coat a shallow, round baking dish, about 10 inches in diameter and 3 inches deep. Distribute the artichoke slices in the bottom of the dish and pour the egg mixture over the top. Bake in a preheated 325° oven for about 20 minutes, or until the eggs are set. Let rest for a few minutes. Cut into wedges.

Asparagi all'Acciughe

A s p a r a g u s   w i t h   A n c h o v y   S a u c e

Serves 4

Thin asparagus is quickly cooked and tossed in a sauce of warmed anchovies and garlic. The bold flavors of the garlic and anchovy give the mild asparagus a pronounced character. Thin asparagus stalks have tender skin, so peeling the base of the stalks may not be necessary.

(Continued)

1 *pound pencil-thin asparagus*

Salt to taste

3 *tablespoons extra-virgin*
  olive oil

3 *garlic cloves, finely chopped*

6 *anchovies*

Lemon wedges

The pale white area at the base of the stalk indicates toughness. Check 1 stalk for tenderness by snapping it back at the base. Usually about an inch or more will break off. This will be your guideline to the tenderness of the asparagus. Gather the asparagus into a bunch and tie with string. Cut across the base of the stalks, removing the tough portion. If the asparagus is a bit thick, use a vegetable peeler to remove the peel about halfway up the stalk.

Blanch the asparagus in plenty of boiling salted water for 2 minutes. Drain well.

In a sauté pan large enough to contain the asparagus, combine the olive oil and garlic, and cook for 2 to 3 minutes over low heat. Add the anchovies, and with a wooden spoon stir the anchovies for 1 to 2 minutes until the anchovies dissolve. Untie the asparagus and add them to the pan. Toss asparagus gently in the oil until the stalks are lightly coated. Serve with lemon wedges on the side.

Indivia Belga in Forno
al Prosciutto

Baked Belgian Endive
Wrapped in Prosciutto

Serves 8

Belgian endive is blanched first to remove excess bitterness, wrapped in salty prosciutto, and baked on a bed of sweet golden sautéed onions. This recipe features a play of contrasts—sweet, salty, and slightly bitter flavors—which merge to form a delectable whole. Can be served as a vegetable side dish or as a light main course.

8 *heads Belgian endive*	3 *tablespoons unsalted butter*
Salt to taste	8 *slices prosciutto*
2 *large onions, thinly sliced*	½ *cup dry white wine*
1 *tablespoon extra-virgin olive oil*	

Blanch the endive in salted boiling water for 3 to 4 minutes, depending on size. Drain endive well in a colander, gently pressing out excess moisture with the back of a wooden spoon. Sauté the onions in the olive oil and butter over low heat until the onions turn golden and tender. Distribute the onions in the bottom of a baking dish just large enough to contain the endive side by side. Wrap each endive in a slice of prosciutto and arrange on top of the onions. Pour the white wine over the endive. Cover with aluminum foil and bake for 20 minutes at 375°, or until the endive is very tender.

Involtini di Melanzane al Forno

Baked Eggplant Rolls with Mozzarella and Mint

Serves 4 to 6

Cooked eggplant is incredibly rich and creamy. It can be roasted, fried, grilled, or braised; each cooking method brings out slightly different nuances of flavor. In this recipe, golden fried eggplant slices are wrapped around fresh mozzarella, grated Pecorino Romano cheese, and chopped fresh mint. The eggplant rolls are moistened with a little tomato-basil sauce and put in the oven just until the cheeses melt. The success of the dish lies in careful selection and handling of ingredients. Slice the eggplant thinly and drain it well on paper towels. Use the freshest mozzarella and good imported Pecorino Romano cheese. Lightly cook the tomato-basil sauce and use only fresh, aromatic herbs.

1 *medium-large firm, glossy eggplant*

Salt

Olive oil for frying

1 *tablespoon extra-virgin olive oil*

1 *garlic clove, minced*

1½ *cups canned imported Italian tomatoes, chopped with their juice*

Handful fresh basil leaves, divided

½ *pound fresh mozzarella*

¼ *cup grated Pecorino Romano cheese*

3 *tablespoons chopped fresh mint leaves*

Trim the stem ends of the eggplant and cut lengthwise into ¼-inch slices. Salt lightly and let drain for 1 hour. Pat eggplant dry with paper towels.

Add enough olive oil to a medium-sized sauté pan to measure ½ inch. Heat the oil until it is hot but not smoking. Fry the eggplant slices, a few at a time, until they are golden on both sides. Drain well on paper towels. Continue frying eggplant slices in batches until all are fried. Place the extra-virgin olive oil and garlic in a small sauté pan. Warm over low heat for a few minutes. Add the tomatoes and their juice, salt to taste, and a few whole basil leaves, and cook over medium heat until the sauce thickens. Shred the mozzarella. On each eggplant slice, place a little shredded mozzarella, a teaspoon or more of grated cheese, and a sprinkling of chopped mint. Roll up each eggplant slice and place in a baking dish just large enough to contain the rolls in 1 layer. Spoon the tomato sauce over the top. Place in a preheated 375° oven and cook for 15 minutes, or until the cheeses melt. Let rest for a few minutes. Chop the remaining basil and sprinkle over the top just before serving.

Melanzane con Mozzarella Affumicata

Japanese Eggplant with Smoked Mozzarella

Serves 6

Fresh eggplant is firm to the touch and has a lustrous skin that ranges in color from mauve to almost black. It is one of the most loved vegetables of

(Continued)

the Italian south. Our recipe calls for the small, delicately shaped Japanese variety. The eggplants are cut in half lengthwise, fried, and then topped with fresh tomato, basil, and smoked mozzarella, and baked in the oven. Arrange on a platter in a sunburst pattern for a beautiful presentation.

6 *Japanese eggplants*

Salt

Olive oil for frying

2 *tablespoons extra-virgin olive oil*

2 *garlic cloves, peeled and thinly sliced*

2 *large, ripe tomatoes, peeled, seeded, and coarsely chopped*

10 *fresh basil leaves, divided*

⅛ *pound smoked mozzarella, shredded*

Trim the tops of the eggplants and cut in half lengthwise. Salt the cut sides and let drain for 30 minutes. Pat dry. Heat enough olive oil in a frying pan to measure ¼ inch. When the oil is hot but not smoking, fry the eggplant halves on both sides until cut sides are golden and eggplant is tender. Fry in batches and do not crowd the pan. Drain thoroughly on paper towels. In a small sauté pan combine the extra-virgin olive oil and garlic. Cook over low heat for 1 to 2 minutes, add the tomatoes, a few basil leaves, and salt to taste, and simmer for 15 minutes or until a sauce forms. Arrange the eggplant halves, cut side up, in a baking dish. Spoon tomato sauce over the top and sprinkle with the shredded mozzarella. Bake at 350° for about 15 minutes, or until the cheese melts. Chop the remaining basil leaves coarsely, and sprinkle over the top. Serve hot or let cool to room temperature.

Fave Stufate con Mortadella

Fava Beans Cooked with Mortadella

Serves 4

Fava beans require a bit of labor to transform them into a delectable dish—you must shell the beans, then peel each one—but lovers of this vegetable do it willingly. Here tender fresh fava beans are lightly braised in olive oil, fresh oregano, and thin slivers of mortadella.

4½ *pounds fava beans in the pod*

2 *slices mortadella*

3 *tablespoons extra-virgin olive oil, plus extra for drizzling*

1 *sprig fresh oregano*

Salt and freshly ground black pepper to taste

Remove the fava beans from the pods. Carefully peel the waxy skin from each bean. Cut the mortadella into fine julienne strips.

Place the olive oil and oregano in a medium-sized sauté pan. Add the mortadella strips and cook over low heat for 2 to 3 minutes. Add the fava beans, salt to taste, and 3 to 4 tablespoons of water. Cook covered over medium-low heat until the beans are tender and the water has evaporated, about 5 minutes. Remove the lid and continue to cook for about 5 minutes more over low heat, stirring often. If the beans begin to stick to the pan, add a little water. Before serving, drizzle with olive oil, and grind a little fresh pepper over the top.

Finocchio all'Aglio e Acciughe

Fennel with Golden Garlic and Anchovy

Serves 4 to 6

Fennel is given a preliminary cooking in boiling water and then tossed in olive oil with browned whole garlic cloves and anchovies. The combination of flavors is amazing—the light, sweet fennel and deep, rich golden garlic cloves and anchovies. The garlic cloves should be served with the dish. They are delicious.

3 medium fennel bulbs
Salt to taste
¼ cup extra-virgin olive oil

4-6 garlic cloves, peeled and lightly crushed
3 anchovies

Trim the stalks and root ends of the fennel. Cut away any bruised or wilted parts. Slice the fennel bulbs lengthwise about ¼ inch thick. Bring a large pot of water to a boil. Add salt to taste and when the water returns to the boil, drop in the fennel slices. Cook until crisp but tender, about 5 minutes. Drain the fennel and place in one layer on paper towels to absorb excess water. In a large sauté pan, heat the olive oil with the garlic cloves over medium heat. When the garlic is golden, add the anchovies and stir until anchovies melt. Add the drained fennel and cook over low heat for about 5 minutes to let the flavors blend.

Finocchi in Umido
Braised Fennel

Serves 4 to 6

Fennel is one of the most intriguing vegetables. Eaten raw, it is incredibly delicious—crisp, sweet, juicy, with a licorice-like flavor. When cooked, fennel completely changes its character becoming more subtle—tender, almost creamy, and mildly sweet. In this recipe, fennel is braised in fresh tomatoes and aromatic bay leaves for an interesting flavor contrast.

3 *medium fennel bulbs*

3 *tablespoons extra-virgin olive oil*

1 *large onion, peeled and cut into medium dice*

2 *large tomatoes, peeled, seeded, and chopped*

4 *bay leaves*

Salt and freshly ground black pepper to taste

Trim the stalks and root ends of the fennel. Cut away from the bulbs any wilted or bruised parts. Cut bulbs in quarters lengthwise. Place the olive oil in a medium-sized braising pan. Add the onions and sauté over low heat until tender, about 12 minutes. Add the fennel and sauté over medium heat until lightly colored. Add the tomatoes, bay leaves, and salt and pepper to taste. Cook until fennel is tender when pierced with a knife.

Lenticchie al Prosciutto Cotto
e Erbe Invernale

Lentils with Ham and Winter Herbs

Serves 4 to 6

Lentils simmered with aromatic bay leaves, rosemary, sage, and finely diced ham produce a warming, cold-weather side dish or a first course that can be served with bruschetta. Lentils are inexpensive, cook quickly, and are nourishing to body and soul. Their fine taste and texture, pronounced fragrance, and earthy, dark color seem particularly well suited to wintery nights.

5 tablespoons extra-virgin olive oil, divided

1 onion, peeled and finely diced

2 garlic cloves, peeled and finely chopped

2 bay leaves

1 small sprig fresh rosemary, leaves chopped

1 sprig fresh sage, leaves chopped

¼ pound Black Forest ham, cut ¼ inch thick, diced

1½ cups lentils

3–4 canned imported Italian tomatoes, seeded and chopped

Salt and freshly ground black pepper to taste

3 tablespoons finely chopped Italian parsley

Place 3 tablespoons of the olive oil in a medium-sized saucepan. Add the onion, garlic, and herbs, and sauté over low heat until the onion turns tender and translucent. Add the ham and sauté for about 2 to 3 minutes.

Wash the lentils, drain them, and add to the saucepan. Toss the lentils until they are lightly coated with oil. Add the tomatoes, salt and pepper to taste, and enough water to cover. Bring to a boil, then regulate the heat to a steady simmer. Place the lid askew on the pan and cook the lentils until they are tender but not mushy, about 20 minutes or longer, depending on the age of the lentils. There should be a small amount of liquid left in the pot. If there is too much liquid, boil it off. If the lentils dry out while cooking, add more water until the lentils are cooked.

Just before serving, turn off the heat and add the remaining 2 tablespoons of olive oil and the chopped parsley. Stir and let rest covered for 1 to 2 minutes.

Cipolline Dorate

Golden Onions

Serves 4

Italians grow a small, flat, yellow onion that can sometimes be found here in specialty produce stores. These onions are called barlettas, and they are the onions of choice for this recipe. If barlettas are not available, ordinary boiling onions or pearl onions will work perfectly well. Here the onions are first sautéed in butter with pancetta, then braised in broth until tender.

1 *pound small yellow or white onions*

3 *tablespoons unsalted butter*

2 *slices pancetta, chopped*

1 *cup beef broth*

1 *bay leaf*

Salt to taste

Blanch the onions in boiling water for 1 minute. Drain and peel. Combine the butter and pancetta in a medium-sized braising pan, and sauté over low heat until the pancetta renders some of its fat, about 5 minutes. Add the onions and sauté over medium heat until the onions are a light gold color. Add the broth and bay leaf, and salt to taste. Simmer until the onions are tender and the broth has evaporated. The amount of cooking time will vary according to the size of onion. Test the onions with the tip of a paring knife. They should be tender but still hold their shape.

Peperoni Imbottiti

Stuffed Yellow Peppers

Serves 6

Yellow peppers, with their bright golden-yellow color and lustrous skin, are among the most beautiful vegetables. Served raw, they are crisp and juicy. When the peppers are cooked, their flesh softens to release wonderfully honeyed juices. In our recipe, the sweetness of the peppers is counterbalanced by the piquant tang of anchovies, capers, and olives. Serve warm or at room temperature. Peperoni Imbottiti make a great addition to an antipasto buffet.

6 *yellow peppers, large and thick-fleshed*

½ *cup bread crumbs*

4 *anchovy fillets, chopped to a paste*

3 *tablespoons capers*

12 *green olives, pitted and coarsely chopped*

Salt and freshly ground black pepper to taste

3 *tablespoons chopped Italian parsley, plus extra for garnish*

Extra-virgin olive oil

Cut peppers in half lengthwise and carefully remove the seeds and membranes. Combine the remaining ingredients with enough olive oil to form a paste. Arrange the pepper halves, cut side up, in a baking dish and distribute the bread crumb mixture evenly over the peppers. Top each pepper half with a few drops of oil. Bake in a preheated 325° oven for 20 minutes or until the peppers are tender. Serve either warm or at room temperature, sprinkled with extra chopped parsley.

Peperoni Gialli Ripieni di Pasta

Yellow Peppers Stuffed with Pasta

Serves 6

Peppers make great containers for stuffings. And what better filling could there be than a mixture of short pasta, tomatoes, herbs, and Pecorino Romano cheese?

6 *small yellow peppers*

½ *pound imported tubetti*

¼ *cup extra-virgin olive oil, divided, plus additional for oiling baking dish and for drizzling on peppers*

1 *pound tomatoes, peeled, seeded, and chopped*

2 *cloves garlic, finely chopped*

Small handful chopped fresh mint

1 *bunch Italian parsley, leaves chopped*

¼ *cup grated Pecorino Romano cheese, plus additional for sprinkling on top of peppers*

Salt and freshly ground black pepper to taste

Cut the tops off the peppers and remove the cores, seeds, and membranes. Reserve the tops. Cook the tubetti in abundant salted boiling water until cooked about halfway, or very al dente. Drain well and toss with 1 tablespoon of olive oil. Place 3 tablespoons of oil, tomatoes, and garlic in a medium-sized sauté pan and cook over high heat for 10 minutes, or until the sauce thickens. Let cool. Toss the cooked pasta in tomato sauce and add the mint, parsley, ¼ cup grated Pecorino Romano cheese, and salt and pepper to taste. Lightly oil a baking dish just large enough to contain the peppers without crowding them. Lightly moisten the peppers inside and out with oil, and arrange in the baking dish. Salt the interiors of the peppers. Spoon the tomato-pasta mixture into the pepper cases. Drizzle peppers with a teaspoon or so of oil and sprinkle with extra grated cheese. Place the reserved tops on the peppers. Bake in a preheated 375° oven for 30 minutes, or until the peppers are just tender and the pasta is cooked al dente. Serve hot or at room temperature.

Piselli al Prosciutto

Peas with Prosciutto

Serves 4

This classic Italian vegetable dish calls for tender, tiny fresh peas and beautifully pink, buttery prosciutto. The peas are quickly cooked in butter-sweetened onion and a small amount of broth. At the last moment, julienne strips of prosciutto are stirred in and lightly cooked.

3 *pounds fresh peas, unshelled weight*

¼ *cup unsalted butter*

1 *small onion, finely diced*

½ *cup beef broth (additional may be required)*

Salt and freshly ground black pepper to taste

4 *large, thin slices prosciutto, cut crosswise into julienne strips*

Shell the peas. In a small saucepan melt the butter over low heat. Add the onion and sauté slowly until it is tender and transparent. Add the peas, broth, and salt and pepper to taste. Cook over medium heat until peas are tender. The cooking time will vary depending on the size of the peas. Older peas require more time to cook, so increase the amount of broth. Just before the peas are ready, stir in the prosciutto and cook briefly. Serve immediately.

Patate in Tegame

Baked Sliced Potatoes with Tomato and Oregano

Serves 4

The humble potato is the essence of rustic cooking—as connected to the earth as any food can be. In Italian marketplaces, freshly dug potatoes still have earth from the fields clinging to them, giving off a warm, fertile smell. In this recipe their mild, sweet flavor is accented by sharp Pecorino Romano cheese and pungent dried Mediterranean oregano. The potatoes look especially appealing if baked in an earthenware dish that can be brought to the table. Serve as an accompaniment to simple grilled meat or fish.

1 *pound boiling potatoes*

1 *pound red, ripe tomatoes*

3 *tablespoons extra-virgin olive oil, divided*

Salt to taste

2 *cloves garlic, peeled and thinly sliced*

1 *teaspoon dried oregano*

3 *tablespoons grated Pecorino Romano cheese*

Scrub the potatoes and slice them about ⅛ inch thick. Core the tomatoes and coarsely chop, reserving the juices. Select a gratin dish large enough to accommodate all the potato slices in one layer with only slight overlapping. Oil the gratin dish with 1 tablespoon of the olive oil. Distribute the potato slices evenly in the dish. Sprinkle the garlic over the potatoes, and top with the chopped tomatoes and reserved juices. Season with salt to taste. Drizzle with the remaining oil and sprinkle with the oregano and the cheese. Bake in a preheated 375° oven for 45 minutes, or until the potatoes are tender and the top is lightly crusted. If dish looks dry, add a few tablespoons of water during cooking.

Pizza di Patate

Potato Pizza

Serves 4 to 6

This is a traditional recipe from Puglia with a slight twist on the toppings. Boiled and mashed potatoes are shaped into a pizza-like crust and topped with cheeses and herbs. Avoid toppings that are watery and that would cause the crust to become soggy. Another crucial factor in getting a crisp crust is to limit the number of times you poke the potatoes during boiling. If too much water seeps into the potatoes, the crust will be too soft. Select one potato as a tester and start testing only when you are sure they are almost done.

2 *pounds russet potatoes of similar size*

¼ *cup extra-virgin olive oil, divided, plus extra for pizza pan*

Salt to taste

2 *tablespoons toasted bread crumbs*

¼ *pound shredded smoked mozzarella*

¼ *cup grated Pecorino Romano cheese*

2 *medium tomatoes, seeded and cut into small dice*

1 *teaspoon dried oregano*

Boil the potatoes in salted water to cover until tender. Drain and when cool enough to handle, peel them. Put potatoes through a ricer. Add 3 tablespoons of the olive oil and salt to taste. Very lightly grease a 12-inch pizza pan with the oil. Sprinkle with the toasted bread crumbs. Spread the potato mixture over the pan to form a thin crust that is slightly thicker at the edges. Distribute the smoked mozzarella, and sprinkle with the grated cheeses, tomato, and oregano. Drizzle with the remaining olive oil. Bake at 450° for 20 minutes, or until the crust is golden.

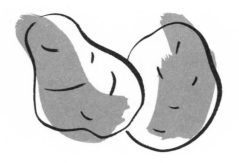

Tiella del Sud

Baked Sliced Potatoes,
Peppers, and Tomatoes

Serves 4 to 6

This is a good example of a simple, earthy dish with all the exuberant color and flavor of vegetables from the south of Italy. Ripe, flavorful tomatoes are essential to its preparation, as are thick-fleshed, deep-colored peppers. The juices this dish produces call for the best coarse textured and flavorful bread you can find to sop up every delectable drop.

1 *pound boiling potatoes*

2 *sweet peppers, either red or yellow, or 1 of each*

3 *large red, ripe tomatoes*

¼ *cup extra-virgin olive oil*

Salt and freshly ground black pepper to taste

3 *garlic cloves, peeled and coarsely chopped*

10 *fresh basil leaves, coarsely chopped*

2 *teaspoons dried oregano*

Wash the potatoes well and slice thinly. Cut the peppers lengthwise and remove the cores and seeds. Slice into strips about ½ inch thick. Core the tomatoes and slice horizontally approximately ¼ inch thick, reserving the juice. Use some of the olive oil to grease the bottom of a gratin dish large enough to contain all the ingredients to a depth of about 2 inches. In the dish arrange a layer of potatoes, a layer of peppers, and then a layer of tomatoes. Season with salt and pepper to taste and sprinkle with garlic, basil, and oregano. Continue layering until all the ingredients are used up. Pour the reserved juice from the tomatoes over the mixture. Drizzle with the remaining olive oil. Bake in a preheated 400° oven for about 45 minutes, or until the potatoes are tender. If the mixture appears too dry, add a few tablespoons of water as it cooks.

Spinaci Saltati al Prosciutto

Sautéed Spinach with Prosciutto

Serves 4

Beautiful, glossy, and bright green sautéed spinach is tossed with julienned pink prosciutto. This versatile side dish looks lovely on the plate. Take care not to overcook the spinach.

2 *pounds fresh, tender spinach*

Salt to taste

¼ *cup extra-virgin olive oil*

2 *garlic cloves, peeled and chopped*

4 *slices prosciutto, cut into julienne*

Remove any tough stems from the spinach. Wash well in 3 changes of cold water to remove all traces of sand and dirt. Drain, and place spinach and all the water that clings to it in a pot large enough to contain it and cook over medium heat, covered, until spinach just wilts. Drain well in a colander, gently pressing out excess water with the back of a wooden spoon. In a medium-sized sauté pan combine the olive oil and garlic. Cook over low heat for 2 to 3 minutes. Add the prosciutto and cook another 1 to 2 minutes. Add the spinach and salt to taste. Toss gently over medium-low heat until spinach is hot.

Pomodori Piccanti al Forno

Spicy Baked Tomato Halves

Serves 4

Use slightly underripe tomatoes for this dish. They hold their shape better when baked. Tomatoes that are streaked with a little green have an appealing tart edge that contrasts nicely with the sweetness of the fresh herbs. Capers and diced salame add punch. These stuffed tomatoes are good to serve as a side dish with many simple grilled meats and fish.

4 *large, slightly underripe*
tomatoes

Salt to taste

2 *garlic cloves, peeled and*
minced

¼ *cup chopped Italian parsley*

1 *bunch fresh basil, leaves*
coarsely chopped

2 *tablespoons capers*

¼ *cup diced spicy salame*

Salt and freshly ground black
pepper to taste

2 *tablespoons toasted bread*
crumbs

¼ *cup extra-virgin olive oil*

Cut the tomatoes in half horizontally and remove all the seeds. Sprinkle the inside of each tomato half with salt and let stand about 15 to 20 minutes.

(Continued)

Place the tomatoes, cut side down, on paper towels until excess moisture is absorbed.

In a small bowl combine the garlic, parsley, basil, capers, and salame. Add a little salt and pepper to taste. Stuff the herb mixture into the tomato halves and sprinkle with the bread crumbs. Using about 1 tablespoon of the olive oil, lightly oil a baking dish large enough to contain the tomato halves in one layer. Arrange the tomato halves in the baking dish and sprinkle with the remaining oil. Bake in a preheated 400° oven for about 5 to 10 minutes, or until tomatoes soften slightly. Serve warm or at room temperature.

Fagiolini Gialli al Pancetta

Wax Beans with Pancetta

Serves 4

Tender wax beans, a lovely shade of yellow tinged with spring green, are blanched first and then tossed with lightly sautéed small pink squares of pancetta, chopped parsley, and garlic.

1 *pound fresh wax beans*

Salt to taste

2 *tablespoons extra-virgin olive oil*

3 *slices pancetta (about 3 ounces), coarsely chopped*

3 *tablespoons chopped Italian parsley*

Trim the beans by snapping or cutting off the ends. Blanch the beans in abundant salted boiling water until tender but crisp, about 5 to 10 minutes, depending on tenderness. Drain in a colander.

In a medium-sized sauté pan combine the olive oil and pancetta. Sauté over low heat until the pancetta colors lightly and renders some of its fat, about 5 minutes. Add the beans, parsley, and salt to taste, and toss them in the oil and pancetta. Cook over medium-low heat for about 10 minutes, or until the beans are cooked through and the flavors have mingled.

Zucchine Ripiene

Stuffed Scaloppine Squash

Serves 6

Scaloppine squash are small, round zucchini with a scalloped edge. They are sweet and firm of flesh. They make most attractive containers for stuffing, and are a very pretty accompaniment to all kinds of main dishes. Ours are filled with a mixture of aromatic basil, lemon rind, bread crumbs, and sharp Pecorino Romano cheese.

6 scaloppine squash of approximately equal size

6 tablespoons extra-virgin olive oil, divided

⅓ cup bread crumbs

¼ cup grated Pecorino Romano cheese

2 eggs, lightly beaten

¼ cup chopped fresh basil

Grated peel of ½ lemon

Salt and freshly ground black pepper to taste

Cut a thin slice off the tops of the zucchini and discard. Scoop out the interior of the zucchini, leaving a wall about ¼ inch thick. Reserve the scooped-out pulp. Blanch the shells in salted boiling water for 2 to 3 minutes, and drain. Chop the zucchini pulp and sauté in 3 tablespoons of the olive oil. Place in a small bowl and mix with the bread crumbs, cheese, eggs, basil, lemon peel, and salt and pepper to taste. Lightly salt the interior of the zucchini shells and fill with the bread-crumb mixture. Drizzle with the remaining olive oil. Bake at 350° for about 20 minutes, or until the filling is firm and the zucchini is tender. Serve warm or at room temperature.

Zucchine Saltate al Basilico
e Pecorino

Sautéed Zucchini with Basil and Pecorino Romano Cheese

Serves 4

The simplest dishes are often the best. Small, tender zucchini are cut into coins, tossed in hot oil, and then sprinkled with cheese and basil. Do not use large zucchini as they are full of water and seeds. Small zucchini have seeds that are barely developed, and their flesh is very compact. Look for those that are 5 inches long or smaller, firm to the touch, and smooth-skinned. This dish makes a delightful first course served with Crostini (see page 45).

2 *pounds small, fresh zucchini*

6 *tablespoons extra-virgin olive oil*

2 *cloves garlic, peeled and minced*

3 *tablespoons grated Pecorino Romano cheese*

Salt and freshly ground black pepper to taste

10 *large fresh basil leaves, torn*

1 *recipe Crostini (see page 45), optional*

Wash the zucchini well to remove all traces of dirt. When their skins feel smooth to the touch, dry them well. Trim the ends and slice zucchini into rounds about ¼ inch thick. In a large sauté pan, heat the olive oil. Add the zucchini, and over high heat toss them until tender but slightly crisp. In the final minute or so of cooking, add the garlic and toss with the zucchini. Off the heat, toss with the cheese, salt, and pepper. Scatter the basil over the top. Serve garnished with Crostini, if desired.

Zucchine in Tegame con Panna

Gratinéed Zucchini with
Fresh Tomatoes and Cream

Serves 6

An elegant presentation with cream adding the special note. Fried zucchini slices are layered with tomatoes and basil and topped with fresh cream and Parmesan cheese. The dish is baked in the oven until the cream topping turns golden.

1½ pounds medium zucchini

Salt to taste

Olive oil for frying

1 cup cream

6 tablespoons grated Parmesan cheese

4 medium tomatoes, sliced ¼ inch thick

1 bunch fresh basil leaves, coarsely chopped

Slice the zucchini lengthwise about ¼ inch thick. Lightly salt them and let drain for about 30 minutes. Pat dry. In a large skillet heat the olive oil to a depth of ¼ inch. When the oil is hot but not smoking, fry the zucchini slices, a few at a time, turning them so that both sides become golden. Remove from the pan and let zucchini drain well on paper towels. In a small bowl combine the cream and Parmesan cheese. Select a gratin dish that is large enough to contain the ingredients to a depth of 2 inches. Place a layer of zucchini in the bottom. Spoon over the zucchini a little of the cream and Parmesan mixture. Top with a few tomato slices and some of the chopped basil. Continue layering all the ingredients, finishing with a thick layer of the cream and Parmesan mixture. Cook in a preheated 350° oven until the cream is hot and bubbling and lightly golden. Let dish rest for a few minutes before serving.

Pesce e Frutti di Mare

Fish and Shellfish

Italy is a narrow peninsula surrounded by the sea, so it isn't surprising that fresh seafood is an intrinsic part of Italian cooking. Everyone who has traveled to Italy remembers that first bowl of tiny fresh clams in broth, or plate of fresh shrimp in the shell grilled over coals. In America, finding fresh seafood may be difficult, especially if you are far from the coasts, but it is well worth the effort.

Nothing surpasses a whole grilled fish, Italian-style, bathed in olive oil and lemon and seasoned with fresh herbs. Seafood soups, made with shellfish or a mixture of fish and shellfish, briny and exhilarating, are another glory of the Italian kitchen. Fried calamari, that most addictive of seafood, with its crunchy exterior and soft, melting flesh, is another favorite, found in every seaside restaurant. We offer recipes for these classic dishes, as well as for new variations on themes such as seafood carpaccios, braised shrimp on a bed of raw arugula, and marinated grilled squid on bruschetta.

For our recipes, we have selected fish and shellfish that are most widely available here and have their counterparts in Italian cooking, such as tuna, swordfish, and various shellfish. When you are in the mood to cook seafood, head to the fish market to see what fresh catch piques your interest, and proceed from there. To capture the true taste of Italian seafood, let the fish market be your inspiration.

Pesce al Burro e Vino

Whole Fish Baked in Butter and Wine

Serves 4

The delicate flavor of whole red snapper is enriched by butter, with dry white wine adding a bracing note. Simple dishes like this one help us rediscover the true taste of food.

A 2½-pound whole red snapper or similar fish	*3 tablespoons unsalted butter, divided*
Salt to taste	*¾ cup dry white wine*

Wash the fish well and dry it. Make 3 diagonal cuts along both sides of the fish. Season it inside and out with salt to taste. Place 2 tablespoons of the butter inside the cavity of the fish. Use the remaining butter to coat the bottom of a baking dish just large enough to contain the fish comfortably. Place the fish in the baking dish and pour the white wine over the top. Cover with aluminum foil and bake for about 20 minutes at 375°. Remove the fish from the baking dish and reserve the juices. Carefully fillet the fish. Arrange on individual plates and spoon the juices over the top.

Carpaccio di Salmone

Salmon Carpaccio

Serves 6 as a luncheon dish or 12 as an appetizer

Salmon Carpaccio is "cooked" by being marinated in lemon juice, olive oil, and red onion. Served with a complementary topping of fennel, green onion, and tomato, it makes a lovely, light luncheon dish or a great appetizer.

Juice of 2 lemons

1 tablespoon extra-virgin olive oil

½ red onion, peeled and finely chopped

Freshly ground black pepper to taste

1 pound salmon fillet

1 fennel bulb, sliced very thin

4 green onions, sliced very thin

1 tomato, peeled, seeded, and diced

Salt and freshly ground black pepper to taste

¼ cup extra-virgin olive oil

Lemon wedges

Make a marinade by combining the first 4 ingredients. Cut the salmon into four 4-ounce pieces, or six 2½-ounce pieces. Gently pound the salmon between 2 sheets of oiled parchment paper until very thin. Lay the fish in a glass, stainless-steel, or enamel baking pan, and cover with the marinade. Refrigerate for at least 4 hours.

While the fish is marinating, make the topping for the Carpaccio by combining the fennel, green onions, tomato, seasonings, and olive oil.

Before serving, lift the salmon from the marinade and arrange on individual plates. Spoon topping onto each serving and garnish with lemon wedges.

Carpaccio di Tonno

Tuna Carpaccio

Serves 6 as a luncheon dish or 12 as an appetizer

The meaty flavor and texture of fresh tuna truly make it suitable for a dish that is usually made with beef. The tuna is marinated with the sharp bite of mustard and shallots, then topped with spicy radishes and smooth borlotti beans.

Juice of 3 lemons

1 teaspoon Dijon mustard

2 tablespoons extra-virgin olive oil

1 shallot, peeled and minced

Salt and freshly ground black pepper to taste

1 pound fresh tuna

16 radishes, sliced very thin

1½ cups borlotti beans

½ cup extra-virgin olive oil

Lemon wedges

Make a marinade by combining the first 5 ingredients. Cut the tuna into four 4-ounce pieces, or six 2½-ounce pieces. Gently pound the tuna between 2 sheets of oiled parchment paper until very thin. Place the fish in a glass, stainless-steel, or enamel baking pan, and cover with the marinade. Refrigerate for at least 4 hours.

While the fish is marinating, make the topping for the Carpaccio by combining the remaining ingredients except for the lemon wedges.

Before serving, lift the tuna from the marinade and arrange on individual plates. Spoon topping on each serving and garnish with lemon wedges.

Trance alla Griglia

Grilled Fish Steaks
with Marinade

Serves 4

We frequently serve meals whose centerpiece is this simple preparation of swordfish or tuna steaks. The fish is not marinated before grilling. Instead, a light marinade of extra-virgin olive oil, lemon juice, and herbs is used to baste the fish during cooking. A final touch: we lavishly brush the steaks with the marinade when they are arranged on the serving platter. We recommend using rosemary and parsley for tuna, and parsley and oregano for swordfish. Use fish steaks that are thin, preferably not more than ½ inch thick. Tuna and swordfish should take only 1 to 2 minutes per side to cook. Tuna, especially, has a tendency to become tough if the steak is thicker than ½ inch since it would require longer cooking.

4 ½-inch-wide tuna or swordfish steaks

1 cup extra-virgin olive oil

¼ cup fresh lemon juice

Small handful coarsely chopped Italian parsley

1 sprig fresh rosemary, leaves only, minced (for tuna)

4 sprigs fresh oregano, leaves only, coarsely chopped, or 1 teaspoon dried oregano (for swordfish)

Salt and freshly ground black pepper to taste

In a small bowl mix together the olive oil, lemon juice, herbs, and salt and pepper to taste. Let marinade steep at least 15 minutes.

Heat a charcoal or gas grill or ridged stovetop griddle until very hot.

(Continued)

Lightly rub the grill with an oil-soaked towel to prevent fish from sticking. Lightly brush each fish steak with oil and place on the grill. As the fish cooks, baste it with the marinade. Cook 1 to 2 minutes per side, or until the fish feels firm when pressed with a finger.

When fish is cooked, remove it from the grill and place it on a large serving platter. While the fish is still very hot, lavishly brush it with the marinade. Serve with lemon wedges.

Pesce alla Griglia

Grilled Whole Fish with Herb Paste

Serves 4

Grilling is one of the simplest and most flavorful ways to cook fish. There are many methods of preparing it. You can marinate the fish briefly in a little oil, lemon, and herbs, then grill it and brush with the marinade. Or you can stuff the fish with whole herbs, lemon, and perhaps a little garlic before grilling, or you can take marination one step further as in this recipe. First make a highly aromatic herb paste and rub it into the fish cavity and into slashes on either side of the fish. Marinate the fish in the paste for a bit, then grill it and brush occasionally with additional oil. The paste infuses the herbal flavor deep into the delicate flesh. The only accompaniment should be some lemon wedges. The secret to grilling fish without tearing the skin is twofold. First, the grill must be very, very hot. Then you must wait long enough before turning the fish so that a crust forms on the skin. Small, single-serving fish are often hard to find, although most Asian fish markets have a good selection. You can substitute a large 4-pound fish if small ones are unavailable.

4 *small fish, approximately 1 pound each or less (red snapper, striped bass, New Zealand snapper), gutted, scaled, but with the heads left on*

1 *garlic clove, peeled*

25 *fresh basil leaves*

1 *sprig fresh rosemary, leaves only, very finely chopped*

¼ cup coarsely chopped Italian parsley

1–2 *teaspoons coarse salt or to taste*

Freshly ground black pepper to taste

Extra-virgin olive oil

Lemon wedges

Place the garlic and all the herbs on a chopping board, and using a chef's knife chop the herbs together coarsely. Add the salt and pepper, and continue to chop very fine until the herbs begin to form a paste. Drizzle some olive oil over the herbs and, using the flat side of the knife, work the oil into the herbs to form a smooth herbal mixture.

Make 4 shallow slashes on each side of the fish. With your fingers, work the herb paste into the slashes, rubbing some into the cavity as well. Lay the fish on a platter to marinate for about ½ hour.

Heat a charcoal or gas grill or ridged stovetop griddle until very hot. Carefully lay the fish onto the grill. Cook the fish until a thin crust forms on the skin, which enables you to turn the fish with a spatula. As the fish cooks, baste it with a little oil. Cook the fish until done, approximately 3 to 4 minutes per side. Serve on individual plates garnished with lemon wedges.

Pesce alla Griglia con
Salsa di Prezzemolo e Pinoli

Grilled White Fish with Parsley and Pine Nut Sauce

Serves 4

This brilliant-green sauce has a bracing flavor mellowed by creamy-textured pine nuts. It is especially delicious spooned over grilled white-fleshed fish fillets, such as halibut, sea bass, or whitefish. The sauce can be made several hours in advance.

Large handful Italian parsley, leaves only

3 garlic cloves, peeled

¼ cup pine nuts

Salt to taste

Extra-virgin olive oil

4 6–7-ounce fish fillets

Finely chop the parsley, garlic, and pine nuts by hand or pound into a rough pesto using a mortar and pestle. Add salt. Place in a small bowl and add enough olive oil to form a fairly liquid pesto. Set aside.

Heat a charcoal or gas grill or ridged stovetop griddle until very hot. Lightly rub the grill with an oil-soaked towel to prevent fish from sticking. Lightly brush each fish fillet with oil and place on the grill. Cook the fish approximately 2 to 3 minutes per side, or until it feels firm when you press it with your finger.

As fish is cooked, remove it from the grill and place on individual plates. Spoon the sauce over the fish fillets and serve.

Trota all'Erbe

Trout Stuffed with Herb Sprigs

Serves 4

Fresh trout has a delicate flavor that takes well to fresh herbs and garlic. Here it is moistened with extra-virgin olive oil and lemon, stuffed with a trio of herbs and very thinly sliced garlic, drizzled with a touch of white wine, sealed in foil, and baked briefly. The result is a highly aromatic and moist dish with delectable juices for dipping bread.

4 whole trout, cleaned and scaled

Aluminum foil

½ cup extra-virgin olive oil

Salt and freshly ground black pepper

Juice of 2 lemons

4 garlic cloves, thinly sliced

4 small sprigs fresh rosemary

4 sprigs Italian parsley

4 sprigs fresh mint

¼ cup imported white wine vinegar

(Continued)

Arrange the trout on 4 large squares of aluminum foil that will later be folded to form packets. Rub trout with olive oil inside and out. Generously season with salt and pepper. Drizzle lemon juice on fish inside and out. Stuff the interior of the trout with the garlic slices and whole herbs, arranging the sprigs along the length of the fish. Fold the trout closed so that the edges meet. (For a more pronounced herbal flavor, place the trout on a platter and add the olive oil, lemon juice, salt, pepper, herbs, and garlic as described above. Cover trout with plastic wrap and marinate for 1 to 2 hours before placing it in the foil packets and then proceed with the recipe.)

Drizzle 1 tablespoon of the wine vinegar on the trout in each packet, and fold packets securely so that no juices escape. Place packets on a baking sheet and cook at 400° for about 10 minutes per inch of thickness of trout, or until fish is just opaque. Transfer trout and all their juices to individual plates. If desired, make shallow cuts in the skin along the heads and tails, and remove skin from the top of each trout before serving.

Trota al Prosciutto e Salvia

Trout Stuffed with Prosciutto and Sage

Serves 4

Mild and sweet-fleshed whole trout are stuffed with strips of prosciutto and sage leaves, which impart a rich flavor and strongly herbal aroma.

4 *whole trout, cleaned and scaled*

¼ *cup extra-virgin olive oil*

Salt and freshly ground black pepper to taste

4 *slices prosciutto*

12 *fresh sage leaves*

¼ *cup dry white wine*

Place the trout in a baking dish and rub with the olive oil. Season trout inside and out with salt and pepper to taste. Insert a slice of prosciutto along the length of each trout. Arrange 3 sage leaves inside each fish. Sprinkle with the white wine. Bake at 375° for 10 minutes per inch of thickness. Transfer trout to a serving dish along with all their juices. Remove the skin from the top of each trout before serving.

Pesce in Carpione

Marinated Whitefish with Pine Nuts

Serves 4 to 6

This dish comes from a long tradition of using acidic marinades to preserve fish, a simple technique that results in an explosion of flavor. The sweetness of the onion and raisin and the bite of the vinegar, mustard, and raw shallot permeate the fish to create the perfect refreshing summertime entrée.

⅓ cup golden raisins

1½ onions, peeled and sliced very thin

2 tablespoons extra-virgin olive oil

¾ cup white wine vinegar

1 tablespoon Dijon mustard

1 shallot, peeled and minced

2 garlic cloves, peeled and minced

Juice of ½ lemon

¼ cup extra-virgin olive oil

Salt and freshly ground black pepper to taste

Vegetable oil for frying

1 pound whitefish fillet, cut into 4 or 6 equal portions

1 cup all-purpose unbleached flour

Salt

⅓ cup pine nuts

Rinse the raisins in cold water and remove any hard ones, then soak them in warm water to cover for about 15 minutes. Drain and set aside. Meanwhile, sauté the onions in the olive oil over moderate heat for about 20 minutes, stirring occasionally. The onions should be very tender and sweet. Raise the heat and add the vinegar to the onions and simmer for a few minutes to reduce slightly. Add the raisins and remove from the heat.

Make a marinade with the mustard, shallot, garlic, lemon juice, and olive oil. Season with salt and pepper to taste. Heat about 1 inch of vegetable oil in a frying pan until very hot but not smoking. Lightly dust the fish in the flour and fry in the oil until golden. Drain on paper towels. Place the fish in a shallow glass dish and top with the raisins, pine nuts, and onions. Pour the vinaigrette over the fish-and-onion mixture and cover with plastic wrap. Let the fish marinate in the refrigerator for at least 3 hours, preferably overnight. Bring back to room temperature before serving.

Gamberi alla Romana

Shrimp Roman Style

Serves 4

We were introduced to this dish several summers ago in Rome while dining *all'aperto* on a terrace overlooking Roman ruins. The fragrance and spice of crushed black pepper permeates the shrimp as they marinate.

2 *pounds large shrimp*

6 *tablespoons extra-virgin olive oil*

1 *teaspoon coarsely crushed black peppercorns*

Juice of ½ lemon

Salt to taste

Lemon wedges

Peel and devein the shrimp (see page 289). Let drain well in a colander and pat dry with paper towels. Place the shrimp in a shallow bowl. Add the olive oil, crushed peppercorns, lemon juice, and salt to taste, and gently toss. Let marinate for 1 hour at room temperature or several hours refrigerated. If the shrimp are refrigerated, return them to room temperature.

(Continued)

Lift the shrimp out of the marinade. Some black pepper will cling to them, but let the excess oil drain. Have 4 skewers handy. Thread the shrimp on the skewers. Grill over high heat until the shrimp is just opaque, about 1 minute on each side. Lightly salt each side after grilling. Serve with lemon wedges.

Gamberi al Pomodoro e Rucola

Shrimp with Tomato and Arugula

Serves 4 to 6

Raw arugula is the peppery base for sweet, tender shrimp, which are briefly cooked in a light tomato sauce. An unusual dish that is almost a warm salad.

1½ pounds large shrimp

¼ cup extra-virgin olive oil

3 garlic cloves, peeled and minced

½ teaspoon red chile pepper flakes

2 anchovies, chopped

1½ pounds Roma tomatoes, peeled, seeded, and chopped

Salt and freshly ground black pepper to taste

2 cups coarsely chopped arugula

Lemon wedges

Shell and devein the shrimp (see page 289). Set aside to drain. Combine the oil, garlic, and red chile pepper in a medium-sized sauté pan. Cook over low heat for 2 to 3 minutes until the garlic releases its aroma. Add the anchovies and continue to cook over low heat until they dissolve into the oil. Add the tomatoes and salt and pepper to taste. Raise the heat to medium high and cook until juices thicken, about 10 minutes. Lower the heat, add the shrimp, and cook for 2 to 3 minutes, or until the shrimp is just opaque. If the sauce is too runny, lift out the shrimp, raise the heat to high, and reduce sauce quickly. Arrange the arugula on a platter and spoon over it the tomato and shrimp mixture. Garnish with lemon wedges.

Gamberi Saltati al Rosmarino
Sautéed Shrimp with Rosemary

Serves 4

In this recipe the shrimp are deveined, but their shells are left on so they stay moist as they cook. The aromatic marinade consists of rosemary, bay leaves, lemon juice, and black pepper. Sucking on the flavorful shells is an integral part of the eating experience, a little messy but very satisfying.

¼ cup extra-virgin olive oil

4 small sprigs fresh rosemary

2 large garlic cloves, sliced

4 bay leaves, broken in half

1½ pounds large shrimp

Juice of ½ lemon

Salt and freshly ground black pepper to taste

Lemon wedges

Combine the olive oil, rosemary, garlic, and bay leaves in a small sauté pan. Warm the ingredients over low heat for 2 to 3 minutes. Let cool. Meanwhile, devein the shrimp by making a shallow cut along the curved

(Continued)

side of the shell and discarding the black vein that runs along its length. Rinse under cold running water. Drain the shrimp and dry well. Place in a shallow dish. Pour the contents of the sauté pan over the shrimp. Add the lemon juice, salt, and a generous amount of freshly ground pepper. Toss the shrimp so that it is coated with the marinade. Let the shrimp marinate for at least 1 hour but preferably for several hours, tossing the mixture from time to time. If you plan to marinate the shrimp for longer than 1 hour, refrigerate them and return them to room temperature before continuing with the recipe.

Transfer the ingredients to a large sauté pan and cook over high heat until shrimp is just opaque. Lightly salt and serve with lemon wedges.

Fritto di Gamberi, Zucchine, e Fiori di Zucca

Mixed Fry of Shrimp, Zucchini, and Zucchini Flowers

Serves 4

Fritto misto is a mixture of vegetables, seafoods, meats, or even cheeses, dipped in a batter or in eggs and bread crumbs, and fried in hot olive oil. It is a method of cooking dear to the heart of Italians. When the frying is done properly, nothing can match sitting down to a plate of fritto misto.

To fry food correctly, the oil must be fresh and there must be plenty of it. The pan should never be crowded. An even, high heat should be maintained but kept below the smoking point. The food should be dry before being dipped in batter or breaded. Breading or battering should be done in small batches. And once fried, all the food should be well drained on paper towels. The end product is crisp, clean tasting, and full of flavor, very different from fried food as most Americans know it. There are certain combinations that are traditional, such as fritto misto made of seafood. The following version combines shrimp, zucchini, and zucchini flowers. The shrimp are dredged in flour before frying and the vegetables are dipped in a batter, or *pastella*.

2 *cups all-purpose, unbleached flour for the batter*	12 *large, fresh zucchini flowers*
1 *cup water (or ½ cup water and ½ cup beer)*	1 *cup all-purpose unbleached flour for shrimp*
1 *pound large shrimp*	*Olive oil for frying*
4 *medium-small zucchini*	*Salt to taste*
	Lemon wedges

To make the batter, beat together with a fork 2 cups of flour and the water, or water and beer, until smooth. Set aside for 10 minutes.

Peel and devein the shrimp (see page 289). Pat dry. Scrub the zucchini well and dry. Cut the zucchini in half lengthwise and then again in half lengthwise. Cut the long strips in half to form short batons. Remove the pistils from inside the zucchini flowers. Very gently dip the flowers in cool water to clean them. Dry on paper towels. Spread the 1 cup flour on a dinner plate.

In 2 separate sauté pans, pour enough oil to come up the sides ¼-inch. Heat the olive oil until very hot but not smoking. Lightly dredge the shrimp in enough flour for 1 batch at a time. Fry until golden on both sides. Transfer to a plate lined with paper towels, add salt to taste, and let drain.

(Continued)

Meanwhile, dip the zucchini and zucchini flowers in the batter and let excess drain off. Again, batter only as much of the food as you can fry at one time. In the second pan fry the zucchini and zucchini flowers in batches until golden on both sides. Transfer to another plate lined with paper towels, add salt, and let drain. When ready to serve, arrange the shrimp, zucchini, and zucchini flowers on a serving platter. Garnish with lemon wedges.

Tonno al Pomodoro, Olive e Basilico

Tuna Steaks in Fresh Tomato, Olive, and Basil Sauce

Serves 4

Fresh tuna is so rich tasting and satisfying, no wonder it has become popular here. The major pitfall in preparing tuna is to overcook it, since it has a tendency to dry out quickly. Braising is a cooking method often used with tuna to ensure the fish stays moist. In this recipe the tuna is first floured lightly, then fried quickly in hot olive oil to seal in the flavor and juices. Then it is braised in a fresh tomato sauce to complete the cooking. It is all done quickly, and with a light hand, to keep the flavors alive.

½ *cup extra-virgin olive oil, divided*

3 *garlic cloves, peeled and finely chopped*

1 *small onion, peeled and finely diced*

1½ *pounds Roma tomatoes, peeled, seeded, and diced*

Salt to taste

10 *oil-cured black olives, pitted and quartered*

8 *fresh basil leaves, coarsely chopped*

4 *slices tuna, cut 1-inch thick*

3 *tablespoons unbleached flour*

Salt and freshly ground black pepper to taste

Place 4 tablespoons of the oil, garlic, and onion in a medium-sized braising pan large enough to hold the tuna. Cook over low heat until the onions are tender and translucent. Add the tomatoes and salt to taste, and cook over medium-high heat until a sauce forms, about 10 minutes. A few minutes before the sauce is ready, add the olives and stir. Off the heat, stir in the basil leaves.

Dredge the tuna very lightly in the flour, shaking off the excess. Heat the remaining olive oil in a sauté pan and fry the tuna quickly, about 1 minute on each side. Season with salt and pepper to taste.

Transfer the tuna to the braising pan containing the sauce. Spoon the sauce over the tuna. Cover and cook over medium-low heat for about 4 minutes, or until the tuna is just cooked all the way through.

Involtini di Pesce Spada

Grilled Swordfish Rolls

Serves 6

Swordfish is one of the glories of Sicilian cooking. In the central market-place in Palermo, whole fish, their swords jutting out in front, are brought in fresh from the open sea. The fishmongers cut off slices for their customers. This Sicilian dish combines tender swordfish with tangy provolone, a cheese associated with the Italian south. When the hot grilled swordfish rolls are placed on top of the bay leaves, the warm leaves subtly infuse the fish with their perfume.

6 slices swordfish, cut ½ inch thick, plus ½ pound swordfish

½ medium onion, finely diced

¼ cup chopped Italian parsley

¼ cup extra-virgin olive oil, plus additional for brushing on rolls

¼ cup toasted bread crumbs

1 egg, lightly beaten

¼ pound provolone, diced

Salt and freshly ground black pepper to taste

10 bay leaves

Lemon wedges

Place plastic wrap over the swordfish slices and gently pound with a flat metal pounder or your fist until the slices are about ¼ inch thick. Take care not to tear the fish, as it is very soft. Cut each slice in half to form 2 rectangles. Trim the edges if necessary. Reserve the trimmings. Finely dice the remaining ½ pound of swordfish and the swordfish trimmings.

In a medium-sized sauté pan cook the onion and parsley in the olive oil over low heat until the onion softens. Add the chopped swordfish pieces and cook until they are just opaque. Add the bread crumbs, stir well, and cook for 2 to 3 minutes. Place in a small bowl and let cool. Add the egg and mix well. Stir in the diced provolone. Season with salt and pepper to taste. Place about 1 heaping tablespoon of the mixture on the edge of each piece of swordfish. Roll up the fish and secure with toothpicks. Brush with olive oil and season with salt and pepper to taste. Grill the rolls over medium-high heat or broil them, turning only 2 or 3 times, until the swordfish is just cooked. Arrange the bay leaves on a platter and place swordfish rolls on top. Garnish with lemon wedges.

Calamari Fritti

F r i e d   S q u i d

Italian "potato chips." Once you start eating good fried calamari it's hard to stop. To avoid tough calamari, taste it frequently during the frying. Every batch requires a slightly different cooking time.

2 *pounds squid*	*Salt*
1 *cup all-purpose flour*	*Lemon Wedges*
Olive oil for frying	

To clean the squid, carefully pull the head and tentacles from the body sac. Cut the tentacles above the eyes. Pop out the little ball or beak in the

(Continued)

center of the tentacles. Discard it and the innards. Pull out the quill-shaped bone in the body sac and discard. Peel off the skin. Thoroughly rinse the interior of the body and the tentacles. Drain.

Cut the body sacs crosswise into ¼-inch-thick rings. Wash and dry the squid carefully. Place the squid and flour in a sieve and shake to distribute and flour it evenly. Discard the excess flour.

Pour the olive oil to the depth of 1 inch in a large skillet. Heat the oil until hot. Add the squid a few pieces at a time and fry until golden. Using a slotted spoon, remove the squid from the skillet and drain on paper towels. Sprinkle the fried squid with salt and serve on a large platter accompanied by lemon wedges.

Bruschetta con Calamari alla Griglia

Grilled Country Bread with Grilled Squid Salad

Serves 6 to 8

Grilling the squid first, then marinating it makes for a meltingly tender dish. Here grilled squid is marinated in olive oil, lemon juice, and mint. Just before serving, diced tomatoes are tossed with the squid and spooned over toasted bread. The bread soaks up all the mint-scented juices. Seafood Bruschetta makes a very satisfying luncheon dish, but you could also cut the Bruschetta in half and serve it as an appetizer.

2 pounds squid

Extra-virgin olive oil

Juice of 2–3 lemons

Small handful fresh mint,
  chopped

Salt and freshly ground black
  pepper to taste

3 tomatoes, diced

6–8 thick slices Tuscan bread

3 garlic cloves, peeled and
  crushed

To clean the squid, carefully pull the head and tentacles from the body sac. Cut the tentacles above the eyes. Pop out the little ball or beak in the center of the tentacles. Discard it and the innards. Pull out the quill-shaped bone in the body sac and discard. Peel off the skin. Thoroughly rinse the interior of the body and the tentacles. Drain.

Slit each squid sac down one side so that it opens flat. Score each flat piece with a sharp knife. Heat a charcoal or gas grill or a ridged stovetop griddle until very hot. Lightly rub the squid with the olive oil. Grill the squid sacs and tentacles until marks appear, about 4 to 5 minutes total. The flat pieces will curl up into little cylinders.

Remove the squid from the grill, then place in a small glass, enamel, or stainless-steel bowl. Add the lemon juice, olive oil to taste, mint, and salt and pepper to taste. Let marinate, preferably in a cool spot out of the refrigerator, for at least 1 hour. Just before serving, add tomatoes and mix with the marinated squid.

Grill the bread for Bruschetta (see page 39), rub with the garlic, and arrange bread on a serving platter. Spoon the marinated squid and the accompanying juices onto the grilled bread. Drizzle additional olive oil over the Bruschetta, if desired.

Calamari Ripieni di Gamberi

Braised Squid Stuffed with Shrimp

Serves 4 to 6

Squid is stuffed with finely chopped shrimp, more squid, herbs, and Parmesan cheese, then it is braised in white wine, lemon juice, and olive oil. The dish can be served hot or at room temperature, cut into slices or left whole. Serve with some of the pan juices and lemon wedges.

12 *large squid*

6 *shrimp, peeled and deveined*

3 *tablespoons extra-virgin olive oil*

2 *garlic cloves, peeled and minced*

1 *cup dry, coarse bread crumbs*

½ *cup chopped Italian parsley, divided*

¼ *cup fresh basil, chopped*

½ *cup Parmesan cheese*

1 *egg, lightly beaten*

Salt and freshly ground black pepper to taste

Extra-virgin olive oil

½ *cup dry white wine*

Juice of 1 lemon

2 *garlic cloves, peeled and sliced*

Lemon wedges

To clean the squid, carefully pull the head and tentacles from the body sac. Cut the tentacles above the eyes. Pop out the little ball or beak in the center of the tentacles. Discard it and the innards. Pull out the quill-shaped bone in the body sac and discard. Peel off the skin. Thoroughly rinse the interior of the body and the tentacles. Drain.

Chop the squid tentacles and shrimp very fine. In a small bowl mix together the chopped squid and shrimp and add the olive oil, garlic, bread crumbs, half the parsley, basil, and the Parmesan cheese. Add the egg and stir until the mixture is smooth. Carefully fill each squid sac ¾ full with the stuffing. Close the open end of the sac with a toothpick.

To cook the squid, place them in a skillet just large enough to hold them in one layer. Add enough olive oil to completely coat the bottom of the skillet. Add the white wine, lemon juice, remaining parsley, and sliced garlic. Bring the liquid to a simmer and cover the skillet. Braise the squid for approximately 45 minutes, or until tender when pierced with a fork. Serve with lemon wedges.

Calamari in Umido

Squid Braised in Tomato and Red Chile

Serves 4

Squid, with its translucent skin, mottled pink and purple markings, and long trailing tentacles, has always been a popular seafood in Italy. Squid is now available cleaned, stripped of all its deep-sea and otherworldly aspects, which saves time and eliminates a task that may have turned off many a prospective squid lover. This lean and tender seafood has a delicious, delicate flavor. It must either be cooked for just a few minutes over high heat until opaque or braised slowly until it is meltingly tender. In this dish Crostini soak up the juices and make it a satisfying main course.

(Continued)

2 pounds cleaned squid

3 cloves garlic, peeled and minced

½ teaspoon red chile pepper flakes

½ cup extra-virgin olive oil

½ cup dry white wine

1½ pounds ripe tomatoes, peeled, seeded, and chopped

Salt to taste

1 recipe Crostini (see page 45)

Chopped Italian parsley for garnish

Lemon wedges

Even if you purchase squid cleaned, check each one carefully. See page 295 for directions on how to clean squid. Thoroughly rinse out the interior of each squid. Cut the body sac into ¼-inch-thick rings and leave the tentacles whole, or if the tentacles are large, cut them in half lengthwise. Sauté the garlic and red chile pepper flakes in the olive oil over low heat for 2 to 3 minutes. Add the squid and toss it in the oil. Add the white wine and bring to a boil. Let boil a few minutes. Add the chopped tomatoes and salt to taste, cover, and cook over medium-low heat until the squid is tender, 15 to 30 minutes or longer. Meanwhile, prepare the Crostini. Distribute the squid and juices in shallow soup bowls. Top with a few Crostini per bowl. Sprinkle with chopped parsley. Serve with lemon wedges and with additional crostini in a small basket.

Canestrelli al Orígano e Limone

Sautéed Scallops with
Oregano and Lemon

Serves 4

Sweet scallops are sautéed with aromatic oregano and hot red chile pepper flakes. Off the heat, lemon juice is added. The scallops and the delicious cooking juices are spooned over grilled bread.

1 *recipe Bruschetta (see page 39), using 4 slices of bread*

¼ *cup extra-virgin olive oil*

2 *large garlic cloves, peeled and crushed*

1½ *pound bay scallops, washed and well drained*

½ *teaspoon red chile pepper flakes*

3 *small sprigs fresh oregano, leaves finely chopped, or 1 teaspoon dried oregano*

Salt and freshly ground black pepper to taste

Juice of ½ lemon

Make the Bruschetta (see page 39) and keep warm. Place the olive oil in a large sauté pan. Add the garlic and sauté over medium heat. When the garlic is golden, discard it. Add the scallops, red chile pepper flakes, oregano, and salt and pepper to taste. Sauté over medium heat for about 4 minutes, or until scallops are barely opaque. Remove the pan from the heat, add the lemon juice, and stir once or twice. Place 1 slice of Bruschetta in the bottom of each of 4 shallow soup bowls. Ladle the scallops and juices over the bread.

Zuppa di Cozze

Mussel Soup

Serves 4

Mussels are generally free of sand and do not need to be soaked in water. Just scrub them well and remove the tuft of fibers, or beard, that protrudes from the side of the shell. The mussels are prepared *al bianco*, white, so-named because no tomatoes are used in the soup. Remember to remove the mussels from the pan as they open; overcooking them even a little robs them of their juiciness.

4 *pounds mussels*	½ *teaspoon red chile pepper flakes*
1 *recipe Bruschetta (see page 39), using 4 slices of bread*	¼ *cup chopped Italian parsley*
¼ *cup extra-virgin olive oil*	1 *cup dry white wine*
3 *garlic cloves, peeled and minced*	*Freshly ground black pepper to taste*

Wash and scrub the mussels well under cold running water. Remove the beards by pulling them free from the shell or by cutting them off. Discard any mussels that are open or cracked. Make the Bruschetta and keep warm. Put the olive oil, garlic, red chile pepper flakes, and parsley in a sauté pan or braising pan large enough to contain all the mussels no more than 2 or 3 layers deep. Sauté for a few minutes over low heat. Add the white wine and bring to a boil. Add the mussels, cover, and cook over high heat until the mussels open. Use a slotted spoon to transfer the mussels to a large bowl as they open. Place the Bruschetta in the bottom of 4 shallow soup bowls. Ladle the broth over the bread and distribute the mussels. Grind pepper on top.

Minestra di Cozze e Vongole

Mussel and Clam Stew

Serves 4 to 6

One of our favorite fish soups. A *soffritto* of onion and celery add sweetness to this easy-to-make yet impressive dish.

3 *pounds small clams*

2 *pounds mussels*

Extra-virgin olive oil

1 *large onion, peeled and chopped*

2 *celery stalks, minced*

3 *garlic cloves, peeled and minced*

1½ *cups tomato puree*

2 *cups dry white wine*

Handful chopped Italian parsley

Freshly ground black pepper to taste

To clean the clams, soak them well in a large bowl of heavily salted water, or in the sink, for at least 15 minutes. Lift the clams out of the water and

(Continued)

rinse them under cold running water. Repeat the soaking and rinsing once again.

To clean the mussels, scrub them well under cold running water. Remove all traces of grit. Remove the beard by moving it back and forth until it gives way. Discard any shells that are open or cracked.

Pour enough olive oil in a large, heavy skillet to cover the bottom by ¼ inch. Cook the onion and celery over moderate heat until soft. Add the garlic and cook until it gives off its characteristic aroma, then add the tomato puree and stir. Let the tomato-onion mixture cook for 2 minutes, then add the clams, mussels, and white wine. Cover the skillet and cook the shellfish over high heat just until they begin to open. Add the parsley and pepper, cover, and continue cooking until all the shells have opened. Serve immediately with good crusty bread.

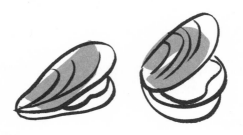

Brodo di Pesce

Fish Broth

Makes approximately 3 quarts

A light, sweet broth for making delicious fish soups or seafood risotti. For the best broth, ask your fishmonger for the bones from halibut, whitefish, and sea bass. Fish broth requires only twenty minutes to cook. Longer cooking sours the flavor.

12 *mussels, cleaned*

½ *cup extra-virgin olive oil*

1 *onion, peeled and coarsely chopped*

1 *fennel bulb with tops, chopped*

1 *celery stalk, coarsely chopped*

1 *large carrot, coarsely chopped*

1 *large leek, coarsely chopped*

1 *tomato, diced*

2 *garlic cloves, peeled and chopped*

2 *bay leaves*

Handful coarsely chopped Italian parsley

10 *black peppercorns*

5 *pounds fish bones*

½ *cup dry white wine*

Juice of 1 lemon

3 *quarts water*

To clean the mussels, scrub them well under cold running water. Remove all traces of grit. Remove the beard by moving it back and forth until it gives way. Discard any shells that are open or cracked. Set mussels aside.

Heat the olive oil in a large stockpot. Add the vegetables and herbs, and fry over moderate heat for approximately 5 minutes, or just until vegetables begin to wilt. Add the fish bones and cook about 8 minutes, or until any flesh remaining on the bones turns white. Make sure all sides of the bones get cooked.

Add the mussels to the stockpot and cook about 2 minutes. Add the white wine to deglaze the pan. Cook over high heat until the alcohol evaporates. Add the lemon juice and water. Bring to a simmer and gently cook for 20 minutes. Strain the broth.

Zuppa di Pesce

Fish Soup

Serves 6 to 8

There are few dishes easier to prepare and that have such a visual impact at the table. Presented in a beautiful white or terracotta bowl the pearlescent black mussels, earthy gray-brown clams, and delicate pink shrimp all look beautiful floating in a fragrant broth redolent of the sea. Use whatever shellfish and/or fish is available. Vary the combinations each time you make this recipe. The soup is most flavorful when it is made with unshelled shrimp and very small whole fish or crosswise slices of larger fish. If you wish a soup that is easier to eat, it's okay to first shell the shrimp and use large pieces of fish fillets. This soup takes only minutes to cook, so be careful not to overcook the ingredients.

1 *pound small clams*

½ *pound mussels*

1 *pound squid*

Extra-virgin olive oil

6 *garlic cloves, peeled and sliced*

2 *pinches red chile pepper flakes*

¼ *cup tomato paste diluted with 1 cup water*

20 *large shrimp, left whole or shelled and deveined*

1 *pound fish (swordfish, tuna, seabass), cut into large chunks*

3 *cups Brodo di Pesce (see page 304)*

Handful chopped Italian parsley

1 *recipe Crostini (see page 45)*

To clean the clams, soak them well in a large bowl of heavily salted water, or in the sink, for at least 15 minutes. Lift the clams out of the water and rinse them under cold running water. Repeat the soaking and rinsing.

To clean the mussels, scrub them well under cold running water. Remove all traces of grit. Remove the beard by moving it back and forth until it gives way. Discard any shells that are open or cracked.

To clean the squid, carefully pull the head and tentacles from the body sac. Cut the tentacles above the eyes. Pop out the little ball or beak in the center of the tentacles. Discard it and the innards. Pull out the quill-shaped bone in the body sac and discard. Peel off the skin. Thoroughly rinse the interior of the body and the tentacles. Drain. Cut into ¼-inch-thick rings.

Pour enough olive oil in a large heavy skillet to cover the bottom by ¼ inch. Add the garlic and red pepper flakes, and cook for a few seconds. Add the diluted tomato paste and cook for 2 minutes. Add the clams, mussels, and shrimp (if still in the shell). Cover the skillet and cook briefly over high heat, just until shells open. Add the squid, shrimp (if shelled), fish, fish broth, and parsley, and cook over low heat until fish and shrimp are tender. Serve soup in large individual bowls over large Crostini.

Pollame

e Carne

Poultry and Meat

In Italy meat is a precious commodity, so it's no wonder that it is treated so respectfully. One has only to stroll by the window of a butcher to see beautiful cuts of meat, carefully trimmed, lovingly displayed, roasts neatly tied with string and braided with a sprig or two of fresh herbs. Since meat is eaten less often than fish, vegetables, and grains, it has a special status in Italian cooking. It is associated with special occasions, family gatherings, feasting, and times of plenty. It also recalls the ancient tradition of cooking wild game over blazing hot coals, a rustic tradition that finds expression today in simple grilled meat and poultry dishes found all over Italy.

The recipes in this chapter have been culled from this varied repertoire and range from simple grilled sausage morsels and roast chicken stuffed with country-style cured meats and pungent rosemary and sage, to more modern dishes like chicken scaloppine topped with julienned fennel and sun-dried tomatoes; veal and beef carpaccios with arugula, olives, and herbs; and lamb chops seasoned with sweet, aromatic balsamic vinegar.

Pollo alla Fiorentina

C h i c k e n   B r e a s t   S a u t é e d   i n   B u t t e r

Serves 4

This is a characteristically simple yet elegant Tuscan way to cook chicken breasts. The sweet butter gently enhances the delicate, light flavor of the chicken. As with all simple dishes, the quality of the individual ingredients makes the difference between the insipid and the inspired. If possible, buy free-range chicken, and use the best and freshest unsalted butter available. Pounding the chicken breasts until they are about ½ inch thick allows them to cook quickly so that the meat remains moist.

2 *whole chicken breasts, split, skinned, and boned*

3 *tablespoons unbleached white flour*

6 *tablespoons unsalted butter*

Salt

Wash the chicken breasts and dry them well. Trim away any traces of fat. Pound each breast carefully with a flat-surfaced meat pounder until the meat is about ½ inch thick or less. Chicken can be butterflied where it is extra-thick. To butterfly the chicken breast, hold a knife horizontally and cut a slit into the thick area up to but not through the edge of the meat. Spread open the breast and gently pound it to an even thickness. Place the flour on a plate and lightly dredge the chicken breasts in the flour, shaking off the excess.

Place the butter in a large sauté pan and raise heat to medium low. Add the chicken breasts, cook for 3 to 4 minutes on one side. Turn them over, salt the cooked side, and continue to cook for 3 to 4 minutes more, or until the chicken is springy to the touch. Turn the chicken again, and salt the other side. Spoon the juices from the pan over the top of the chicken breasts and serve.

Scaloppine di Pollo

Herbed Chicken Scallops

Serves 4 to 6

A quick, simple flavorful recipe that can change according to the topping or garnish you choose. The chicken takes on more flavor the longer it marinates, so this dish is perfect to prepare in advance. The actual cooking time is less than 5 minutes. We give you the basic recipe for marinating and cooking the chicken breasts. Also included are two recipes for garnishes that can top the chicken, but do not limit yourself to these. Try a basil pesto (see *Pasta Fresca*, page 92) or an olive pesto (see *Cucina Fresca*, page 276), or simply top the chicken with diced tomato and arugula.

3 *whole chicken breasts, split, skinned, boned, and pounded to ¼-inch thickness*

½ *cup extra-virgin olive oil*

Juice of 1 lemon

3 *garlic cloves, peeled and crushed*

1 *shallot, peeled and minced*

3 *sprigs fresh oregano, chopped*

3 *sprigs fresh thyme, chopped*

¼ *cup dry white wine*

Place the chicken breasts in a shallow glass bowl and cover with the remaining ingredients. Marinate for at least 4 hours in the refrigerator.

Heat a griddle or sauté pan until it is red hot. Grill or sauté the marinated breasts approximately 2 minutes per side, or just until done. Do not overcook. Serve the chicken with just lemon wedges or with either of the following toppings.

RED PEPPER AND LEEK
TOPING:

3 tablespoons extra-virgin
olive oil

3 red peppers, seeds and
membranes removed, cut into
cubes

4 leeks, washed and sliced thin

½ cup dry white wine

1 cup chicken broth

4 sprigs fresh oregano, chopped

Salt and freshly ground black
pepper to taste

Heat the oil in a sauté pan. Add the peppers and leeks, and cook until soft, being careful not to brown the vegetables. Add the white wine, let reduce for 1 minute, and add the broth. Let cook for a few minutes until liquid is slightly reduced. Add the herbs and season with salt and pepper to taste.

CELERY, BLACK OLIVE,
AND FENNEL TOPPING:

3 tablespoons extra-virgin
olive oil

½ red onion, peeled and minced

2 stalks celery, diced

2 bulbs fennel, tough outer
leaves removed, cut into dice

¼ cup dry white wine

½ cup chicken broth

10 Calamata olives, pitted and
chopped

5 sun-dried tomatoes, chopped

2 tablespoons balsamic vinegar

6 fresh basil leaves, julienned

Salt and freshly ground black
pepper to taste

Heat the olive oil in a sauté pan. Add the onion, celery, and fennel, and cook until soft. Add the white wine and cook until reduced by half. Add the broth, olives, and sun-dried tomatoes, and cook for a few minutes. Off the heat, add the vinegar, basil, and salt and pepper to taste.

Petto di Pollo con Salsa Verde

Thinly Sliced Chicken Breast with Green Sauce

Serves 4

Italians love raw parsley sauces. Finely chopped flat-leaf parsley and extra-virgin olive oil form the basis of this recipe, but there are many variations. Capers and anchovies can be added to the sauce. Vinegar is generally an ingredient when the sauce is paired with meats, and lemon juice is most often used with fish. Fresh basil and finely chopped garlic can flavor the sauce. Sometimes bread or hard-cooked egg yolk is used as a binder.

In this recipe tender chicken breasts are poached in aromatic vegetables, then thinly sliced, and served with a fresh green sauce made of parsley, basil, capers, and anchovies, with a touch of vinegar for piquancy.

TO POACH THE CHICKEN:

1 *small onion, quartered*

1 *carrot, cut into* 3 *to* 4 *pieces*

1 *celery stalk, cut into* 3 *to* 4 *pieces*

A *few parsley sprigs*

2 *whole chicken breasts, split and boned*

Salt

FOR THE GREEN SAUCE:

½ *cup finely chopped Italian parsley*

Handful fresh basil leaves, chopped

2 *garlic cloves, peeled and minced*

3 *anchovies, chopped to a paste*

2 *tablespoons capers, chopped*

¾ *cup extra-virgin olive oil*

3 *tablespoons imported red wine vinegar*

Salt and freshly ground black pepper to taste

In a saucepan place the onion, carrot, celery, parsley sprigs, and enough water to cover the chicken later. Bring to a boil. Add the chicken breasts and salt to taste, and cook at a brisk simmer until they are tender, about 10 to 15 minutes. Remove chicken from the poaching liquid. Remove the skin and let chicken cool a while. Cut chicken into thin slices. Arrange slices on a platter, and if preparing in advance, cover with plastic wrap, and set aside.

In a small bowl combine the chopped parsley, basil, garlic, anchovies, and capers. Stir in the olive oil and vinegar, and season with salt and pepper to taste.

To serve, spoon the parsley sauce over the top of the sliced chicken. If preparing the chicken in advance, add the sauce just before serving to maintain its bright green color.

Scaloppine di Pollo con Salsa Cruda

Chicken Scallops with Tomato and Arugula Salad

Serves 4

One of our favorite ways to serve chicken. The light rosemary-scented breading keeps the chicken breasts moist. For a topping we add a salad of chopped tomato and arugula for the fresh flavor and brilliant color it adds.

(Continued)

2 *whole chicken breasts, split, skinned, and boned, excess fat removed.*

2 *eggs*

1 *cup bread crumbs*

1 *tablespoon minced fresh rosemary*

Salt and freshly ground black pepper to taste

Olive oil for frying

5–6 *Roma tomatoes, cut into small dice*

¼ *cup chopped arugula*

2 *tablespoons extra-virgin olive oil*

Lemon wedges

Butterfly the thick areas of the chicken breasts. Gently pound the breasts to flatten them. Lightly beat the eggs in a shallow bowl. Combine the bread crumbs and rosemary, and season with salt and pepper to taste. Spread the bread-crumb mixture on a plate. Pour enough olive oil in a medium-sized sauté pan to measure ¼ inch up the side of the pan. Heat the oil until hot but not smoking. Dip the chicken breasts in the beaten egg and let the excess drain off. Coat with bread crumbs, shaking off the excess. Sauté the chicken in the olive oil until golden on both sides, about 4 to 5 minutes. Transfer to paper towels, salt to taste, and let drain. Combine the tomatoes and arugula with the extra-virgin olive oil and season with salt to taste. Arrange the chicken breasts on a platter and spoon the tomato mixture in a ribbon along one side. Garnish with lemon wedges.

Fritto Misto di Pollo e Carciofi

Mixed Fry of Chicken and Artichoke

Serves 4

Strips of chicken breast and trimmed baby artichokes are dipped in egg and bread crumbs, and fried in fresh olive oil until crisp and golden. A few lettuce leaves and lemon wedges make a fresh-looking garnish.

1 *lemon, cut in half*

16 *baby artichokes*

2 *whole chicken breasts, split, skinned, and boned*

1 *cup bread crumbs*

3 *eggs*

Olive oil for frying

Salt to taste

Leaves of radicchio or butter lettuce

Use ½ the lemon to rub the cut portion of the artichoke. Fill a large bowl with water and squeeze into it the juice from the other lemon half. Clean artichokes as instructed on page 246. Small artichokes generally have not developed chokes, so omit that step unless necessary. Cut each artichoke in half, and immerse artichokes immediately into the lemon water to prevent darkening. Drain the artichokes in a colander. Blanch in salted boiling water for 1 to 2 minutes and drain.

Cut each chicken breast into 5 long strips. Spread the bread crumbs on a plate. Beat the eggs in a shallow soup bowl. In a medium-sized sauté pan heat enough olive oil to measure ¼ inch up the side of the pan. When the oil is hot but not smoking, dip a few chicken strips into the beaten egg, let excess drip off, then lightly coat with bread crumbs, shaking off the excess. Fry strips in the hot oil until they are golden on both sides. Place on paper towels, salt to taste, and let drain. Using the same method, fry the arti-

(Continued)

chokes until they are all a light golden brown. Transfer chicken and artichokes to a platter and garnish with the radicchio or butter lettuce leaves
and lemon wedges.

Pollo Fritto al Limone

F r i e d   L e m o n - M a r i n a t e d   C h i c k e n

Serves 4

In this recipe chicken pieces are marinated in lemon juice, dredged in flour,
and fried in hot olive oil. Fried chicken sounds very American, but frying
is a cooking technique used often in Italy, and Italians have developed a
vast repertoire of fried dishes.

1 *frying chicken, cut up, breasts cut into thirds*	3 *tablespoons extra-virgin olive oil*
Salt and freshly ground black pepper to taste	*Olive oil for frying*
	Unbleached flour
Juice of 1 large lemon	*Lemon wedges*

Season the chicken pieces with salt and a generous amount of freshly
ground pepper, and place in a shallow dish. Drizzle with the lemon juice
and extra-virgin olive oil. Turn the pieces over in the marinade a few times
to coat the chicken evenly. Cover the dish and let chicken marinate in the
refrigerator for 2 to 3 hours, or overnight, and toss occasionally.

In a large frying pan pour the olive oil to a depth of ¼ inch. Heat the oil
until it is very hot but not smoking. Place some flour on a dinner plate.
Remove the marinated chicken from the refrigerator and pat dry with paper towels. Dredge in flour, shaking off the excess. Place the chicken pieces
in the hot oil and quickly fry on all sides. Reduce the heat to medium and

cook about 15 minutes or longer, or until chicken feels springy to the touch and is golden brown. Drain on paper towels. For the chicken pieces to fry properly, the pan must not be too crowded. If necessary, fry the chicken in 2 batches. Serve with lemon wedges on the side.

Spiedini di Pollo

S k e w e r e d   C h i c k e n   W r a p p e d
i n   P r o s c i u t t o

Serves 4

Chunks of chicken breast are wrapped in prosciutto and threaded on skewers along with cubes of rustic bread and rosemary sprigs. The prosciutto gives the chicken a woodsy flavor and keeps it moist; the bread becomes crisp and golden; and the aromatic rosemary perfumes the whole. Everyone raves about this dish.

2 *whole chicken breasts, split, skinned, and boned*

12 *slices prosciutto, cut in half*

28 *pieces rustic bread, cut into 1-inch dice*

24 *small sprigs fresh rosemary*

Extra-virgin olive oil

Salt and freshly ground black pepper to taste

(Continued)

Separate the tenderloin from the chicken breasts. Cut the tenderloin in half; cut each breast into 4 pieces. Wrap each piece in a slice of prosciutto. Have 4 skewers ready. Thread a cube of bread on each one; then next to it add a sprig of rosemary, then a piece of chicken, then another cube of bread. Continue alternating the ingredients using 6 pieces of chicken, 7 cubes of bread, and 6 sprigs of rosemary for each skewer. Brush the skewers with olive oil and season with salt and pepper to taste. Grill or broil until chicken is just firm to the touch and a little springy.

Pollastrini alla Diavola

Grilled Game Hens in Lemon and Black Pepper

Serves 4

Game hens are split down the back, opened flat, and marinated in extra-virgin olive oil, lemon, and crushed black peppercorns. Then they are grilled, either on an outdoor grill or on a *gratella*, a cast-iron stovetop grill widely used in Italy and available here in gourmet cookware stores. A broiler also works quite well. The game hen cooks quickly, remains juicy all the way through, and turns golden brown and crisp on the outside. We had the definitive version of this dish in a restaurant in Frascati with bruschetta and prosciutto as an antipasto, a lettuce salad afterward, and cool white wine.

4 *game hens*

Extra-virgin olive oil, enough to generously moisten game hens

1 *tablespoon coarsely crushed black pepper, plus a*

peppermill filled with black peppercorns

Juice of 1 lemon

Salt

Lemon wedges

Split the game hens down the back and remove the backbones. Place the hens in a large dish. Rub the hens with the olive oil, sprinkle with the crushed pepper, and drizzle lemon juice over the top. Turn the hens over to distribute marinade evenly, cover, and marinate in the refrigerator for at least 1 hour but preferably for several hours. Return to room temperature.

Heat the grill until very hot, or preheat the broiler. Drain the excess marinade from the hens and place them on the grill or *gratella*, or in a broiler pan. Cook for 10 minutes on each side, salting the cooked side only. Test for doneness by inserting a knife in the thickest part of the flesh. The juices should run clear. Transfer to a serving dish. Grind pepper over the game hens and serve with lemon wedges.

Pollo Arrostito alla Toscana

Tuscan-Style Roast Chicken

Serves 4

This roast chicken has a wild taste that is reminiscent of game, owing to the pungent rosemary and sage and the savory trio of pancetta, prosciutto, and ham.

1 *chicken, about 2½ to 3 pounds*

1 *slice pancetta, about ¼ inch thick*

1 *slice prosciutto, about ⅛ inch thick*

1 *slice Black Forest ham, about ¼ inch thick*

Salt and freshly ground black pepper to taste

1 *sprig fresh rosemary*

1 *sprig fresh sage*

3 *tablespoons unsalted butter, divided*

Wash the chicken inside and out and dry well. Cut the pancetta and prosciutto into small strips. Dice the ham. Season the interior of the chicken with salt and pepper to taste. Place the pancetta, prosciutto, ham, herbs, and 2 tablespoons of the butter in the cavity of the chicken. Rub the remaining butter on the chicken skin and salt the exterior. Truss the chicken.

Preheat the oven to 350°. Place the chicken, breast side down, on a roasting pan in the upper third of the oven. After 15 minutes, turn the chicken so that the breast faces up. Cook for another 15 minutes, then raise the heat to 425°, and cook for an additional 20 minutes. Baste with the juices as it cooks. Transfer the chicken to a serving dish. Tip the roasting pan and spoon off the fat from the juices. Carve the chicken and serve with its savory juices.

Pollo alla Romana

Chicken Roman Style

Serves 4

One of the most popular ways to serve chicken through the sultry summer months in Rome, this beautiful warm-weather dish features strips of bright red and yellow peppers, fresh tomatoes, prosciutto, and basil. It is often served at room temperature, allowing the sweet flavors of the peppers and onions to emerge. In our recipe the peppers are roasted first and added to the dish when the chicken is almost done so that the pepper strips retain some of their crunch. Large meaty peppers that stay crisp when roasted are best for this dish.

1 *chicken, 2½–3 pounds*

3 *tablespoons extra-virgin olive oil*

Salt and freshly ground black pepper to taste

1 *medium onion, peeled and thinly sliced*

1 *large garlic clove, peeled and minced*

⅛ *pound prosciutto, cut into strips*

1 *pound Roma tomatoes, peeled, seeded, and coarsely chopped*

10 *fresh basil leaves, torn into large pieces*

1 *large red pepper*

1 *large yellow pepper*

1 *tablespoon balsamic vinegar*

Cut up the chicken into serving pieces, cutting each breast in half. Wash chicken pieces well and dry thoroughly. Heat the olive oil in a skillet. Place the chicken pieces in the skillet, skin side down. Brown on both sides. Transfer chicken to a platter and season with salt and pepper to taste. Keep warm. In the same skillet sauté the onion, garlic, and prosciutto until the onion becomes tender, about 10 minutes. Add the chicken pieces and

(Continued)

turn to coat with the onion mixture. Add the tomatoes, basil, and salt and pepper to taste. Cover and cook for about 30 minutes, turning the chicken 2 or 3 times. Meanwhile, roast the peppers over a gas flame or in the broiler. When peppers are cool enough to handle, peel them, cut them in half, and remove the seeds and membranes. Slice peppers into ½-inch strips. A few minutes before the chicken is ready, add the roasted pepper strips and the balsamic vinegar and stir. The chicken is cooked when the meat is very tender when pierced with a fork. Serve hot or at room temperature.

Pollo Piccante

Piquant Chicken

Serves 4

Black olives, capers, and garlic infuse this spicy dish with their deep, seductive flavors.

1 *chicken, about 2½ pounds*

¼ *cup extra-virgin olive oil*

2 *garlic cloves, peeled and lightly crushed*

Salt and freshly ground black pepper to taste

Handful Italian parsley, chopped and divided

½ *teaspoon red chile pepper flakes*

½ *cup white wine*

2 *tablespoons capers*

12 *oil-cured black olives, pitted and quartered*

Cut up the chicken into serving pieces, cutting each breast in half. Wash well and dry thoroughly. Combine the olive oil and garlic in a large skillet. Sauté garlic over medium heat until it is golden. Lift out the garlic. To the skillet add the chicken, skin side down, and sauté over medium heat until it is golden brown on both sides. Season with salt and pepper. Sprinkle the chicken with half the parsley and the red chile pepper flakes, and toss. Add the white wine, bring to a boil, and cook at medium-high heat for 3 to 4 minutes. Add the capers and black olives. Stir well. Cover and cook until the chicken is tender, about 30 minutes, or until meat is easily pierced by a fork. Lift out the chicken and arrange on a platter. Tip the skillet and spoon off all the fat. Pour over the chicken all the juices, olives, and capers from the pan, and sprinkle with the remaining parsley.

Carpaccio di Vitello

Veal Carpaccio with Radicchio

Serves 6 to 8

In this dish, the height of rustic chic, thin slices of veal are topped with radicchio and Pecorino Romano cheese, then drizzled with extra-virgin olive oil. Ask your butcher to completely clean the tenderloin of any fat or sinew. Uncooked veal is slightly less tender than beef because it lacks marbling, so it is important to pound the meat very thin. Many butchers will do this for you too.

1 *pound veal tenderloin, trimmed of all fat and sinew*

2 *small heads radicchio, chopped*

½ *cup shaved Pecorino Romano cheese*

Freshly ground black pepper

Extra-virgin olive oil

Lemon wedges

Cut the tenderloin into ¾-inch-thick pieces and gently pound them until they are very thin. Place the veal onto serving dishes and top with the chopped radicchio and cheese shavings. Drizzle the olive oil over the meat and liberally grind black pepper over all. Garnish with lemon wedges.

Lombata di Vitello

Grilled Marinated Veal Chop

Serves 4

A classic grilled veal chop redolent of rosemary and garlic simply cannot be beat. Try to find a reliable source for properly ranched veal. Veal from range-fed animals has more flavor, better texture, and is less watery. The color of the meat is pinker, but this is a small price to pay for a more humane treatment of the calf. Use loin chops with the filet. Veal T-bone steaks are also very impressive.

4 *large veal loin chops, 1½–2 inches thick*	*Olive oil*
8 *garlic cloves, peeled*	*Coarse salt*
12 *sprigs fresh rosemary, divided*	*Lemon wedges*
	Extra-virgin olive oil

Smash each peeled garlic clove with the side of a large knife. Place half the garlic and half the rosemary in a glass or stainless-steel baking dish. Lay the veal chops on top of the herbs. Cover the chops with the remaining garlic and 4 more sprigs of fresh rosemary. Pour enough olive oil over the chops to just coat them. If the meat is well covered with oil it can marinate for several days. The longer it marinates, the more intense the wild flavor of the rosemary becomes.

Remove the chops from the marinade and carefully wipe off the oil. Although it is possible to pan fry or broil these chops, the best flavor is obtained by grilling the chops. Place them on a rack over hot, glowing wood charcoal, turning once. To cook the meat medium rare takes approximately 10 to 12 minutes total. Remove the chops to a serving platter and garnish with the remaining fresh rosemary sprigs and lemon wedges. Sprinkle coarse salt and drizzle a little extra-virgin olive oil over the chops just before serving.

Scaloppine di Vitello alla Griglia
Grilled Veal Cutlets

Serves 4 to 6

This is the way veal cutlets are prepared in Palermo, a delicious and less caloric alternative to the traditional breaded and fried veal cutlets.

1½ *pounds veal cutlets,*
pounded thin

3 *tablespoons extra-virgin*
olive oil

1 *cup homemade bread crumbs*
(see page 159)

Salt and freshly ground black
pepper to taste

Lemon wedges

Rub the veal cutlets with the olive oil. Place the bread crumbs on a platter and season with salt and pepper to taste. Coat the cutlets on both sides with the bread crumbs. Heat a charcoal or gas grill or ridged stovetop griddle until very hot. Grill for about 1 minute on each side. Some of the bread crumbs will become a little charred, but that is the desired effect. Serve immediately with lemon wedges on the side.

Tagliata di Vitello ai Funghi

Veal Scallops with Wild Mushroom Sauté

Serves 4 to 6

In this dish sautéed mushrooms are spooned over seared veal scallops, a treatment we prefer to veal drenched in a liquid sauce. The deep flavor of the mushrooms penetrates the veal very quickly.

2½ *pounds veal tenderloin, trimmed of all fat and sinew*

¼ *cup extra-virgin olive oil*

2 *garlic cloves, peeled and minced*

2 *sprigs fresh sage, leaves only*

2 *sprigs fresh thyme, leaves only*

¼ *pound shiitake mushrooms or chanterelles, or a mixture of both, trimmed and sliced*

¼ *pound white mushrooms, trimmed and sliced*

Coarse salt and freshly ground black pepper to taste

Extra-virgin olive oil

Lemon wedges

Cut the veal into 3-ounce medallions and place between two pieces of oiled parchment paper. Pound the meat gently into scallops, approximately ¼ inch thick.

Place the olive oil in a skillet and heat the garlic. Add the herbs and mushrooms. Fry the mushrooms over moderate heat until they are tender. Add salt and pepper to taste. Set aside.

Pour enough olive oil in a heavy skillet so that a thin film covers the entire surface. Heat the skillet until it is very hot. Working quickly, sear the veal scallops very briefly on each side so that they do not overcook. As they cook, remove them from the heat and place on a platter. Lightly season the scallops with salt and pepper. Quickly reheat the herbed mushrooms, if necessary, and spoon them over the veal. Garnish with lemon wedges and serve.

Polpette in Spiedini alla Siciliana

Skewered Veal Meatballs

Serves 4

This dish is beautiful—all golden and crusty. Mild veal is teamed with sharp Pecorino Romano cheese and assertively flavored sage. Accompanied by good sturdy country bread, it is a satisfying dish that uses only a small amount of meat. The veal meatballs are moist and soft, so we find it's easier to cook them by placing the skewers directly on a baking sheet under the broiler rather than on a grill.

(Continued)

1 *pound ground veal*

2 *cloves garlic, peeled and minced*

2 *tablespoons chopped Italian parsley*

2 *eggs, lightly beaten*

3 *tablespoons bread crumbs*

¼ *cup grated Pecorino Romano cheese*

24 *pieces country bread, cut into 1-inch cubes*

10 *fresh sage leaves, torn in half*

Extra-virgin olive oil

Salt and freshly ground black pepper to taste

Combine the veal, garlic, parsley, eggs, bread crumbs, and Pecorino Romano cheese. Form mixture into about 20 meatballs, each about ¾ inch in diameter. Have 4 skewers handy. On each skewer, thread 1 cube of bread, ½ sage leaf, and 1 meatball. Continue alternating ingredients, finishing with a cube of bread. Each skewer should have 6 cubes of bread and 5 meatballs. Brush with olive oil and season with salt and pepper to taste. Place the skewers on a baking sheet and place under a hot broiler. Turn the skewers to brown veal on all sides and broil until the meatballs are just firm to the touch. If the bread starts to burn before the veal is cooked, cover with foil and finish up the cooking in the oven.

Polpette di Vitello alla Romana

Veal Meatballs with Fresh Marjoram and Tomatoes

Serves 4

These main-dish meatballs have nothing in common with the steam-table variety in tomato sauce that have long prevailed in Italian delicatessens. If the word "meatball" troubles you, call them polpette and you'll probably feel infinitely better. An integral part of Italian cooking, true polpette are formed into small rounds, sometimes as small as marbles, and made with ground veal, or a combination of veal and beef. In this recipe delicate veal meatballs are simmered in a light, briefly cooked tomato sauce. Marjoram provides its heady perfume. Serve with plenty of good bread for dipping into the savory juices.

1 *thick slice bread, crust removed*

⅓ *cup milk*

1 *pound ground veal*

2 *garlic cloves, peeled and minced*

2 *eggs, lightly beaten*

Grated peel of ½ lemon

¼ *cup grated Parmesan cheese*

2 *tablespoons chopped fresh marjoram leaves, divided*

Salt and freshly ground black pepper to taste

All-purpose unbleached flour

6 *tablespoons extra-virgin olive oil*

½ *28-ounce can imported Italian tomatoes, seeded and chopped, with juice*

Soak the bread in the milk until milk is absorbed. Squeeze out the excess moisture. In a bowl combine the bread, veal, garlic, eggs, lemon peel, Par-

(Continued)

mesan cheese, half the marjoram, and salt and pepper to taste. Form mixture into meatballs about 1 inch in diameter. Roll them in flour and shake off the excess. Place the olive oil in a large skillet. When the oil is hot, add all the meatballs and brown them gently over medium heat. Tip the skillet and drain off all but 3 tablespoons of the cooking fat. Add the chopped tomatoes, remaining marjoram, and salt to taste. Simmer for 10 minutes, or until the sauce thickens. Grind a little fresh black pepper over the top.

Spiedini di Salsicce

Grilled Skewered Sausages

Serves 4

This is a very simple, incredibly flavorful, dish in which chunks of sausage and country bread are threaded on skewers and grilled. You may be tempted to dress it up with herbs or pieces of vegetables, but we think adding anything would interfere with the rustic poetry of the dish. Because the sausage is so rich, it goes well with a fresh green salad and a few crisp little radishes or slivers of raw fennel.

4 *fresh sweet Italian sausages*   *Extra-virgin olive oil*

24 *pieces country bread, cut into 1-inch cubes*

Pierce the sausages with a fork in several places. Boil them in water to cover for about 10 minutes. Drain and cut each sausage into 5 pieces. Have 4 skewers ready. Thread the bread and sausages on the skewers, starting with a cube of bread. There should be 5 pieces of sausage and 6 pieces of bread per skewer. Very lightly brush with the olive oil. Heat a charcoal or gas grill or broiler until very hot. Grill the skewers until the bread and sausage are golden and crusty on the outside.

Spiedini di Agnello e Salsiccia

Lamb and Sausage Skewers

Serves 4

Fresh lettuces are a welcome foil to the rich flavors of grilled lamb and sausage, as are red radishes, which make a crisp and peppery edible garnish.

¾ pound boned lamb

¾ pound sweet Italian sausage

Extra-virgin olive oil

Salt and freshly ground black pepper to taste

1 small head radicchio, torn into bite-sized pieces

Large handful mâche, leaves separated

1 small head curly endive, pale yellow leaves at center only, torn into bite-sized pieces

1 bunch small radishes, wilted leaves removed

Lemon wedges

Cut the lamb into bite-sized pieces. Cut the sausage into slightly larger pieces. Have 4 skewers ready. Alternate the lamb and sausage on the skew-

(Continued)

ers. Brush with the olive oil and season with salt and pepper to taste. Heat a charcoal or gas grill or broiler until very hot. Grill meats over medium heat until sausage is cooked through and lamb is crusty on the outside but pink inside. Brush with oil to keep meats moist, if necessary. Arrange the lettuces on a serving platter. Place the skewered meats over the lettuces and garnish with radishes. Serve with lemon wedges.

Salsicce al Sugo d'Arancia

Sausages Braised in Tomato with Orange Juice

Serves 4

Sausages are braised in fresh tomatoes with aromatic orange juice as a surprising final touch.

3 *tablespoons extra-virgin olive oil*

4 *sweet Italian sausages, each cut in half*

Juice of ½ *lemon*

1 *pound tomatoes, peeled, seeded, and chopped*

4 *fresh basil leaves, coarsely chopped*

Salt and freshly ground black pepper to taste

½ *cup dry white wine*

Juice of 1 *medium orange*

Place the olive oil in a sauté pan large enough to contain the sausages in one layer. Heat the oil, add the sausages, and turn up the heat to medium. Prick the sausages in several places with a fork, and cook until sausages are nicely browned. Add the lemon juice to deglaze pan, and scrape the bottom of the pan with a wooden spoon. Add the tomatoes, basil, and salt and pepper to taste. Raise the heat to high and cook for 5 minutes. Add the white wine and cook until the wine evaporates. Tip the pan and remove any fat that has separated from the sauce. Add the juice from the orange and cook for 4 to 5 minutes to concentrate the flavors.

Lenticchie, Verdura, e Salsicce

Lentils, Greens, and Sausages

Serves 6

Three good flavors made better by their proximity to one another. This is winter food that speaks to the soul.

2 *cups lentils*	1 *bay leaf*
Salt	½ *cup extra-virgin olive oil*
6 *garlic cloves, peeled, divided*	*Salt and freshly ground black pepper to taste*
1 *celery stalk, cut into short lengths*	
1 *carrot, cut into short lengths*	1 *pound rapini, trimmed*
	6 *sweet Italian sausages*

Pick over the lentils and wash under cold water. In a small stockpot combine lentils with salt, 2 garlic cloves, celery, carrot, and bay leaf, and enough water to cover lentils generously. Bring to a boil, turn down heat, and cook at a steady simmer until vegetables are tender. The amount of time varies greatly, depending on the freshness of the lentils. Add water if necessary during cooking. When the lentils are tender but still intact, drain. Discard the vegetables, garlic, and bay leaf. Drizzle lentils with a few tablespoons of the olive oil and season with salt and pepper to taste.

(Continued)

Cut the rapini into thick strips and cook in an abundant amount of salted boiling water until tender but not mushy. Drain.

Coarsely chop the remaining garlic. Place the remaining oil and the chopped garlic in a medium-sized sauté pan and cook very gently until the garlic turns opaque and the oil is highly flavored. The garlic must not brown. Add the lentils and the greens, and toss. Cook over medium-low heat for 4 to 5 minutes to allow the flavors to mingle. Add a few tablespoons of water if the mixture becomes dry.

Meanwhile, place the sausages in a skillet over medium heat. Prick the sausages all over with a fork. Add enough water to come up ½ inch on the sides of the pan, and cook the sausages until the water evaporates. Cook the sausages in the oil that remains, turning them so they brown on all sides.

Cut the sausages in half lengthwise. Serve 2 halves per person along with some of the lentils and greens.

Costolette di Agnello
all'Aceto Balsamico

Rosemary-Scented Lamb Chops
with Balsamic Vinegar

Serves 4

Cooking lamb with vinegar is an old Roman tradition, as in the famous abbacchio alla Romana, young lamb, Roman style. In this modern preparation, we broil lamb chops and pour over them a *salsina,* or little sauce, made with the pan drippings and balsamic vinegar. The unique flavor of the balsamic vinegar is a good counterpoint to the richness of the lamb.

4 *loin lamb chops*

2 *sprigs rosemary*

2 *garlic cloves, peeled and lightly smashed*

Salt and freshly ground black pepper to taste

¾ *cup balsamic vinegar*

Rub the lamb chops all over with the rosemary and garlic so they are well scented.

Remove the lining from the broiler pan. Preheat the broiler so that it is very hot. Place the lamb chops in the unlined broiler pan. Broil the chops, turning once or twice, so that they are crusty on the outside and barely pink in the center, 8 to 10 minutes total.

Place the chops on a serving platter, and season them with salt and pepper to taste, and keep warm. Meanwhile, place the broiler pan with the drippings on the burner. Add the balsamic vinegar and deglaze the pan over moderate heat, being careful to scrape up all the crusty bits that are stuck to the bottom of the pan. When the pan juices and vinegar have reduced and have thickened a little, quickly pour the sauce over the chops. Serve immediately.

Agnello allo Zenzero e Rosmarino

Leg of Lamb with Ginger and Rosemary

Serves 6 to 8

Lamb has a pronounced flavor, distinct from any other meat. Fragrant, assertive ginger, rosemary, and garlic are a good match for the lamb. Ginger may seem uncharacteristic of Italian cooking, but it does play a small role.

1 *leg of lamb, about 5 pounds, boned and butterflied*

3 *garlic cloves, peeled and cut into slivers*

2 *sprigs fresh rosemary, leaves finely chopped*

1 *teaspoon ground ginger*

Salt and freshly ground black pepper to taste

½ *cup dry white wine*

Several hours before cooking, make slits in the lamb and insert garlic slivers. Combine the rosemary, ginger, and salt and pepper to taste, and rub the mixture all over the lamb. Cover the meat lightly with plastic wrap and refrigerate. Return to room temperature before proceeding with the recipe.

Place the lamb on a roasting pan in a preheated 400° oven. Baste lamb with white wine as the meat begins to brown. Cook for about 40 minutes for rare and about 1 hour for well-done. Rare lamb will register 160° on a meat thermometer, and well done will be 175°. Let lamb rest in a warm place for about 10 minutes before carving it.

Carpaccio

Thinly Sliced Raw Beef Filet with Arugula

Serves 6 to 8

Many chefs freeze beef tenderloin so that they can slice it paper thin on an electric slicer. We prefer to make this dish with a slightly thicker slice of meat and see no reason to put a beautiful, costly piece of beef in the freezer. Your butcher will prepare the thin beef scallops upon request.

1 *pound beef tenderloin, trimmed of all fat and sinew*

2 *bunches arugula, stems removed, leaves chopped*

¼ *cup capers*

⅓ *cup Parmesan cheese shavings*

Extra-virgin olive oil

Freshly ground black pepper to taste

Lemon wedges

Cut the tenderloin into ¾-inch-thick pieces and pound gently until they are very thin. Arrange the beef on serving plates and top with the arugula, capers, and Parmesan cheese shavings. Drizzle with the olive oil and liberally dust with pepper to taste. Garnish with lemon wedges.

Tagliata all'Erbe

Thin Beef Scallops with Herbs

Serves 6

*T*agliata, Italian for cut, usually refers to a thin cut of beef that is quickly grilled or sautéed and seasoned with olive oil and fresh herbs after cooking. This recipe for tagliata topped with fresh rosemary and sage comes from a successful Milanese bistro, La Libera, in the Soho-like Brera district. Ask your butcher to prepare the beef scallops for you, if you prefer.

2½ pounds beef tenderloin, trimmed of all fat and sinew

8 sprigs fresh rosemary, divided

1 bunch fresh sage

Coarse salt and freshly ground black pepper to taste

Extra-virgin olive oil

Cut the beef into 3-ounce medallions and place between two pieces of oiled parchment paper. Pound the medallions gently until they become scallops approximately ¼-inch thick.

Carefully wash and dry the herbs. Remove the leaves from 1 sprig of rosemary, leaving the rest for garnish. Using a sharp knife, finely chop the rosemary leaves. Finely chop 6 large sage leaves. Mix the chopped herbs in a small bowl.

Heat a cast iron griddle or large heavy skillet over high heat. Lightly oil the griddle or skillet using an oiled cloth. Working quickly, sear the beef scallops briefly so that they are still very rare. As they cook, remove them from the heat to a serving platter. Quickly sprinkle the scallops with salt and pepper. Top the meat with the chopped herbs and a drizzle of extra-virgin olive oil. Garnish with the remaining fresh herbs and serve.

Tagliata con Olive

Seared Beef Filet with Olives, Tomato, and Arugula

Serves 6

In this version of tagliata, the strong tastes of arugula and olives accent the mellow flavor of the beef.

2½ pounds beef tenderloin, trimmed of all fat and sinew

½ cup Calamata olives, pitted and cut into quarters lengthwise

2 large red, ripe tomatoes, stem ends removed, finely diced

1 bunch fresh oregano, leaves only, coarsely chopped, or 2 teaspoons dried oregano

Coarse salt and freshly ground black pepper to taste

3 bunches arugula, tough stems discarded

Extra-virgin olive oil

Cut the beef into 3-ounce medallions and place between two pieces of oiled parchment paper. Pound the meat gently into scallops, approximately ¼ inch thick.

In a small bowl combine the olives, tomatoes, oregano, salt and pepper to taste, and set aside at room temperature.

Line a serving platter with the arugula. Heat a cast-iron griddle or large, heavy skillet over high heat. Lightly oil the griddle or skillet using an oiled cloth. Working quickly, sear the beef scallops briefly so that they are still very rare. As they cook, remove them from the heat to the arugula-lined serving platter. Lightly season the meat with salt and pepper to taste. Spoon the tomato-olive mixture over the meat. Drizzle with olive oil to taste.

Filetto al Limone e Pepe
alla Griglia

Grilled Beef
Filets Marinated in Lemon
and Black Pepper

Serves 4

The beef is marinated in lemon and abundant black pepper, then grilled. A simple preparation that highlights the flavor of the beef.

1½ pounds beef tenderloin, cut into 4 medallions

3 tablespoons extra-virgin olive oil

Juice of 1 lemon, plus 4 lemon wedges for garnish

Coarsely ground black pepper

Salt to taste

Wash the beef and dry well. Place the olive oil, lemon juice, and a generous amount of fresh coarsely ground black pepper on a plate that is large enough to contain the beef medallions side by side. Turn the beef over several times in the marinade to coat the meat on both sides. Cover and marinate in the refrigerator for 2 hours, turning frequently. Return the meat to room temperature. Heat a charcoal or gas grill. Drain the marinade and grill the medallions over medium-high heat until deep brown grill marks form on the exterior of the meat and the center is rosy pink. Remove meat from the grill and salt both sides. Let rest for a few minutes. Serve garnished with lemon wedges.

Involtini di Carne alla Siciliana

Grilled Beef Rolls Stuffed with Pine Nuts and Raisins

Serves 4

In this Sicilian specialty, thin slices of beef are stuffed with Pecorino Romano cheese, pine nuts, raisins, and bread crumbs. The meat must be sliced thin, then pounded even thinner, to create these little rolls, which are threaded on skewers, interspersed with small onions and bay leaves, and grilled quickly over a hot fire.

1½ *pounds top round, sliced into 4 long slices, ¼ inch thick*

½ *small onion, finely diced, sautéed in 1 tablespoon extra-virgin olive oil until tender*

¼ *cup toasted bread crumbs*

2 *tablespoons chopped Italian parsley*

3 *tablespoons raisins, soaked in hot water until plump*

3 *tablespoons lightly toasted pine nuts*

3 *tablespoons grated Pecorino Romano cheese*

¼ *cup extra-virgin olive oil, divided*

Salt and freshly ground black pepper to taste

12 *small boiling onions, blanched and peeled*

12 *bay leaves*

Pound the beef slices with a flat meat pounder until slices are very thin. Take care not to tear the meat. Cut each slice in half so that each one

(Continued)

yields 2 rectangles. In a small bowl combine the onions, bread crumbs, parsley, raisins, pine nuts, and Pecorino Romano cheese. Lay flat the beef slices, coat with 2 tablespoons of the olive oil, and season with salt and pepper to taste. Divide the mixture evenly among the slices, placing a portion on the short end of each rectangle. Roll up the meat and secure with string to form a package. Have 4 skewers ready. On each skewer thread an onion and a bay leaf, then a meat roll, an onion and bay leaf, another meat roll, another bay leaf, and finish with an onion. Use the remaining olive oil to lightly moisten the threaded skewers. Grill or broil until the meat is crusty outside but pink inside.

Manzo Bollito al Limone e Erbe

Boiled Beef Marinated
in Lemon and Herbs

Serves 4 to 6

Thinly sliced boiled beef is turned into a summery dish when marinated in lemon, herbs, and capers. Serve as a main dish for lunch or dinner or as an antipasto.

2 *pounds brisket, bottom round, or rump roast*

Salt

½ *cup extra-virgin olive oil*

Juice of 1 lemon, about ¼ *cup*

Freshly ground black pepper to taste

3 *tablespoons chopped Italian parsley*

Small handful fresh basil leaves, cut into julienne

2 *heaping tablespoons small capers*

1 *bunch tender, small radishes with fresh-looking leaves*

Select a pot large enough to contain the meat. Add enough water to the pot to cover the meat. Bring the water to a boil. Add the beef and reduce the heat to a steady, slow simmer. Add about 1 teaspoon salt, cover, and let meat cook slowly for about 2½ hours. Lift the meat out of the liquid and place on a cutting board. Let cool for a few minutes. Reserve the broth for another use. Sprinkle the meat with 1 teaspoon of salt and cut into very thin slices. Arrange slices on a platter so that the edges just overlap.

Place the olive oil in a small bowl. Add the lemon juice and beat with a fork until the oil becomes creamy. Pour mixture over the meat slices. Season with salt and pepper to taste. Sprinkle with the herbs and capers. Cover the platter with plastic wrap and let marinate at room temperature for 1 to 2 hours. Do not refrigerate the meat unless you must prepare it well in advance. If refrigeration is necessary, wrap the meat tightly and return it to room temperature before serving. Trim the radishes, removing any yellowed or wilted leaves. Garnish the platter with the radishes.

Polpettone Estiva

Poached Summer Meat Loaf

Serves 6

Meat loaf isn't just an American tradition. It has a place in Italian cooking, too. This dish, with its colorful pickled-vegetable garnish and bright, fresh parsley sauce, is served at room temperature and is good for a picnic or buffet.

1 *thick slice bread, crusts trimmed*

Milk

1½ *pounds freshly ground lean beef*

⅛ *pound thickly cut salame, cut into small dice*

3 *eggs*

¼ *cup Parmesan cheese*

Small handful chopped Italian parsley

Small handful chopped fresh basil

1 *carrot, peeled and trimmed*

1 *celery stalk, trimmed*

1 *medium onion, peeled and studded with 2 cloves*

Salt and freshly ground black pepper to taste

1 *jar giardiniera (mild), drained and cut into julienne*

1 *recipe green sauce from Petto di Pollo con Salsa Verde (see page 314)*

Soak the bread in the milk to cover until softened. Drain the bread and squeeze out as much liquid as possible. Chop the bread and combine with the beef, salame, eggs, Parmesan cheese, and chopped herbs. Shape the mixture into a loaf and wrap in a double thickness of cheesecloth. Tie the ends with kitchen twine.

Have ready an oval casserole that is large enough for the meat loaf to be immersed in water completely. Fill the casserole with water, and add the carrot, celery, onion, and salt and pepper to taste. Bring to a boil and gently lower the loaf into the water. Reduce the heat to a simmer and cook for about 50 minutes, or until the meat is firm to the touch. Turn off the heat and allow the loaf to cool. Remove it from casserole, drain, and remove the string. Cover the loaf with a dish towel, and weigh it down with heavy cans for about 1 hour. Unwrap the cheesecloth and slice the loaf.

To serve, arrange slices on a platter and surround with the giardiniera. Serve with green sauce on the side.

Dolci

Desserts

A baroque sugar-laden sweet does not automatically end an Italian meal. In fact, in Italy, at home and in restaurants, the most common dessert is seasonal fresh fruit. Usually the fruit is served whole. A bowl of apples, pears, or oranges is presented from which the diner selects one; or a bowl of ice water filled with a bunch of grapes or cherries will be served. Never underestimate the impact a simple presentation of well-chosen fruit can make. Whether you choose beautiful red cherries still dangling from their stems, ripe berries ready to stain the teeth, just-picked luscious figs still warm from the sun, or a never-refrigerated succulent melon full of juice, remember that fruit requires only the care and motivation it takes to discover markets that carry quality produce.

Our first book, *Cucina Fresca*, has many simple fruit recipes. Here we present a few simple fruit desserts, but for those who prefer desserts that are a little more *fatta*, or made, we include some of our favorites. The desserts fall into three categories: first, those simple fruit- or cheese-based sweets that are often eaten at home and are very easy to prepare. Dolci al Cucchiaio, or creamy desserts eaten with a spoon, are one example. Then there are those eaten in *ristoranti* that are more elaborate desserts such as cakes and tarts, often soaked in liqueurs. These are also good eaten for breakfast or as snacks along with a frothy cup of cappuccino. The third category includes desserts that are homespun, rustic cakes that require minimal baking experience.

Insalata di Bosco Misto

Mixed Fresh Berry Salad

Serves 6 to 8

Literally translated, *bosco misto* means mixed woods. This beautiful mixture of berries always conjures up for us an image of sun-dappled European forests and relaxed afternoons of berry picking in the country, which adds to the pleasure of the dish.

1 *pint strawberries, stem ends removed, cut in half lengthwise*

1 *pint blackberries*

1 *pint raspberries*

1 *pint blueberries*

2 *tablespoons sugar*

1 *lemon, zest and juice*

2 *sprigs fresh mint, julienned*

Gently combine all the ingredients and let macerate in the refrigerator for at least 1 hour. Serve chilled.

Macedonia di Frutta

Mixed Fruit Salad

Serves 6 to 8

From a simple combination of mixed fruits, Italians create a dish that brings out the best of each fruit's individual flavor. This is a good way to prepare fruits that may not be beautiful enough to serve whole but still have good flavor.

1 *mango, peeled and sliced*

2 *oranges, peeled and sectioned*

1 *papaya, peeled, pitted, and sliced*

1 *plum, pitted and sliced*

1 *peach, pitted and sliced*

Small bunch grapes, removed from main stem

2 *limes, zest and juice*

2 *tablespoons sugar*

Combine all ingredients and macerate in the refrigerator for at least 1 hour. Serve chilled.

Fichi al Sapore di Miele
H o n e y - W i n e   B r a i s e d   F i g s

Serves 6

A luscious warm topping for ice cream or to eat out of a wineglass. When fresh figs are in season, substitute them for the dried variety.

1½ pounds dried figs or fresh figs

1-liter bottle dessert wine

Zest of 2 oranges

4–6 tablespoons honey

1 cinnamon stick

1 tablespoon fennel seeds

¼ teaspoon freshly ground black pepper

5 tablespoons orange juice

Vanilla ice cream

Soak the dried figs in the wine overnight in a glass, stainless-steel, or enamel bowl. If using fresh figs, omit this step.

In a large nonaluminum saucepan combine the figs, wine, and all the remaining ingredients except for the orange juice and ice cream. Simmer over medium heat until the figs are tender and the sauce has been reduced by half. If using fresh figs, simply simmer them gently as directed until tender. Remove from the pan with a slotted spoon and simmer wine until reduced by half. Place figs and wine together in a beautiful bowl and serve.

Remove the pan from the heat and add the orange juice. Let figs cool in the wine sauce to warm room temperature.

Serve the figs and sauce over the vanilla ice cream.

Mele al Forno

B a k e d   A p p l e s

Serves 4

Baked apples seem to be a bicontinental comfort food. Simple to make, without pretentions, they are a rich yet healthful way to end a meal or they can be served as a treat at any time of day.

4 *tablespoons unsalted butter,
  divided*

2 *tablespoons sugar*

4 *apples*

¼ *cup walnuts, toasted and
  chopped*

4 *tablespoons cinnamon sugar,
  divided*

Pernod

Preheat the oven to 350°. Using 2 tablespoons of butter, generously grease a baking dish that is just large enough to hold the apples. Sprinkle the dish with sugar.

Core the apples and carefully peel the skin from the top quarters of each apple.

Combine the walnuts, the remaining 2 tablespoons of butter, and 2 tablespoons of cinnamon sugar until the mixture resembles bread crumbs.

Fill the apples with the walnut mixture and place them in the prepared pan. Cover the pan with foil and bake the apples for 10 to 15 minutes, or until tender when pierced with a thin knife or toothpick. Remove the apples from the pan and set aside. Pour the juices from the baking dish into a small saucepan and reduce slightly over high heat. Add a splash of Pernod and reduce again.

Pour the sauce over the apples and sprinkle lightly with the remaining cinnamon sugar.

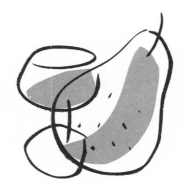

Pere al Mascarpone

Carmelized Pears
with Mascarpone

Serves 6

This dessert is truly an extension of the meal. The pears are barely sweetened, then cooked until just tender. A dollop of mascarpone adds a bit of decadent richness without being too filling.

9 *tablespoons unsalted butter*

6 *Bosc pears, peeled, cored, and sliced into wedges*

¾ *cup sugar*

3 *tablespoons orange zest*

1 *cup dessert wine*

1 *pound mascarpone*

Heat the butter in a sauté pan until it is bubbling. Add the pears and sugar, and cook until the pears are tender. Remove the pears from the pan and caramelize the sugar mixture over high heat. After the sugar has caramelized, add the dessert wine and orange zest and cook until liquid reduces to a thick sauce.

Serve the pears warm or at room temperature with the caramel sauce and a large dollop of mascarpone on top.

Tiramisù

Serves 8 to 10

The name means "pick-me-up." Without a doubt one of the most popular Italian desserts in America. Every Italian restaurant seems to have its own version of this luscious specialty. Tiramisù traditionally combines the archetypal flavors of coffee and anise with chocolate. Here nuts and or berries are a luscious addition.

1 *quart espresso or very strong coffee*

¼ *cup Sambuca*

1 *tablespoon sugar*

1 *tablespoon coffee extract*

4 *egg yolks*

½ *cup sugar*

2½ *cups mascarpone*

½ *cup heavy cream*

2 *packages Italian ladyfingers*

1 *pint raspberries*

½ *cup hazelnuts, toasted and chopped fine*

6 *ounces semisweet chocolate, grated*

In a saucepan combine the coffee, Sambuca, sugar, and coffee extract, and heat over a low flame until the sugar dissolves.

Using a wire whisk or an electric mixer, beat together the egg yolks and sugar until light and fluffy. Beat in the mascarpone. With the whisk or electric mixer, whip the heavy cream in a small bowl. Using a rubber spatula, gently fold the whipped cream into the mascarpone mixture.

Quickly dip the ladyfingers in the coffee mixture just until they absorb the liquid but before they become soft and fall apart.

In a glass baking dish or bowl, layer the ingredients as follows: Start with the cream mixture, then make a layer of ladyfingers, then a layer of cream, then a layer of raspberries, nuts, and cream. Repeat the layering process, ending with the cream mixture. Sprinkle the grated chocolate over the top and let set in the refrigerator for at least 2 hours or overnight. To serve, cut into small rectangles.

Mascarpone Parfait

Makes 6 parfaits

A variation on the Tiramisù theme, this creamy dessert features the bittersweet yet mellow taste of coffee-soaked Biscotti. The fresh, tart flavor of raspberries lightens the dish. Presenting this parfait in wineglasses adds a festive note.

5–6 *Italian Biscotti (see pages 366–370), broken into small chunks*

½ *cup espresso or very strong coffee*

1¼ *pounds mascarpone*

3 *eggs*

3 *ounces sugar*

1 *cup heavy cream*

1 *pint fresh raspberries*

Fresh mint leaves (optional)

Combine the biscotti chunks and coffee in a small bowl and let soak. Meanwhile, using a wire whisk or an electric mixer, whip together the mascarpone, eggs, and sugar in a medium-sized bowl. Set aside. With the wire whisk or electric mixer, whip the heavy cream in a small bowl. Using a rubber spatula, gently fold the whipped cream into the mascarpone mixture.

In each of 6 wine or parfait glasses, make a layer of coffee mixture, then a layer of berries, then a layer of the whipped cream-mascarpone mixture. The creamed mascarpone can either be piped into the glass with a pastry bag or gently spooned in. Layer the ingredients again, and top the parfait with a raspberry and a sprig of mint, if desired. Serve immediately.

Budino di Mascarpone con Cioccolata

C h o c o l a t e   M a s c a r p o n e   P u d d i n g

Serves 12

This comforting Budino is the Italian version of chocolate pudding, made more luscious by the addition of mascarpone and Marsala.

4 *egg yolks*	½ *pound mascarpone*
½ *cup sugar*	¼ *cup Marsala*
½ *teaspoon vanilla*	½ *cup whipped cream*
¼ *cup unsweetened cocoa*	¾ *cup walnuts, toasted*

In a large metal bowl beat the egg yolks and sugar until light and fluffy. Place the bowl over a saucepan, half filled with simmering water, and whisk until "ribbons" form. Still whisking, add the vanilla, cocoa, and mascarpone. Beat until smooth. Slowly add the Marsala, whisking constantly until the mixture thickens. Remove from the heat and spoon into pudding bowls, about ½ cup each. Chill until set. Pipe the whipped cream on top and sprinkle with the nuts.

Budino di Ricotta

Ricotta Pudding

Serves 8 to 10

A lovely pudding with the delicate, milky taste of ricotta. If you wish, serve it with a simple raspberry puree. The scarlet of the raspberries is a striking contrast to the snowy white pudding.

2 *pounds ricotta*	¼ *teaspoon cinnamon*
1 *egg yolk*	2 *tablespoons lemon zest*
½ *cup sugar*	3 *egg whites*
1 *teaspoon vanilla*	*Pinch of salt*
¼ *teaspoon almond extract*	¼ *teaspoon cream of tartar*

Place the ricotta in a cheesecloth or muslin-lined strainer and set it over the sink. Let drain overnight.

Preheat the oven to 325°. Butter a medium-sized loaf pan. Set aside. Prepare a water bath by half filling a rectangular baking tray with water. The loaf pan containing the pudding will be placed in it to bake evenly and gently.

In a food processor or with an electric mixer, process or beat the ricotta, egg yolk, sugar, extracts, and cinnamon until very smooth and light. Add the lemon zest. Transfer to a large mixing bowl.

Whip the egg whites with the salt and cream of tartar until stiff. Beat ¼ of the egg whites into the ricotta mixture; then with a rubber spatula gently fold in the remaining whites. Gently pour the mixture into the prepared loaf pan, and set the pan into the water bath. Bake the pudding for approximately 35 to 40 minutes, or when a toothpick or thin knife inserted in the center is dry when removed. Let cool before serving.

Crostata di Pinoli

Pine Nut Tart

Serves 8 to 10

This tart is very special. Lighter and less filling than a full-fledged cheese-cake, it nevertheless satisfies that urge for a bit of richness at the end of a meal. The characteristically crunchy pine nuts add their warm flavor.

2 cups all-purpose unbleached flour

½ cup sugar

⅓ cup pine nuts, toasted and chopped very fine

6 ounces unsalted butter, melted

½ cup water

1½ cup sugar

6 ounces cream cheese

1 cup ricotta

3 egg yolks and 2 whole eggs

2 ounces pine nuts

FOR THE CRUST:

Preheat the oven to 350°. Mix the flour, sugar, and chopped pine nuts together in a small bowl. Add the melted butter and, using a rubber spatula, gently mix remaining ingredients together. Press into a 10-inch by 3-inch tart pan or springform pan with a removable bottom. Chill in the refrigerator for a few minutes, then place a round of aluminum foil or parchment paper over the pastry and fill to the top with dried beans or rice. Bake for 15 minutes, then remove the beans or rice and parchment, and bake for an additional 10 minutes or until golden brown. Cool in the pan.

FOR THE FILLING:

In a heavy-bottomed saucepan boil the water and sugar for 2 minutes to make a sugar syrup. Set aside. In a food processor cream together the cheeses and egg yolks. With the machine still running, slowly pour in the syrup.

Pour the cheese mixture into the prepared pastry shell. Sprinkle the whole pine nuts evenly over the top. Bake the tart for 30 to 40 minutes, or until golden but still a bit soft in the middle. Cool to room temperature on a cooling rack.

Semolina Cake

This version of pan di Spagna is the perfect accompaniment for a rich caffè latte or foamy cappuccino in the morning or midafternoon. It is simply flavored with flowery almond extract, not too sweet, just the thing to start the day.

¾ *cup all-purpose flour*

½ *cup semolina*

2½ *teaspoons baking powder*

½ *teaspoon salt*

¾ *cup unsalted butter*

1 *cup sugar*

3 *eggs*

6 *yolks*

3 *tablespoons almond extract*

Zest of 1 lemon

½ *cup walnuts, toasted*

Preheat the oven to 375°. Lightly butter an 8-inch round baking pan and, if desired, line it with a circle of parchment paper.

In a large bowl sift together the flour, semolina, baking powder, and salt. Set aside.

Using an electric mixer, cream together the butter and sugar until light colored and fluffy. Slowly add the whole eggs and the egg yolks, 1 at a time, until they are completely incorporated into the butter mixture. Then add the almond extract, lemon zest, and sifted dry ingredients. Mix just until the flour is absorbed. Do not overmix or the cake will not be as light. Fold in the walnuts with a rubber spatula.

Pour the batter into the prepared pan and bake in the center of the oven for approximately 50 minutes, or until a toothpick or thin knife, when inserted into the cake, comes out clean. Let cool before serving. Slice in generous wedges and serve.

Torta Extra-Vergine

Olive Oil Cake

Serves 8 to 10

This simple cake is similar in texture to pound cake. An unusual and healthy alternative to other baking fats, extra-virgin olive oil lends its characteristic fruity aroma to this satisfying snacking cake.

2 *oranges*

2 *lemons*

4 *eggs*

¾ *cup sugar*

1 *cup all-purpose unbleached flour*

3 *teaspoons baking powder*

½ *teaspoon salt*

⅔ *cup extra-virgin olive oil*

½ *cup almonds, toasted and chopped fine*

Powdered sugar

Preheat the oven to 350°. In a saucepan simmer the whole oranges and lemons in water for about ½ hour, or until very soft. Drain and cool the fruit. Scoop out and discard the pulp, and in a food processor pulverize the skin completely until it is a very fine puree.

Using an electric mixer, beat the eggs and slowly add the sugar, beating until fluffy and pale yellow. Mix together the flour, baking powder, and salt. Add the flour mixture to the eggs, alternating with the olive oil, finishing with the flour. Fold in the almonds and the pureed citrus skins.

Pour the batter into an 8-inch springform pan. Bake for approximately 50 minutes, or until a toothpick, when inserted into the cake, comes out clean. Sprinkle the top generously with powdered sugar. Cool on a cooling rack.

Torta Primavera

Simple Pound Cake with Fruit

Serves 8 to 10

This moist, not too sweet cake is filled with raspberries and topped with poached pear slices. A good picnic dessert with rustic charm.

2 cups Biscotti (see page 370) or any crisp cookie, crushed

¾ cup unsalted butter, melted

1¼ cup raspberry jam

2 tablespoons water

1 pint raspberries

7 tablespoons unsalted butter

½ cup sugar

2 eggs

2 egg yolks

1 orange, zest and juice

½ teaspoon vanilla

1⅓ cup pastry flour

1½ teaspoons baking powder

4 pears, peeled, cored, sliced, and poached

Powdered sugar

PREHEAT THE OVEN TO 350°.

To make the crust: Combine the biscotti crumbs with the melted butter. Press the crumb crust into a 10-inch springform baking pan.

TO MAKE THE GLAZE:

Bring the jam and water to a boil and cook for 2 minutes until jam is melted and smooth. Brush the glaze on top of the crust, being sure to reserve some for glazing the finished cake. Cover with the raspberries.

TO MAKE THE CAKE BATTER:

Cream together the butter and sugar until light and fluffy. While beating, add the whole eggs and the yolks, 1 at a time, until well incorporated. Add the orange zest and juice and the vanilla, and continue mixing. Combine the flour and baking powder, and fold into the egg mixture. Do not over-work or the cake will not be as light as desired. Pour the batter over the berries. Carefully arrange the pear slices over the batter in a flower-petal arrangement. Bake the torta for 40 to 50 minutes. Glaze the top with the remaining berry glaze. Dust with powdered sugar.

Biscotti

The Italian word for cookies, *biscotti*, means twice-cooked. Traditionally the dough is formed into a narrow log, baked, cooled, and cut, then baked again. This results in a cookie whose consistency varies from hard to very hard and is just right to dip into liqueurs, red wine, or caffè latte. There are as many recipes for biscotti as there are Italian families, who tend to pass the recipes down from mother to daughter. Typical biscotti ingredients are nuts, anise or fennel seeds, lemon or orange zest, chocolate, raisins, candied fruit, and sometimes even black pepper. Biscotti can be made either with butter, which makes them very short, or with no fat at all. Naturally, each recipe has its own charm and its own adherents. The three recipes that follow give a good sense of the differences among biscotti. The first recipe is for a buttery, rich cookie, spicy with freshly ground black pepper. It is well suited to a late-afternoon snack accompanied by cappuccino. The next recipe is for a very hard, dry, traditional cookie packed with hazelnuts that is made to be dipped into Vin Santo, the famous Tuscan desert wine. The last recipe is a more modern combination of chocolate, nuts, and raisins. Try them all and decide yourself which biscotti will become your family recipe.

Walnut Almond Biscotti

Makes 24 cookies

1¾ cups all-purpose unbleached
  flour

½ teaspoon baking soda

½ teaspoon baking powder

⅛ teaspoon salt

1½ teaspoons freshly ground
  black pepper

½ cup unsalted butter

1 cup sugar

2 large eggs

Zests of 1 orange and 1 lemon

1½ teaspoons vanilla extract

¼ teaspoon almond extract

1½ cup walnuts, toasted and
  chopped

Preheat the oven to 350°. Sift together the flour, baking soda, baking powder, salt, and pepper. In a large bowl mix together the butter and sugar
until light and fluffy. Add the eggs, beating them in 1 at a time. Add the
orange and lemon zests and the vanilla and almond extracts. Fold in the
sifted dry ingredients and nuts, being careful not to overmix.

Shape the dough into a flattish log approximately 3 inches wide and a
length that comfortably fits your baking sheet. If necessary, make 2 logs.
Lay the logs on a greased cookie sheet and bake in the oven for approximately 20 minutes. Remove from the oven and let cool. Using a serrated
bread knife, cut the log or logs crosswise into ¾-inch-wide pieces. Lay the
cookies cut side down on a greased cookie sheet and bake again at 350°
until golden brown, about 15 minutes. Remove from the oven and let cool.
Store in tins.

Cantucci

Hazelnut Biscotti

Makes approximately 24 cookies

These classic hard Italian Biscotti, made without butter or oil, are made to dip into Vin Santo. Store them in tins and they will last at least a month.

4 *cups all-purpose flour*

2 *cups sugar*

2 *teaspoons baking powder*

6 *eggs*

4 *tablespoons Frangelico (a hazelnut liqueur)*

2 *teaspoons almond extract*

2 *teaspoons vanilla extract*

2 *cups roasted hazelnuts, coarsely chopped*

To make Biscotti using a food processor, combine the dry ingredients in the bowl, using the steel blade. In a separate small bowl combine the eggs, Frangelico, and extracts. Add the liquid ingredients to the dry ingredients in a steady stream while the processor is on. Process just until a stiff dough is formed. Add the hazelnuts and pulse the machine just enough to mix the nuts into the dough.

To make the Biscotti by hand, combine the unsifted dry ingredients in a bowl, using a rubber spatula. In a separate small bowl combine the eggs, Frangelico, and extracts. Beat the liquid ingredients into the dry ingredients, using a wooden spoon. The dough will be very stiff. Stir the nuts into the dough.

Shape the dough into a flattish log approximately 3 inches wide and a length that comfortably fits your baking sheets. If necessary, make 2 logs. Lay the logs on a greased cookie sheet and bake in a preheated 350° oven for approximately 20 minutes. Remove from the oven and let cool until comfortable to the touch. Using a serrated bread knife, cut the log crosswise into ¾-inch-wide pieces. If desired, cut the pieces on a slight diagonal. Lay the cookies cut side down on a greased cookie sheet and bake again at 350° for approximately 15 minutes, or until golden brown. Remove from the oven and let cool. Store in tins.

Biscotti al Anice e Cioccolata

Anise-Scented Chocolate Cookies

Makes approximately 24 pieces

These Biscotti are for those times when you want a taste of chocolate but not too much sweetness.

3 *teaspoons anise seed*

¼ *cup dry vermouth*

10 *ounces unsalted butter*

1½ *cups sugar*

6 *eggs*

6 *cups all-purpose flour*

3 *teaspoons baking powder*

2 *teaspoons salt*

1½ *cups walnuts, coarsely chopped*

2 *cups chocolate chips*

Soak the anise seed in the vermouth overnight.

Preheat the oven to 350°.

Using an electric mixer or a wooden spoon, cream butter and sugar until light and fluffy. Beat the eggs in a small bowl. Mix the flour and baking powder well with a rubber spatula. Alternately add the eggs and dry ingredients to the creamed butter and sugar. Beat in the anise seed, walnuts, and chocolate chips.

Shape the dough into a flattish log approximately 3 inches wide and a length that comfortably fits your baking sheets. If necessary, make 2 logs. Lay the logs on a greased cookie sheet and bake in the oven for approximately 20 minutes. Remove from the oven and let cool until you can comfortably touch the logs. Using a serrated bread knife, cut the log crosswise into ¾-inch-wide pieces. If you wish, cut the pieces on a slight diagonal. Lay the cookies cut side down on a greased cookie sheet and bake again at 350° for approximately 15 minutes or until golden brown. Remove from the oven and let cool. Store in tins.

Granita di Caffè

E s p r e s s o   I c e

Serves 4

The classic Italian refresher. The best Granita di Caffè is served with unsweetened whipped cream, which takes the bitter edge off the lightly sweetened coffee.

2 *cups hot, strong espresso*

¼ *cup sugar*

1 *teaspoon coffee extract (optional)*
Unsweetened whipped cream

Combine the hot coffee with the sugar and the optional coffee extract. Stir to dissolve sugar.

Pour the coffee mixture into a large bowl and put bowl in the freezer for approximately 20 minutes. Remove the bowl and beat the coffee mixture, taking care to scrape down any crystallized coffee on the sides of the bowl into the mixture. Return the mixture to the freezer and continue the beating process every 15 minutes or so until you have a bowl of coarse coffee-ice crystals, the texture of a rough sorbet.

Serve in wineglasses with plenty of unsweetened whipped cream.

Frittelle di Polenta

Polenta Fritters

Serves 6 to 8

Based on a recipe from Luigi Carnacina and Vincenzo Buonassisi's book on polenta, this homey dessert featuring polenta made with raisins and pine nuts, and sweetened with sugar, is unusual, beautiful, and especially festive. The polenta is cooled and cut into cubes, then dipped into batter and fried. Like many Italian fried-dough desserts, the fritters are sprinkled with powdered sugar before serving.

1 *recipe Polenta (see page 232 or page 233)*

½ *cup golden raisins*

½ *cup dark raisins*

½ *cup pine nuts*

½ *cup sugar*

2 *cups milk, approximately*

½ *cup all-purpose flour*

1 *tablespoon sugar*

Pinch of salt

Water

Olive oil for frying

Powdered sugar

Cook Polenta according to the traditional or instant recipe, adding the raisins, pine nuts, and ½ cup sugar. When the Polenta is properly cooked, pour into 2 or more baking dishes to the depth of ½ inch. Set aside to cool and harden.

When the polenta is cool and firm, cut it into ½-inch cubes. Place in a bowl and cover with milk. Let soak for 1 hour.

Meanwhile, combine the flour, 1 tablespoon sugar, salt, and enough water to form a thick batter.

Drain the polenta and carefully fold the cubes into the batter. Heat the olive oil to a depth of 2 inches in a large skillet. Drop large tablespoons of battered polenta cubes into the hot oil. Fry until golden, turning fritters frequently. Remove from the skillet using a slotted spoon and drain on paper towels. Dust the fritters with powdered sugar and serve hot on a large platter.

Gelato Affogato

Vanilla Ice Cream Drowned with Espresso

Few desserts are as much fun to eat as a dish of creamy ice cream covered with a special topping. This recipe, featuring vanilla ice cream drenched in espresso, is our favorite and, of course, it is the simplest.

Vanilla ice cream *Freshly made hot espresso*

Spoon the ice cream into wineglasses. Pour the equivalent of a demitasse of espresso over each portion of ice cream. Serve immediately.

Uva Passa al Rhum

Raisins Macerated in Dark Rum

Serves 6

Many *gelaterie* in Italy make a flavor called Malaga that blends the sweet creaminess of ice cream with macerated raisins. In lieu of a neighborhood ice cream store that makes this stupendous flavor, we have come up with this topping. Serve with the best vanilla ice cream you can find.

½ *cup golden raisins*   1 *cup Meyers's rum*
½ *cup dark raisins*

Combine all ingredients and macerate at least 2 hours. Serve over ice cream.

Index